Workshop on Graph-based Methods for Natural Language Processing 2010

(TextGraphs-5)

Held at ACL 2010

Uppsala, Sweden
16 July 2010

ISBN: 978-1-61738-822-4

Printed from e-media with permission by:

Curran Associates, Inc.
57 Morehouse Lane
Red Hook, NY 12571

CURRAN ASSOCIATES INC. proceedings.com

Some format issues inherent in the e-media version may also appear in this print version.

Printed by Curran Associates, Inc. (2010)

Association for Computational Linguistics
209 N. Eighth Street
Stroudsburg, Pennsylvania 18360

Phone: 1-570-476-8006
Fax: 1-570-476-0860

acl@aclweb.org

Additional copies of this publication are available from:

Curran Associates, Inc.
57 Morehouse Lane
Red Hook, NY 12571 USA
Phone: 845-758-0400
Fax: 845-758-2634
Email: curran@proceedings.com
Web: www.proceedings.com

Introduction

Recent years have shown an increased amount of interest in applying graph theoretic models to computational linguistics. Both graph theory and computational linguistics are well studied disciplines, which have traditionally been perceived as distinct, embracing different algorithms, different applications, and different potential end-users. However, as recent research work has shown, the two seemingly distinct disciplines are in fact intimately connected, with a large variety of Natural Language Processing (NLP) applications adopting efficient and elegant solutions from graph-theoretical framework.

The TextGraphs workshop series addresses a broad spectrum of research areas and brings together specialists working on graph-based models and algorithms for natural language processing and computational linguistics, as well as on the theoretical foundations of related graph-based methods. This workshop is aimed at fostering an exchange of ideas by facilitating a discussion about both the techniques and the theoretical justification of the empirical results among the NLP community members. Spawning a deeper understanding of the basic theoretical principles involved, such interaction is vital to the further progress of graph-based NLP applications.

In addition to the general goal of employing graph-theoretical methods for text processing tasks, this year we invited papers on a special theme "Graph Methods for Opinion analysis". One of the motivations for our special theme was that graphical approaches become very pertinent as the field of opinion mining advances towards deeper analysis and more complex systems. We wanted to encourage publication of early results, position papers and initiate discussions of issues in this area.

This volume contains papers accepted for publication for TextGraphs-5 2010 Workshop on Graph- Based Algorithms for Natural Language Processing. TextGraphs-5 was held on 16th of July 2010 in Uppsala, Sweden at ACL 2010, the 48th Annual Meeting of the Association for Computational Linguistics. This was the fifth workshop in this series, building on the successes of previous workshops that were held at HLT-NAACL (2006, 2007), Coling (2008) and ACL (2009).

We issued calls for both regular, short and position papers. Six regular and ten short papers were accepted for presentation, based on the careful reviews of our program committee. We are very thankful to the incredible program committee, whose detailed comments and useful suggestions have benefited the papers and helped us to create a great program. We are particularly grateful for the timely reviews, especially considering that we had a tight schedule.

The articles apply graph methods to a variety of NLP problems such as Word Sense Disambiguation (De Cao et al., Fagerlund et al., Biemannl), Topic Segmentation (Ambwani and Davis), Summarization (Jorge and Pardo, Fukumoto and Suzuki), Language Evolution (Enright), Language Acquisition (German et al.), Language Resources (Archer), Lexical Networks (Oliveira and Gomes, Görnerup and Karlgren) and Clustering (Wieling and Nerbonne, Chen and Ji). Additionally, we have selected three papers for our special theme: Zontone et al. use graph theoretic dominant set clustering algorithm for the annotation of images with sentiment scores, Amancio et al. employ complex network features to distinguish between positive and negative opinions, and Tatzl and Waldhauser offer a formalization that could help to automate opinion extraction within the Media Content Analysis framework.

Last but not the least, having a prominent researcher as the invited speaker significantly added to the success of our workshop. We would like to thank Professor Edwin Hancock from the

University of York for his captivating talk on graph-based machine learning algorithms. We are also grateful to the European Community project, EternalS: "Trustworthy Eternal Systems via Evolving Software, Data and Knowledge" (project number FP7 247758) for sponsoring our invited speaker.

Enjoy the workshop!

The organizers

Carmen Banea, Alessandro Moschitti, Swapna Somasundaran and Fabio Massimo Zanzotto

Upsala, July 2010

Organizers:

Carmen Banea, University of North Texas, US
Alessandro Moschitti, University of Trento, Italy
Swapna Somasundaran, University of Pittsburgh, US
Fabio Massimo Zanzotto, University of Rome, Italy

Program Committee:

Andras Csomai, Google Inc.
Andrea Esuli, Italian National Research Council, Italy
Andrea Passerini, Trento University, Italy
Andrew Goldberg, University of Wisconsin, US
Animesh Mukherjee, ISI Foundation, Turin, Italy
Carlo Strapparava, Istituto per la Ricerca Scientifica e Tecnologica, Italy
Dragomir R. Radev, University of Michigan, US
Eduard Hovy, Information Sciences Institute, US
Fabrizio Sebastiani, Istituto di Scienza e Tecnologia dell'Informazione, Italy
Giuseppe Carenini, University of British Columbia, Canada
Hiroya Takamura, Tokyo Institute of Technology, Japan
Lillian Lee, Cornell University, US
Lise Getoor, University of Maryland, US
Lluis Marquez Villodre, Universidad Politecnica de Catalunya, Spain
Michael Gamon, Microsoft Research, Redmond
Michael Strube, EML research, Germany
Monojit Choudhury, Microsoft Research, India
Richard Johansson, Trento University
Robero Basili, University of Rome, Italy
Roi Blanco, Yahoo!, Spain
Smaranda Muresan, Rutgers University, US
Sofus Macskassy, Fetch Technologies El Segundo, US
Stefan Siersdorfer, L3S Research Center, Hannover, Germany
Theresa Wilson, University of Edinburgh, Germany
Thomas Gartner, Fraunhofer Institute for Intelligent Analysis and Information Systems, Germany
Ulf Brefeld, Yahoo!, Spain
Veselin Stoyanov, Cornell University, US
William Cohen, Carnegie Mellon University, US
Xiaojin Zhu, University of Wisconsin, US
Yejin Choi, Cornell University, US

Invited Speaker:

Edwin R. Hancock, University of York, UK

Table of Contents

TextGraphs-5 Program

Friday July 16, 2010

12:40–13:50 Lunch break

Session 3: Lexical Similarity and Its application

13:50–14:10 *Cross-Lingual Comparison between Distributionally Determined Word Similarity Networks*
Olof Görnerup and Jussi Karlgren

14:10–14:30 *Co-Occurrence Cluster Features for Lexical Substitutions in Context*
Chris Biemann

14:30–14:50 *Contextually-Mediated Semantic Similarity Graphs for Topic Segmentation*
Geetu Ambwani and Anthony Davis

14:50–15:10 *MuLLinG: MultiLevel Linguistic Graphs for Knowledge Extraction*
Vincent Archer

15:10–15:30 *Experiments with CST-Based Multidocument Summarization*
Maria Lucia Castro Jorge and Thiago Pardo

15:30–16:00 Coffee Break

Special Session on Opinion Mining

16:00–16:20 *Distinguishing between Positive and Negative Opinions with Complex Network Features*
Diego Raphael Amancio, Renato Fabbri, Osvaldo Novais Oliveira Jr., Maria das Graças Volpe Nunes and Luciano da Fontoura Costa

16:20–16:40 *Image and Collateral Text in Support of Auto-Annotation and Sentiment Analysis*
Pamela Zontone, Giulia Boato, Jonathon Hare, Paul Lewis, Stefan Siersdorfer and Enrico Minack

16:40–17:00 *Aggregating Opinions: Explorations into Graphs and Media Content Analysis*
Gabriele Tatzl and Christoph Waldhauser

(continued)

Session 5: Spectral Approaches

17:00–17:20 *Eliminating Redundancy by Spectral Relaxation for Multi-Document Summarization*
Fumiyo Fukumoto, Akina Sakai and Yoshimi Suzuki

17:20–17:40 *Computing Word Senses by Semantic Mirroring and Spectral Graph Partitioning*
Martin Fagerlund, Magnus Merkel, Lars Eldén and Lars Ahrenberg

17:40–18:00 Final Wrap-up

Graph-based Clustering for Computational Linguistics: A Survey

Zheng Chen
The Graduate Center
The City University of New York
zchen1@gc.cuny.edu

Heng Ji
Queens College and The Graduate Center
The City University of New York
hengji@cs.qc.cuny.edu

Abstract

In this survey we overview graph-based clustering and its applications in computational linguistics. We summarize graph-based clustering as a five-part story: *hypothesis, modeling, measure, algorithm* and *evaluation*. We then survey three typical NLP problems in which graph-based clustering approaches have been successfully applied. Finally, we comment on the strengths and weaknesses of graph-based clustering and envision that graph-based clustering is a promising solution for some emerging NLP problems.

1 Introduction

In the passing years, there has been a tremendous body of work on graph-based clustering, either done by theoreticians or practitioners. Theoreticians have been extensively investigating cluster properties, quality measures and various clustering algorithms by taking advantage of elegant mathematical structures built in graph theory. Practitioners have been investigating the graph clustering algorithms for specific applications and claiming their effectiveness by taking advantage of the underlying structure or other known characteristics of the data. Although graph-based clustering has gained increasing attentions from Computational Linguistic (CL) community (especially through the series of TextGraphs workshops), it is studied case by case and as far as we know, we have not seen much work on comparative study of various graph-based clustering algorithms for certain NLP problems. The major goal of this survey is to "bridge" the gap between theoretical aspect and practical aspect in graph-based clustering, especially for computational linguistics.

From the theoretical aspect, we state that the following five-part story describes the general methodology of graph-based clustering:
(1) Hypothesis. The hypothesis is that a graph can be partitioned into densely connected subgraphs that are sparsely connected to each other.
(2) Modeling. It deals with the problem of transforming data into a graph or modeling the real application as a graph.
(3) Measure. A quality measure is an objective function that rates the quality of a clustering.
(4) Algorithm. An algorithm is to exactly or approximately optimize the quality measure.
(5) Evaluation. Various metrics can be used to evaluate the performance of clustering by comparing with a "ground truth" clustering.

From the practical aspect, we focus on three typical NLP applications, including coreference resolution, word clustering and word sense disambiguation, in which graph-based clustering approaches have been successfully applied and achieved competitive performance.

2 Graph-based Clustering Methodology

We start with the basic clustering problem. Let $X = \{x_1, \dots, x_N\}$ be a set of data points, $S = (s_{ij})_{i,j=1,\dots,N}$ be the similarity matrix in which each element indicates the similarity $s_{ij} \geq 0$ between two data points x_i and x_j. A nice way to represent the data is to construct a graph on which each vertex represents a data point and the edge weight carries the similarity of two vertices. The clustering problem in graph perspective is then formulated as partitioning the graph into subgraphs such that the edges in the same subgraph have high weights and the edges between different subgraphs have low weights. In the next section, we define essential graph notation to facilitate discussions in the rest of this survey.

Proceedings of the 2010 Workshop on Graph-based Methods for Natural Language Processing, ACL 2010, pages 1–9,
Uppsala, Sweden, 16 July 2010.

2.1 Graph Notation

A graph is a triple $G=(V,E,W)$ where $V = \{v_1, \dots, v_N\}$ is a set of vertices, $E \subseteq V \times V$ is a set of edges, and $W = (w_{ij})_{i,j=1,\dots,N}$ is called *adjacency matrix* in which each element indicates a non-negative weight ($w_{ij} \geq 0$) between two vertices v_i and v_j.

In this survey we target at hard clustering problem which means we partition vertices of the graph into non-overlapping clusters, i.e., let $C = (C_1, \dots, C_K)$ be a partition of V such that
(1) $C_i \neq \emptyset$ for $i \in \{1, \dots, K\}$.
(2) $C_i \cap C_j = \emptyset$ for $i, j \in \{1, \dots, K\}$ and $i \neq j$
(3) $C_1 \cup \dots \cup C_K = V$

2.2 Hypothesis

The hypothesis behind graph-based clustering can be stated in the following ways:

(1) The graph consists of dense subgraphs such that a dense subgraph contains more well-connected internal edges connecting the vertices in the subgraph than cutting edges connecting the vertices across subgraphs.
(2) A random walk that visits a subgraph will likely stay in the subgraph until many of its vertices have been visited (Dongen, 2000).
(3) Among all shortest paths between all pairs of vertices, links between different dense subgraphs are likely to be in many shortest paths (Dongen, 2000).

2.3 Modeling

Modeling addresses the problem of transforming the problem into graph structure, specifically, designating the meaning of vertices and edges in the graph, computing the edge weights for weighted graph, and constructing the graph. Luxburg (2006) stated three most common methods to construct a graph: *ε-neighborhood graph, k-nearest neighbor graph,* and *fully connected graph.* Luxburg analyzed different behaviors of the three graph construction methods, and stated that some graph-cluster algorithms (e.g., spectral clustering) can be quite sensitive to the choice of graphs and parameters ($\boldsymbol{\varepsilon}$ and $\boldsymbol{k}$). As a general recommendation, Luxburg suggested exploiting *k-nearest neighbor graph* as the first choice, which is less vulnerable to the choices of parameters than other graphs. Unfortunately, theoretical justifications on the choices of graphs and parameters do not exist and as a result, the problem has been ignored by practitioners.

2.4 Measure

A measure is an objective function that rates the quality of a clustering, thus called *quality measure*. By optimizing the quality measure, we can obtain the "optimal" clustering.

It is worth noting that *quality measure* should not be confused with *vertex similarity measure* where it is used to compute edge weights. Furthermore, we should distinguish *quality measure* from *evaluation measure* which will be discussed in section 2.6. The main difference is that cluster quality measure directly identifies a clustering that fulfills a desirable property while evaluation measure rates the quality of a clustering by comparing with a ground-truth clustering.

We summarize various quality measures in Table 1, from the basic density measures (*intra-cluster* and *inter-cluster*), to cut-based measures (*ratio cut, ncut, performance, expansion, conductance, bicriteria*), then to the latest proposed measure *modularity*. Each of the measures has strengths and weaknesses as commented in Table 1. Optimizing each of the measures is NP-hard. As a result, many efficient algorithms, which have been claimed to solve the optimal problem with polynomial-time complexity, yield sub-optimal clustering.

2.5 Algorithm

We categorize graph clustering algorithms into two major classes: divisive and agglomerative (Table 2). In the divisive clustering class, we categorize algorithms into several subclasses, namely, *cut-based, spectral clustering, multilevel, random walks, shortest path*. Divisive clustering follows top-down style and recursively splits a graph into subgraphs. In contrast, agglomerative clustering works bottom-up and iteratively merges singleton sets of vertices into subgraphs. The divisive and agglomerative algorithms are also called hierarchical since they produce multi-level clusterings, i.e., one clustering follows the other by refining (divisive) or coarsening (agglomerative). Most graph clustering algorithms ever proposed are divisive. We list the quality measure and the running complexity for each algorithm in Table 2.

Measures	Comments
intra-cluster density inter-cluster density	– Maximizing intra-cluster density is equivalent to minimizing inter-cluster density and vice versa – Drawback: both favor cutting small sets of isolated vertices in the graph (Shi and Malik, 2000)
ratio cut (Hagan and Kahng, 1992) ncut (Shi and Malik, 2000)	– Ratio cut is suitable for unweighted graph, and ncut is a better choice for weighted graph – Overcome the drawback of intra-cluster density or inter-cluster density – Drawback: both favor clusters with equal size
performance (Dongen, 2000; Brandes et al., 2003)	– Performance takes both intra-cluster density and inter-cluster density into considerations simultaneously
expansion, conductance, bicriteria (Kannan et al., 2000)	– Expansion is suitable for unweighted graph, and conductance is a better choice for weighted graph – Both expansion and conductance impose quality within clusters, but not inter-cluster quality; bicriteria takes both into considerations
modularity (Newman and Girvan,2004)	– Evaluates the quality of clustering with respect to a randomized graph – Drawbacks: (1) It requires global knowledge of the graph's topology, i.e., the number of edges. Clauset (2005) proposed an improved measure *Local Modularity*. (2) Resolution limit problem: it fails to identify clusters smaller than a certain scale. Ruan and Zhang (2008) proposed an improved measure *HQcut*. (3) It fails to distinguish good from bad clustering between different graphs with the same modularity value. Chen et al. (2009) proposed an improved measure *Max-Min Modularity*

Table 1. Summary of Quality Measures

Category		Algorithms	optimized measure	running complexity
divisive	cut-based	*Kernighan-Lin algorithm* (Kernighan and Lin, 1970)	*intercluster*	$O(\|V\|^3)$
		cut-clustering algorithm (Flake et al., 2003)	*bicriteria*	$O(\|V\|)$
	spectral	*unnormalized spectral clustering* (Luxburg, 2006)	*ratiocut*	$O(\|V\|\|E\|)$
		normalized spectral clustering I (Luxburg, 2006; Shi and Malik, 2000)	*ncut*	$O(\|V\|\|E\|)$
		normalized spectral clustering II (Luxburg, 2006; Ng, 2002)	*ncut*	$O(\|V\|\|E\|)$
		iterative conductance cutting (ICC) (Kannan et al.,2000)	*conductance*	$O(\|V\|\|E\|)$
		geometric MST clustering (GMC) (Brandes et al., 2007)	*pluggable(any quality measure)*	$O(\|V\|\|E\|)$
		modularity oriented (White and Smyth,2005)	*modularity*	$O(\|V\|\|E\|)$
	multilevel	*multilevel recursive bisection* (Karypis and Kumar, 1999)	*intercluster*	$O(\|V\|logK)$
		multilevel K-way partitioning (Karypis and Kumar, 1999)	*intercluster*	$O(\|V\| + KlogK)$
	random	*Markov Clustering Algorithm (MCL)* (Dongen, 2000)	*performance*	$O(m^2\|V\|)$
	shortest path	*betweenness* (Girvan and Newman, 2003)	*modularity*	$O(\|V\|\|E\|^2)$
		information centrality (Fortunato et al., 2004)	*modularity*	$O(\|V\|\|E\|^3)$
agglomerative		*modularity oriented* (Newman, 2004)	*modularity*	$O(\|V\|\|E\|)$

Table 2. Summary of Graph-based Clustering Algorithms ($|V|$: the number of vertices, $|E|$: the number of edges, K: the number of clusters, m: the number of resources allocated for each vertex)

The first set of algorithms (*cut-based*) is associated with *max-flow min-cut* theorem (Ford and Fulkerson, 1956) which states that "the value of the maximum flow is equal to the cost of the minimum cut". One of the earliest algorithm, *Kernighan-Lin* algorithm (Kernighan and Lin, 1970) splits the graph by performing recursive bisection (split into two parts at a time), aiming to minimize inter-cluster density (cut size). The high complexity of the algorithm ($O(|V|^3)$ makes it less competitive in real applications. Flake et al. (2003) proposed a cut-clustering algorithm which optimizes the bicriterion measure and the complexity is proportional to the number of clusters K using a heuristic, thus the algorithm is competitive in practice.

The second set of algorithms is based on spectral graph theory with Laplacian matrix as the mathematical tool. The connection between clustering and spectrum of Laplacian matrix (L) basically lies in the following important proposition: the multiplicity k of the eigenvalue 0 of L equals to the number of connected components in the graph. Luxburg (2006) and Abney (2007) presented a comprehensive tutorial on spectral clustering. Luxburg (2006) discussed three forms of Laplacian matrices (one unnormalized form and two normalized forms) and their three corresponding spectral clustering algorithms (unnormalized, normalized I and normalized II). Unnormalized clustering aims to optimize *ratiocut* measure while normalized clustering aims to optimize *ncut* measure (Shi and Malik, 2000), thus spectral clustering actually relates with cut-based clustering. The success of spectral clustering is mainly based on the fact that it does not make strong assumptions on the form of the clusters and can solve very general problems like intertwined spirals which k-means clustering handles much worse. Unfortunately, spectral clustering could be unstable under different choices of graphs and parameters as mentioned in section 2.3. Luxburg et al. (2005) compared unnormalized clustering with normalized version and proved that normalized version always converges to a sensible limit clustering while for unnormalized case the same only holds under strong additional assumptions which are not always satisfied. The running complexity of spectral clustering equals to the complexity of computing the eigenvectors of Laplacian matrix which is $O(|V|^3)$. However, when the graph is sparse, the complexity is reduced to $O(|V||E|)$ by applying efficient *Lanczos* algorithm.

The third set of algorithms is based on multilevel graph partitioning paradigm (Karypis and Kumar, 1999) which consists of three phases: coarsening phase, initial partitioning phase and refinement phase. Two approaches have been developed in this category, one is *multilevel recursive bisection* which recursively splits into two parts by performing multilevel paradigm with complexity of $O(|V|logK)$; the other is *multilevel K-way partitioning* which performs coarsening and refinement only once and directly partitions the graph into K clusters with complexity of $O(|V| + KlogK)$. The latter approach is superior to the former one for less running complexity and comparable (sometimes better) clustering quality.

The fourth set of algorithms is based on the second interpretation of the hypothesis in section 2.2, i.e., a random walk is likely to visit many vertices in a cluster before moving to the other cluster. An outstanding approach in this category is presented in Dogen (2000), named Markov clustering algorithm (MCL). The algorithm iteratively applies two operators (expansion and inflation) by matrix computation until convergence. Expansion operator simulates spreading of random walks and inflation models demotion of inter-cluster walks; the sequence matrix computation results in eliminating inter-cluster interactions and leaving only intra-cluster components. The complexity of MCL is $O(m^2|V|)$ where m is the number of resources allocated for each vertex. A key point of random walk is that it is actually linked to spectral clustering (Luxburg, 2006), e.g., *ncut* can be expressed in terms of transition probabilities and optimizing *ncut* can be achieved by computing the stationary distribution of a random walk in the graph.

The final set of algorithms in divisive category is based on the third interpretation of the hypothesis in section 2.2, i.e., the links between clusters are likely to be in the shortest paths. Girvan and Newman (2003) proposed the concept of edge *betweenness* which is the number of shortest paths connecting any pair of vertices that pass through the edge. Their algorithm iteratively removes one of the edges with the highest *betweenness*. The complexity of the algorithm is $O(|V||E|^2)$. Instead of *betweenness*, Fortunato et al. (2004) used *information centrality* for each edge and stated that it performs better than *betweenness* but with a higher complexity of $O(|V||E|^3)$.

The agglomerative category contains much fewer algorithms. Newman (2004) proposed an algorithm that starts each vertex as singletons, and then iteratively merges clusters together in pairs, choosing the join that results in the greatest increase (or smallest decrease) in *modularity* score. The algorithm converges if there is only cluster left in the graph, then from the clustering hierarchy, we choose the clustering with maximum *modularity*. The complexity of the algorithm is $O(|V||E|)$.

The algorithms we surveyed in this section are by no means comprehensive as the field is longstanding and still evolving rapidly. We also refer readers to other informative references, e.g., Schaeffer (2007), Brandes et al. (2007) and Newman (2004).

A natural question arises: "which algorithm should we choose?" A general answer to this question is that no algorithm is a panacea. First, as we mentioned earlier, a clustering algorithm is usually proposed to optimize some quality measure, therefore, it is not fair to compare an algorithm that favors one measure with the other one that favors some other measure. Second, there is not a perfect measure that captures the full characteristics of cluster structures; therefore a perfect algorithm does not exist. Third, there is no definition for so called "best clustering". The "best" depends on applications, data characteristics, and granularity.

2.6 Evaluation

We discussed various quality measures in section 2.4, however, a clustering optimizing some quality measure does not necessarily translate into effectiveness in real applications with respect to the ground truth clustering and thus an evaluation measure plays the role of evaluating how well the clustering matches the gold standard. Two questions arise: (1) what constraints (properties, criteria) should an ideal evaluation measure satisfy? (2) Do the evaluation measures ever proposed satisfy the constraints?

For the first question, there have been several attempts on it: Dom (2001) developed a parametric technique for describing the quality of a clustering and proposed five "desirable properties" based on the parameters; Meila (2003) listed 12 properties associated with the proposed entropy measure; Amigo et al. (2008) proposed four constraints including homogeneity, completeness, rag bag, and cluster size vs. quantity. A parallel comparison shows that the four constraints proposed by Amigo et al. (2008) have advantages over the constraints proposed in the other two papers, for one reason, the four constraints can describe all the important constraints in Dom (2001) and Meila (2003), but the reverse does not hold; for the other reason, the four constraints can be formally verified for each evaluation measure, but it is not true for the constraints in Dom (2001).

Table 3 lists the evaluation measures ever proposed (including those discussed in Amigo et al., 2008 and some other measures known for coreference resolution). To answer the second question proposed in this section, we conclude the findings in Amigo et al. (2008) plus our new findings about MUC and CEAF as follows: (1) all the measures except B-Cubed fail the rag bag constraint and only B-Cubed measure can satisfy all the four constraints; (2) two entropy based measures (VI and V) and MUC only fail the rag bag constraint; (3) all the measures in set mapping category fail completeness constraint (4) all the measures in pair counting category fail cluster size vs. quantity constraint; (5) CEAF, unfortunately, fails homogeneity, completeness, rag bag constraints.

Category	Evaluation Measures
set mapping	purity, inverse purity, F-measure
pair counting	rand index, Jaccard Coefficient, Folks and Mallows FM
entropy	entropy, mutual information, VI, V
editing distance	editing distance
coreference resolution	MUC (Vilain et al.,1995), B-Cubed (Bagga and Baldwin, 1998), CEAF (Luo, 2005)

Table 3. Summary of Evaluation Measures

3 Applying Graph Clustering to NLP

A variety of structures in NLP can be naturally represented as graphs, e.g., co-occurrence graphs, coreference graphs, word/sentence/ document graphs. In recent years, there have been an increasing amount of interests in applying graph-based clustering to some NLP problems, e.g., document clustering (Zhong and Ghosh, 2004), summarization (Zha, 2002), coreference resolution (Nicolae and Nicolae, 2006), word sense disambiguation (Dorow and Widdows, 2003; Véronis, 2004; Agirre et al., 2007), word clustering (Matsuo et al., 2006; Biemann, 2006). Many authors chose one or two their favorite graph clustering algorithms and claimed the effectiveness by comparing with supervised algorithms (which need expensive annotations) or other non-graph clustering algorithms. As far as we know, there is not much work on the comparative study of various graph-based clustering algorithms for certain NLP problems. As mentioned at the end of section 2.5, there is not a graph clustering algorithm that is effective for all applications. However, it is interesting to find out, for a specific NLP problem, if graph clustering methods can be applied, (1) how the parameters in the graph model affects the performance? (2) Does the NLP problem favor some quality measure and some graph clustering algorithm rather than the others? Unfortunately, this survey neither provides answers for these questions; instead, we overview a few NLP case studies in which some graph-based clustering methods have been successfully applied.

3.1 Coreference Resolution

Coreference resolution is typically defined as the problem of partitioning a set of *mentions* into *entities*. An *entity* is an object or a set of objects in the real world such as *person*, *organization*, *facility*, while a *mention* is a textual reference to an entity. The approaches to solving coreference resolution have shifted from earlier linguistics-based (rely on domain knowledge and hand-crafted rules) to machine-learning based approaches. Elango (2005) and Chen (2010) presented a comprehensive survey on this topic. One of the most prevalent approaches for coreference resolution is to follow a two-step procedure: (1) a classification step that computes how likely one mention corefers with the other and (2) a clustering step that groups the mentions into clusters such that all mentions in a cluster refer to the same entity. In the past years, NLP researchers have explored and enriched this methodology from various directions (either in classification or clustering step). Unfortunately, most of the proposed clustering algorithms, e.g., closest-first clustering (Soon et al., 2001), best-first clustering (Ng and Cardie, 2002), suffer from a drawback: an instant decision is made (in greedy style) when considering two mentions are coreferent or not, therefore, the algorithm makes no attempt to search through the space of all possible clusterings, which results in a sub-optimal clustering (Luo et al., 2004). Various approaches have been proposed to alleviate this problem, of which graph clustering methodology is one of the most promising solutions.

The problem of coreference resolution can be modeled as a graph such that the vertex represents a mention, and the edge weight carries the coreference likelihood between two mentions. Nicolae and Nicolae (2006) proposed a new quality measure named BESTCUT which is to optimize the sum of "correctly" placed vertices in the graph. The BESTCUT algorithm works by performing recursive bisection (similar to *Kernighan-Lin* algorithm) and in each iteration, it searches the best cut that leads to partition into halves. They compared BESTCUT algorithm with (Luo et al., 2004)'s Belltree and (Ng and Cardie, 2002)'s Link-Best algorithm and showed that using ground-truth entities, BESTCUT outperforms the other two with statistical significance (4.8% improvement over Belltree and Link-Best algorithm in ECM F-measure). Nevertheless, we believe that the BESTCUT algorithm is not the only choice and the running complexity of BESTCUT,$O(|V||E| + |V|^2 log|V|)$, is not competitive, thus could be improved by other graph clustering algorithms.

Chen and Ji (2009a) applied normalized spectral algorithm to conduct event coreference resolution: partitioning a set of *mentions* into *events*. An *event* is a specific occurrence involving participants. An *event mention* is a textual reference to an event which includes a distinguished *trigger* (the word that most clearly expresses an event occurs) and involving *arguments* (entities/temporal expressions that play certain roles in the event). A graph is similarly constructed as in entity coreference resolution except that it involves quite different feature engineering (most features are related with event *trigger* and *arguments*). The graph clustering approach yields competitive results by comparing with an agglomerative clustering algorithm proposed in (Chen et al., 2009b), unfortunately, a scientific comparison among the algorithms remains unexplored.

3.2 Word Clustering

Word clustering is a problem defined as clustering a set of words (e.g., nouns, verbs) into groups so that similar words are in the same cluster. Word clustering is a major technique that can benefit many NLP tasks, e.g., thesaurus construction, text classification, and word sense disambiguation. Word clustering can be solved by following a two-step procedure: (1) classification step by representing each word as a feature vector and computing the similarity of two words; (2) clustering step which applies some clustering algorithm, e.g., single-link clustering, complete-link clustering, average-link clustering, such that similar words are grouped together.

Matsuo et al. (2006) presented a graph clustering algorithm for word clustering based on word similarity measures by web counts. A word co-occurrence graph is constructed in which the vertex represents a word, and the edge weight is computed by applying some similarity measure (e.g., PMI, χ^2) on a co-occurrence matrix, which is the result of querying a pair of words to a search engine. Then an agglomerative graph clustering algorithm (Newman, 2004), which is surveyed in section 2.5, is applied. They showed that the similarity measure χ^2 performs better than PMI, for one reason, PMI performs worse when a word group contains rare or frequent words, for the other reason, PMI is sensitive to web output inconsistency, e.g., the web count of $w_1$is below the web count of $w_1 AND w_2$ in extreme case. They also showed that their graph clustering algorithm outperforms average-link agglomerative clustering by almost 32% using χ^2 similarity measure. The concern of their approach is the running complexity for constructing co-occurrence matrix, i.e., for n words, $O(n^2)$ queries are required which is intractable for a large graph.

Ichioka and Fukumoto (2008) applied similar approach as Matsuo et al. (2006) for Japanese Onomatopoetic word clustering, and showed that the approach outperforms k-means clustering by 16.2%.

3.3 Word Sense Disambiguation (WSD)

Word sense disambiguation is the problem of identifying which sense of a word (meaning) is conveyed in the context of a sentence, when the word is polysemic. In contrast to supervised WSD which relies on pre-defined list of senses from dictionaries, unsupervised WSD induces word senses directly from the corpus. Among those unsupervised WSD algorithms, graph-based clustering algorithms have been found competitive with supervised methods, and in many cases outperform most vector-based clustering methods.

Dorow and Widdows (2003) built a co-occurrence graph in which each node represents a noun and two nodes have an edge between them if they co-occur more than a given threshold. They then applied Markov Clustering algorithm (MCL) which is surveyed in section 2.5, but cleverly circumvent the problem of choosing the right parameters. Their algorithm not only recognizes senses of polysemic words, but also provides high-level readable cluster name for each sense. Unfortunately, they neither discussed further how to identify the sense of a word in a given context, nor compared their algorithm with other algorithms by conducting experiments.

Véronis (2004) proposed a graph based model named *HyperLex* based on the small-world properties of co-occurrence graphs. Detecting the different senses (uses) of a word reduces to isolating the high-density components (hubs) in the co-occurrence graph. Those hubs are then used to perform WSD. To obtain the hubs, *HyperLex* finds the vertex with highest relative frequency in the graph at each iteration and if it meets some criteria, it is selected as a hub. Agirre (2007) proposed another method based on *PageRank* for finding hubs. *HyperLex* can detect low-frequency senses (as low as 1%) and most importantly, it offers an excellent precision (97% compared to 73% for baseline). Agirre (2007) further conducted extensive experiments by comparing the two graph based models (*HyperLex* and *PageRank*) with other supervised and non-supervised graph methods and concluded that graph based methods perform close to supervised systems in the lexical sample task and yield the second-best WSD systems for the Senseval-3 all-words task.

4 Conclusions

In this survey, we organize the sparse related literature of graph clustering into a structured presentation and summarize the topic as a five part story, namely, hypothesis, modeling, measure, algorithm, and evaluation. The hypothesis serves as a basis for the whole graph clustering methodology, quality measures and graph clustering algorithms construct the backbone of the methodology, modeling acts as the interface between the real application and the methodology, and evaluation deals with utility. We also survey several typical NLP problems, in which graph-based clustering approaches have been successfully applied.

We have the following final comments on the strengths and weaknesses of graph clustering approaches:

(1) Graph is an elegant data structure that can model many real applications with solid mathematical foundations including spectral theory, Markov stochastic process.

(2) Unlike many other clustering algorithms which act greedily towards the final clustering and thus may miss the optimal clustering, graph clustering transforms the clustering problem into optimizing some quality measure. Unfortunately, those optimization problems are NP-Hard, thus, all proposed graph

clustering algorithms only approximately yield "optimal" clustering.

(3) Graph clustering algorithms have been criticized for low speed when working on large scale graph (with millions of vertices). This may not be true since new graph clustering algorithms have been proposed, e.g., the multilevel graph clustering algorithm (Karypis and Kumar, 1999) can partition a graph with one million vertices into 256 clusters in a few seconds on current generation workstations and PCs. Nevertheless, scalability problem of graph clustering algorithm still needs to be explored which is becoming more important in social network study.

We envision that graph clustering methods can lead to promising solutions in the following emerging NLP problems:

(1) Detection of new entity types, relation types and event types (IE area). For example, the eight event types defined in the ACE[1] program may not be enough for wider usage and more event types can be induced by graph clustering on verbs.

(2) Web people search (IR area). The main issue in web people search is the ambiguity of the person name. Thus by extracting attributes (e.g., attended schools, spouse, children, friends) from returned web pages, constructing person graphs (involving those attributes) and applying graph clustering, we are optimistic to achieve a better person search engine.

Acknowledgments

This work was supported by the U.S. National Science Foundation Faculty Early Career Development (CAREER) Award under Grant IIS-0953149, the U.S. Army Research Laboratory under Cooperative Agreement Number W911NF-09-2-0053, Google, Inc., CUNY Research Enhancement Program, Faculty Publication Program and GRTI Program. The views and conclusions contained in this document are those of the authors and should not be interpreted as representing the official policies, either expressed or implied, of the Army Research Laboratory or the U.S. Government. The U.S. Government is authorized to reproduce and distribute reprints for Government purposes notwithstanding any copyright notation here on.

[1] http://www.nist.gov/speech/tests/ace/

References

A. Bagga and B. Baldwin.1998. Algorithms for scoring coreference chains. *Proc. The First International Conference on Language Resources and Evaluation Workshop on Linguistics Coreference.*

A. Clauset. 2005. Finding local community structure in networks. *Physical Review E*, 72:026132.

B. Dom. 2001. An information-theoretic external cluster-validity measure. *IBM Research Report.*

B. Dorow, D. Widdows. 2003. Discovering corpus-specific word-senses. In *Proc. EACL.*

B. W. Kernighan and S. Lin.1970. An efficient heuristic procedur for partitioning graphs. Bell Syst. Techn. J.,Vol. 49, No. 2, pp. 291–307.

C. Biemann. 2006. Chinese Whispers - an Efficient-Graph Clustering Algorithm and its Application to Natural Language Processing Problems. In *Proc. of the HLT-NAACL-06 Workshop on Textgraphs-06.*

C. Nicolae and G. Nicolae. 2006. Bestcut: A graph algorithm for coreference resolution. In *EMNLP*, pages 275–283, Sydney, Australia.

E. Agirre, D. Martinez, O.L. de Lacalle and A.Soroa. 2007. Two graph-based algorithms for state-of-the-art WSD. In *Proc. EMNLP.*

E. Amigo, J. Gonzalo, J. Artiles and F. Verdejo. 2008. A comparison of extrinsic clustering evaluation metrics based on formal constraints. *Information Retrieval.*

E. Terra and C. L. A. Clarke. Frequency Estimates for Statistical Word Similarity Measures. In *Proc. HLT/NAACL 2003.*

G. Karypis and V. Kumar. 1999. Multilevel algorithms for multiconstraint graph partitioning. in *Proceedings of the 36th ACM/IEEE conference on Design automation conference*, (New Orleans, Louisiana), pp. 343 – 348.

G. W. Flake, R. E. Tarjan and K. Tsioutsiouliklis. 2003. Graph clustering and minimum cut trees. *Internet Mathematics*, 1(4):385–408.

H. Zha.2002. Generic summarization and keyphrase extraction using mutual reinforcement principle and sentence clustering. In *Proc. of SIGIR2002*, pp. 113-120.

J. Chen, O. R. Zaïane, R. Goebel. 2009. Detecting Communities in Social Networks Using Max-Min Modularity. *SDM 2009*: 978-989.

J. Ruan and W. Zhang.2008. Identifying network communities with a high resolution. Physical Review E, 77:016104.

J. Shi and J. Malik. 2000. Normalized Cuts and Image Segmentation. *IEEE Trans. Pattern Analysis and Machine Intelligence*, vol. 22, no. 8, pp. 888-905.

J. Véronis. 2004. HyperLex: Lexical Cartography for Information Retrieval. *Computer Speech & Language* 18(3).

K. Ichioka and F. Fukumoto. 2008. Graph-based clustering for semantic classification of onomatopoetic words. In *Proc. of the 3rd Textgraphs Workshop on Graph-based Algorithms for Natural Language Processing.*

L. Hagen and A. B. Kahng. 1992. New spectral methods for ratio cut partitioning and clustering. *IEEE Transactions Computer-Aided Design*, Santa Clara CA, 422-427.

L. R. Ford, D. R. Fulkerson. 1956. Maximal flow through a network. *Canadian Journal of Mathematics* 8: 399–404.

M. E. J. Newman. 2004. Detecting community structure in networks. Eur. Phys. J. B, 38, 321–330.

M. E. J. Newman. 2004. Fast algorithm for detecting community structure in networks. *Phys Rev E.* 69, 2004.

M. E. J. Newman and M. Girvan. 2004. Finding and evaluating community structure in networks. *Phys. Rev. E* 69,026113.

M. Girvan and M. E. J. Newman. 2002. Community structure in social and biological networks. *Proc. Natl. Acad. Sci.* USA 99, 7821-7826.

M. Meila. 2003. Comparing clusterings. In *Proceedings of COLT03.*

M. Vilain, J. Burger, J. Aberdeen, D. Connolly and L. Hirschman.1995. A model-theoretic coreference scoring scheme. In *Proceedings of the Sixth Message Understanding Conference (MUC-6).*

P. Elango. 2005. Coreference Resolution: A Survey. *Technical Report*, University of Wisconsin Madison.

R. Kannan, S. Vempala, and A. Vetta. 2000. On clusterings:good, bad and spectral. In *Proceedings of the 41st Annual Symposium on Foundations of Computer Science.*

S. Abney. 2007. Semi-supervised Learning for Computational Linguistics, Chapman and Hall.

S. E. Schaeffer. 2007. Graph clustering. *Computer Science Review*, 1(1):27–64.

S. Fortunato, V. Latora, and M. Marchiori. 2004. A Method to Find Community Structures Based on Information Centrality. *Phys Rev E.*70, 056104.

S. van Dongen. 2000. Graph Clustering by Flow Simulation. *PhD thesis*, University of Utrecht.

S. White and P. Smyth. 2005. A spectral clustering approach to finding communities in graphs. In *SIAM International Conference on Data Mining.*

U. Brandes, M. Gaertler, and D. Wagner. 2003. Experiments on graph clustering algorithms. *Proc. 11th European Symp. Algorithms, LNCS* 2832:568-579.

U. Brandes, M. Gaertler, and D.Wagner. 2007. Engineering graph clustering: Models and experimental evaluation. *J. Exp. Algorithmics*, 12:1.1.

U. Luxburg, O. Bousquet, M. Belkin. 2005. Limits of spectral clustering. In *L. K. Saul, Y. Weiss and L. Bottou (Eds.), Advances in neural information processing systems* 17. Cambridge, MA: MIT Press.

U. Luxburg.2006. A tutorial on spectral clustering. Technical Report 149, *Max Plank Institute for Biological Cybernetics.*

V. Ng and C. Cardie. 2002. Improving machine learning approaches to coreference resolution. In *Proc. Of the ACL*, pages 104–111.

W. M. Soon, H. T. Ng and D. Lim.2001. A machine learning approach to coreference resolution of noun phrases. *Computational Linguistics*, 27(4):521–544.

X. Luo. 2005. On coreference resolution performance metrics. *Proc. of HLT-EMNLP.*

X. Luo, A. Ittycheriah, H. Jing, N. Kambhatla and S. Roukos. 2004. A mention-synchronous coreference resolution algorithm based on the Bell Tree. In *Proc. of ACL-04*, pp.136–143.

Y. Matsuo, T. Sakaki, K. Uchiyama, and M. Ishizuka. 2006. Graph-based word clustering using web search engine. In *Proc. of EMNLP 2006.*

Z. Chen and H. Ji. 2009a. Graph-based Event Coreference Resolution. In *Proc. ACL-IJCNLP 2009 workshop on TextGraphs-4: Graph-based Methods for Natural Language Processing.*

Z. Chen, H. Ji, R. Haralick. 2009b. A Pairwise Coreference Model, Feature Impact and Evaluation for Event Coreference Resolution. In *Proc. RANLP 2009 workshop on Events in Emerging Text Types.*

Z. Chen. 2010. Graph-based Clustering and its Application in Coreference Resolution. *Technical Report*, the Graduate Center, the City University of New York.

Towards the Automatic Creation of a Wordnet from a Term-based Lexical Network

Hugo Gonçalo Oliveira*
CISUC, University of Coimbra
Portugal
hroliv@dei.uc.pt

Paulo Gomes
CISUC, University of Coimbra
Portugal
pgomes@dei.uc.pt

Abstract

The work described here aims to create a wordnet automatically from a semantic network based on terms. So, a clustering procedure is ran over a synonymy network, in order to obtain synsets. Then, the term arguments of each relational triple are assigned to the latter, originating a wordnet. Experiments towards our goal are reported and their results validated.

1 Introduction

In order perform tasks where understanding the information conveyed by natural language is critical, today's applications demand better access to semantic knowledge. Knowledge about words and their meanings is typically structured in lexical ontologies, such as Princeton WordNet (Fellbaum, 1998), but this kind of resources is most of the times handcrafted, which implies much time-consuming human effort. So, the automatic construction of such resources arises as an alternative, providing less intensive labour, easier maintenance and allowing for higher coverage, as a trade-off for lower, but still acceptable, precision.

This paper is written in the scope of a project where several textual resources are being exploited for the construction of a lexical ontology for Portuguese. We have already made a first approach on the extraction of relational triples from text, where, likewise Hearst (1992), we take advantage of textual patterns indicating semantic relations. However, the extracted triples are held between two terms, which is not enough to build a lexical ontology capable of dealing with ambiguity.

Therefore, we present our current approach towards the automatic integration of lexico-semantic knowledge into a single independent lexical ontology, which will be structured on concepts and adopt a model close to WordNet's. The task of establishing synsets and mapping term-based triples to them is closely related to word sense disambiguation, where the only available context consists of the connections in the term-base network.

After contextualising this work, our approach is described. It involves (i) a clustering procedure for obtaining a thesaurus from a synonymy network, (ii) the augmentation of the later with manually created thesaurus, and (iii) mapping term-based relational triples to the thesaurus, to obtain a wordnet. Then, our experimentation results, as well as their validation, are presented. Briefly, we have tested the proposed approach on a term-based lexical network, extracted automatically from a dictionary. Synsets were validated manually while the attached triples were validated with the help of a web search engine.

2 Context

Our ultimate goal is the automatic construction of a broad-coverage structure of words according to their meanings, also known as a lexical ontology, the first subject of this section. We proceed with a brief overview on work concerned with moving from term-based knowledge to synset-based knowledge, often called ontologising.

2.1 Lexical Ontologies

Despite some terminological issues, lexical ontologies can be seen both as a lexicon and as an ontology (Hirst, 2004) and are significantly different from classic ontologies (Gruber, 1993). They are not based on a specific domain and are intended to provide knowledge structured on lexical items (words) of a language by relating them according to their meaning. Moreover, the main goal of a lexical ontology is to assemble lexical and semantic information, instead of storing common-sense knowledge (Wandmacher et al., 2007).

*supported by FCT scholarship SFRH/BD/44955/2008.

Proceedings of the 2010 Workshop on Graph-based Methods for Natural Language Processing, ACL 2010, pages 10–18,
Uppsala, Sweden, 16 July 2010.

Princeton WordNet (Fellbaum, 1998) is the most representative lexico-semantic resource for English and also the most accepted model of a lexical ontology. It is structured around groups of synonymous words (synsets), which describe concepts, and connections, denoting semantic relations between those groups. The success of WordNet led to the adoption of its model by lexical resources in different languages, such as the ones in the EuroWordNet project (Vossen, 1997), or WordNet.PT (Marrafa, 2002), for Portuguese.

However, the creation of a wordnet, as well as the creation of most ontologies, is typically manual and involves much human effort. Some authors (de Melo and Weikum, 2008) propose translating Princeton WordNet to wordnets in other languages, but if this might be suitable for several applications, a problem arises because different languages represent different socio-cultural realities, do not cover exactly the same part of the lexicon and, even where they seem to be common, several concepts are lexicalised differently (Hirst, 2004).

Another popular alternative is to extract lexico-semantic knowledge and learn lexical ontologies from text. Research on this field is not new and varied methods have been proposed to achieve different steps of this task including the extraction of semantic relations (e.g. (Hearst, 1992) (Girju et al., 2006)) or sets of similar words (e.g. (Lin and Pantel, 2002) (Turney, 2001)).

Whereas the aforementioned works are based on unstructured text, dictionaries started earlier (Calzolari et al., 1973) to be seen as an attractive target for the automatic acquisition of lexico-semantic knowledge. MindNet (Richardson et al., 1998) is both an extraction methodology and a lexical ontology different from a wordnet, since it was created automatically from a dictionary and its structure is based on such resources. Nevertheless, it still connects sense records with semantic relations (e.g. hyponymy, cause, manner).

For Portuguese, PAPEL (Gonçalo Oliveira et al., 2009) is a lexical network consisting of triples denoting semantic relations between words found in a dictionary. Other Portuguese lexical ontologies, created by different means, are reviewed and compared in (Santos et al., 2009) and (Teixeira et al., 2010).

Besides corpora and dictionary processing, in the later years, semi-structured collaborative resources, such as Wikipedia or Wiktionary, have proved to be important sources of lexico-semantic knowledge and have thus been receiving more and more attention by the community (see for instance (Zesch et al., 2008) (Navarro et al., 2009)).

2.2 Other Relevant Work

Most of the methods proposed to extract relations from text have term-based triples as output. Such a triple, *term1* RELATION *term2*, indicates that a possible meaning of *term1* is related to a possible meaning of *term2* by means of a RELATION.

Although it is possible to create a lexical network from the latter, this kind of networks is often impractical for computational applications, such as the ones that deal with inference. For instance, applying a simple transitive rule, a SYNONYM_OF $b \wedge b$ SYNONYM_OF $c \rightarrow a$ SYNONYM_OF c over a set of term-based triples can lead to serious inconsistencies. A curious example in Portuguese, where synonymy between two completely opposite words is inferred, is reported in (Gonçalo Oliveira et al., 2009): *queda* SYNONYM_OF *ruína* $\wedge$ *queda* SYNONYM_OF *habilidade* $\rightarrow$ *ruína* SYNONYM_OF *habilidade*. This happens because natural language is ambiguous, especially when dealing with broad-coverage knowledge. In the given example, *queda* can either mean *downfall* or *aptitude*, while *ruína* means *ruin*, *destruction*, *downfall*.

A possible way to deal with ambiguity is to adopt a wordnet-like structure, where concepts are described by synsets and ambiguous words are included in a synset for each of their meanings. Semantic relations can thereby be unambiguously established between two synsets, and concepts, even though described by groups of words, bring together natural language and knowledge engineering in a suitable representation, for instance, for the Semantic Web (Berners-Lee et al., 2001). Of course that, from a linguistic point of view, word senses are complex and overlapping structures (Kilgarriff, 1997) (Hirst, 2004). So, despite word sense divisions in dictionaries and ontologies being most of the times artificial, this trade-off is needed in order to increase the usability of broad-coverage computational lexical resources.

In order to move from term-based triples to an ontology, Soderland and Mandhani (2007) describe a procedure where, besides other stages, terms in triples are assigned to WordNet synsets. Starting with all the synsets containing a term in a triple, the term is assigned to the synset with higher similarity to the contexts from where the triple was extracted, computed based on the terms in the synset, sibling synsets and direct hyponym synsets.

Two other methods for ontologising term-based triples are presented by Pantel and Pennacchiotti (2008). One assumes that terms with the same relation to a fixed term are more plausible to describe the correct sense, so, to select the correct synset, it exploits triples of the same type sharing one argument. The other method, which seems to perform better, selects suitable synsets using generalisation through hypernymy links in WordNet.

There are other works where WordNet is enriched, for instance with information in its glosses, domain knowledge extracted from text (e.g. (Harabagiu and Moldovan, 2000) (Navigli et al., 2004)) or wikipedia entries (e.g. (Ruiz-Casado et al., 2005)), thus requiring a disambiguation phase where terms are assigned to synsets.

In the construction of a lexical ontology, synonymy plays an important role because it defines the conceptual base of the knowledge to be represented. One of the reasons for using WordNet synsets as a starting point for its representation is that, while it is quite straightforward to define a set of textual patterns indicative of several semantic relations between words (e.g. hyponymy, part-of, cause) with relatively good quality, the same does not apply for synonymy. In opposition to other kinds of relation, synonymous words, despite typically sharing similar neighbourhoods, may not co-occur frequently in unstructured text, especially in the same sentence (Dorow, 2006), leading to few indicative textual patterns. Therefore, most of the works on synonymy extraction from corpora rely on statistics or graph-based methods (e.g. (Lin and Pantel, 2002) (Turney, 2001) (Dorow, 2006)). Nevertheless, methods for synonymy identification based on co-occurrences (e.g. (Turney, 2001)) are more prone to identify similar words or near synonyms than real synonyms.

On the other hand, synonymy instances can be quite easily extracted from resources structured on words and meanings, such as dictionaries, by taking advantage not only of textual patterns, more frequent in those resources (e.g. *também conhecido por/como*, *o mesmo que*, for Portuguese), but also of definitions consisting of only one word or a enumeration, which typically contain synonyms of the defined word. So, as it is possible to create a lexical network from a set of relational triples ($a\ R\ b$), a synonymy network can be created out of synonymy instances (a SYNONYM_OF b). Since these networks tend to have a clustered structure, Gfeller et al. (2005) propose a clustering procedure to improve their utility.

3 Research Goals

The research presented here is in the scope of a project whose final goal is to create a lexical ontology for Portuguese by automatic means. Although there are clear advantages of using resources already structured on words and meanings, dictionaries are static resources which contain limited knowledge and are not always available for this kind of research. On the other hand, there is much text available on the most different subjects, but free text has few boundaries, leading to more ambiguity and parsing issues.

Therefore, it seems natural to create a lexical ontology with knowledge from several textual sources, from (i) high precision structured resources, such as manually created thesaurus, to (ii) semi-structured resources such as dictionaries or collaborative encyclopedias, as well as (iii) unstructured textual corpora. Likewise Wandmacher et al. (2007) propose for creating a lexical ontology for German, these are the general lines we will follow in our research, but for Portuguese.

Considering each resource specificities, including its organisation or the vocabulary used, the extraction procedures might be significantly different, but they should all have one common output: a set of term-based relational triples that will be integrated in a single lexical ontology.

Whereas the lexical network established by the triples could be used, these networks are not suitable for several tasks, as discussed in Section 2.2. A fragment of a synonymy network extracted from a Portuguese dictionary can be seen in Figure 1. Since all the connections imply synonymy, the network suggests that all the words are synonymous, which is not true. For example, the word *copista* may have two very distinct meanings: (a) a person who writes copies of written documents or (b) someone who drinks a lot of wine. On the other hand, other words which may refer to the same concept as, for instance, meaning (a) of *copista*, such as *escrevente*, *escrivão* or *transcritor*.

So, in order to deal with ambiguity in natural

language, we will adopt a wordnet-like structure which enables the establishment of unambiguous semantic relations between synsets.

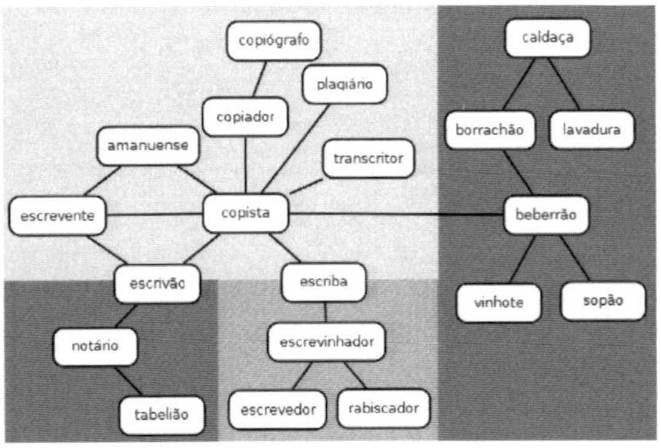

Figure 1: Fragment of a synonymy network.

4 Approach

Considering our goal, a set of term-based triples goes through the following stages: (i) clustering over the synonymy network for the establishment of synsets, to obtain a thesaurus; (ii) augmentation of the thesaurus by merging it with synsets from other resources; (iii) assignment of each argument of a term-based triple (except synonymy) to a synset in the thesaurus, to obtain a wordnet. Note that stages (i) and (ii) are not both mandatory, but at least one must be performed to obtain the synsets.

Looking at some of the works referred in Section 2.2, ours is different because it does not require a conceptual base such as WordNet. Also, it integrates knowledge from different sources and tries to disambiguate each word using only knowledge already extracted and not the context where the word occurs.

4.1 Clustering for a thesaurus

This stage was originally defined after looking at disconnected pieces of a synonymy network extracted from a dictionary, which had a clustered structure apparently suitable for identifying synsets. This is also noticed by Gfeller et al. (2005) who have used the Markov Clustering algorithm (MCL) (van Dongen, 2000) to find clusters in a synonymy network.

Therefore, since MCL had already been applied to problems very close to ours (e.g. (Gfeller et al., 2005), (Dorow, 2006)), it seemed to suit our purpose – it would not only organise a term-based network into a thesaurus, but, if a network extracted from several resources is used, clustering would homogenise the synonymy representation.

MCL finds clusters by simulating random walks within a graph by alternately computing random walks of higher length, and increasing the probabilities of intra-cluster walks. It can be briefly described in five steps: (i) take the adjacency matrix A of the graph; (ii) normalise each column of A to 1 in order to obtain a stochastic matrix S; (iii) compute S^2; (iv) take the γth power of every element of S^2 and normalise each column to 1[1]; (v) go back to (ii) util MCL converges to a matrix idempotent under steps (ii) and (iii).

Since MCL is a hard-clustering algorithm, it assigns each term to only one cluster thus removing ambiguities. To deal with this, Gfeller et al. (2005) propose an extension to MCL for finding unstable nodes in the graph, which frequently denote ambiguous words. This is done by adding random stochastic noise, δ, to the non-zero entries of the adjacency matrix and then running MCL with noise several times. Looking at the clusters obtained by each run, a new matrix can be filled based on the probability of each pair of words belonging to the same cluster.

We have adopted this procedure, with slight differences. First, we observed that, for the network we used, the obtained clusters were closer to the desired results if $-0.5 < \delta < 0.5$. Additionally, in the first step of MCL, we use frequency-weighted adjacency matrixes F, where each element F_{ij} corresponds to the number of existing synonymy instances between i and j. Although using only one dictionary each synonymy instance will be extracted at most two times (*a* SYNONYM_OF *b* and *b* SYNONYM_OF *a*), if more resources are used, it will strengthen the probability that two words appearing frequently as synonyms belong to the same cluster.

Therefore, the clustering stage has the following steps: (i) split the original network into sub-networks, such that there is no path between two elements in different sub-networks, and calculate the frequency-weighted adjacency matrix F of each sub-network; (ii) add stochastic noise to each entry of F, $F_{ij} = F_{ij} + F_{ij} * \delta$; (iii) run MCL, with $\gamma = 1.6$, over F for 30 times; (iv) use the (hard) clustering obtained by each one of the 30 runs to create a new matrix P with the probabil-

[1]Increasing γ (typically $1.5 < \gamma < 2$) increases the granularity of the clusters.

ities of each pair of words in F belonging to the same cluster; (v) create the clusters based on P and on a given threshold $\theta = 0.2$. If $P_{ij} > \theta$, i and j belong to the same cluster; (vi) in order to clean the results, remove: (a) big clusters, B, if there is a group of clusters $C = C_1, C_2, ...C_n$ such that $B = C_1 \cup C_2 \cup ... \cup C_n$; (b) clusters completely included in other clusters. Applying this procedure to the network in Figure 1 results in the four represented clusters. There, ambiguous words *escrivão* and *escriba* are included in two different clusters.

4.2 Merging synsets for thesaurus augmentation

In this stage, other resources with synsets, such as manually created thesaurus, are merged together and then merged with the thesaurus obtained in the previous stage, by the following procedure: (i) define one thesaurus as the basis B and the other as T; (ii) create a new empty thesaurus M and copy all the synsets in B to M; (iii) for each synset $T_i \in T$, find the synsets $B_i \in B$ with higher Jaccard coefficient[2] c, and add them to a set of synsets $J \subset B$. (iv) considering c and J, do one of the following: (a) if $c = 1$, it means that the synset is already in M, so nothing is done; (b) if $c = 0$, T_i is copied to M; (c) if $|J| = 1$, the synset in J is copied to M; (d) if $|J| > 1$, a new set, $n = T_i \cup J'$ where $J' = \cup_{i=0}^{|J|} J_i$, $J_i \in J$, is created, and all elements of J are removed from M.

The synsets of the resulting thesaurus will be used as the conceptual base in which the term-based triples are going to be mapped.

4.3 Assigning terms to synsets

After the previous stages, the following are available: (i) a thesaurus T and (ii) a term-based semantic network, N, where each edge has a type, R, and denotes a semantic relation held between the meaning of the terms in the two nodes it connects. Using T and N, this stage tries to map term-based triples to synset-based triples, or, in other words, assign each term, a and b, in each triple, $(a\ R\ b) \in N$, to suitable synsets. The result is a knowledge base organised as a wordnet.

In order to assign a to a synset A, b is fixed and all the synsets containing a, $S_a \subset T$, are collected. If a is not in the thesaurus, it is assigned to a new synset $A = (a)$. Otherwise, for each synset $S_{ai} \in S_a$, n_{ai} is the number of terms $t \in S_{ai}$ such that $(t\ R\ b)$ holds[3]. Then, $p_{ai} = \frac{n_{ai}}{|S_{ai}|}$ is calculated. Finally, all the synsets with the highest p_{ai} are added to C and (i) if $|C| = 1$, a is assigned to the only synset in C; (ii) if $|C| > 1$, C' is the set of elements of C with the highest n_a and, if $|C'| = 1$, a is assigned the synset in C', unless $p_{ai} < \theta$ [4]; (iii) if it is not possible to assign a synset to a, it remains unassigned. Term b is assigned to a synset using this procedure, but fixing a.

If hypernymy links are already established, semi-mapped triples, where one of the arguments is assigned to a synset and the other is not, $(A\ R\ b)$ or $(a\ R\ B)$, go to a second phase. There, hypernymy is exploited together with the assignment candidates, in C, to help assigning the unassigned term in each semi-mapped triple, or to remove triples that can be inferred. Take for instance $(A\ R\ b)$. If there is one synset $C_i \in C$ with:

- a hypernym synset H, (H HYPERNYM_OF C_i) and a triple $(A\ R\ H)$, b would be assigned to C_i, but, since hyponyms inherit all the properties of their hypernym, the resulting triple can be inferred and is thus ignored:
  $(A\ R\ H) \wedge (H$ HYPERNYM_OF $C_i) \rightarrow (A\ R\ C_i)$[5]

  For example, if H=(*mammal*) and C_i=(*dog*), possible values of A and R are A=(*hair*) R=PART_OF; A=(*animal*) R=HYPERNYM_OF

- a hyponym synset H, (C_i HYPERNYM_OF H) and a triple $(A\ R\ H)$, b is assigned to C_i. Furthermore, if all the hyponyms of C_i, (C_i HYPERNYM_OF I_i), are also related to A in the same way, $(A\ R\ I_i)$, it can be inferred that I_i inherits the relation from C_i. So, all the later triples can be inferred and thus removed.

  For example, if H=(*dog*), I_i=(*cat*), I_j=(*mouse*) and C_i=(*mammal*), possible values of A and R are A=(*hair*) R=PART_OF; A=(*animal*) R=HYPERNYM_OF

[2] $Jaccard(A, B) = A \cap B / A \cup B$

[3] If R is a transitive relation, the procedure may benefit from applying one level of transitivity to the network: $x\ R\ y \wedge y\ R\ z \rightarrow x\ R\ z$. However, since relations are held between terms, some obtained triples might be incorrect. So, although the latter can be used to help selecting a suitable synset, they should not be mapped to synsets themselves.

[4] θ is a threshold defined to avoid that a is assigned to a big synset where a, itself, is the only term related to b

[5] Before applying these rules it is necessary to make sure that all relations are represented only in one way, otherwise they might not work. For instance, if the decision is to represent *part-of* triples in the form *part* PART_OF *whole*, triples *whole* HAS_PART *part* must be reversed. Furthermore, these rules assume that hypernymy relations are all represented *hypernym* HYPERNYM_OF *hyponym* and not *hyponym* HYPONYM_OF *hypernym*.

5 Experimentation

In this section we report experimental results obtained after applying our procedure to part of the lexical network of PAPEL (Gonçalo Oliveira et al., 2009). The clustering procedure was first ran over PAPEL's noun synonymy network in order to obtain the synsets which were later merged with two manually created thesaurus. Finally, hypernym-of, member-of and part-of triples of PAPEL were mapped to the thesaurus by assigning a synset to each term argument.

5.1 Resources used

For experimentation purposes, freely available lexical resources for Portuguese were used. First, the last version of PAPEL, 2.0, a lexical network for Portuguese created automatically from a dictionary, as referred in Section 2. PAPEL 2.0 contains approximately 100,000 words, identified by their orthographical form, and approximately 200,000 term-based triples relating the words by different types of semantic relations.

In order to enrich the thesaurus obtained from PAPEL, TeP (Dias-Da-Silva and de Moraes, 2003) and OpenThesaurus.PT[6] (OT), were used. Both of them are manually created thesaurus, for Brazilian Portuguese and European Portuguese respectively, modelled after Princeton WordNet (Fellbaum, 1998) and thus containing synsets. Besides being the only freely available thesaurus for Portuguese we know about, TeP and OT were used together with PAPEL because, despite representing the same kind of knowledge, they are mostly complementary, which is also observed by (Teixeira et al., 2010) and (Santos et al., 2009).

Note that, for experimentation purposes, we have only used the parts of these resources concerning nouns.

5.2 Thesaurus creation

The first step for applying the clustering procedure is to create PAPEL's synonymy network, which is established by its synonymy instances, a SYNONYM_OF b. After splitting the network into independent disconnected sub-networks, we noticed that it was composed by a huge sub-network, with more than 16,000 nodes, and several very small networks. If ambiguity was not resolved, this would suggest that all the 16,000 words had the same meaning, which is not true.

[6]http://openthesaurus.caixamagica.pt/

		TeP	OT	CLIP	TOP
Words	**Quantity**	17,158	5,819	23,741	30,554
	Ambiguous	5,867	442	12,196	13,294
	Most ambiguous	20	4	47	21
Synsets	**Quantity**	8,254	1,872	7,468	9,960
	Avg. size	3.51	3.37	12.57	6.6
	Biggest	21	14	103	277

Table 1: (Noun) thesaurus in numbers.

		Hypernym_of	Part_of	Member_of
Term-based triples		62,591	2,805	5,929
1st	**Mapped**	27,750	1,460	3,962
	Same synset	233	5	12
	Already present	3,970	40	167
Semi-mapped triples		7,952	262	357
2nd	**Mapped**	88	1	0
	Could be inferred	50	0	0
	Already present	13	0	0
Synset-based triples		23,572	1,416	3,783

Table 2: Results of triples mapping

A small sample of this problem can be observed in Figure 1.

We then ran the clustering procedure and the thesaurus of PAPEL, CLIP, was obtained. Finally, we used TeP as the base thesaurus and merged it, first with OT, and then with CLIP, giving rise to the noun thesaurus we used in the rest of the experimentation, TOP.

Table 1 contains information about each one of the thesaurus, more precisely, the quantity of words, words belonging to more than one synset (ambiguous), the number of synsets where the most ambiguous word occurs, the quantity of synsets, the average synset size (number of words), and the size of the biggest synset[7].

5.3 Mapping the triples

The mapping procedure was applied to all the hypernym-of, part-of and member-of term-based triples of PAPEL, distributed according to Table 2 where additional numbers on the mapping are presented. After the first phase of the mapping, 33,172 triples had both of their terms assigned to a synset, and 10,530 had only one assigned. However, 4,427 were not really added, either because the same synset was assigned to both of the terms or because the triple had already been added after analysing other term-based triple. In the second phase, only 89 new triples were mapped and, from those, 13 had previously been added while other 50 triples were discarded or not attached because they could be inferred. Another interesting fact is that 19,638 triples were attached to a synset with only one term. From those, 5,703 had a synset

[7]Synsets with only one word were ignored in the construction of Table 1.

with only one term in both arguments.

We ended up with a wordnet with 27,637 synsets, 23,572 hypernym-of, 1,416 part-of and 3,783 member-of synset-based triples.

6 Validation of the results

Evaluation of a new broad-coverage ontology is most of the times performed by one of two means: (i) manual evaluation of a representative subset of the results; (ii) automatic comparison with a gold standard. However, while for English most researchers use Princeton WordNet as a gold standard, for other languages it is difficult to find suitable and freely available consensual resources. Considering Portuguese, as we have said earlier, TeP and OT are effectively two manually created thesaurus but, since they are more complementary than overlapping to PAPEL, we thought it would be better to use them to enrich our resource.

There is actually a report (Raman and Bhattacharyya, 2008) with an automatic evaluation of synsets, but we decided no to follow it because this evaluation is heavily based on a dictionary and we do not have unrestricted access to a full and updated dictionary of Portuguese and also, indirectly by PAPEL, a dictionary was one of our main sources of information.

Therefore, our choice relied on manual validation of the synsets of CLIP and TOP. Furthermore, synset-based triples were validated in an alternative automatic way using a web search engine.

6.1 Manual validation of synsets

Ten reviewers took part in the validation of ten random samples with approximately 50 synsets from each thesaurus. We made sure that each synset was not in more than one sample and synsets with more than 50 terms were not validated. Also, in order to measure the reviewer agreement, each sample was analysed by two different reviewers. Given a sample, each reviewer had to classify each synset as: correct (1), if, in some context, all the terms of the synset could have the same meaning, or incorrect (0), if at least one term of the synset could never mean the same as the others. The reviewers were advised to look for the possible meanings of each word in different dictionaries. Still, if they could not find them, or if they did not know how to classify the synset, they had a third option, N/A (2).

In the end, 519 synsets of CLIP and 480 of TOP were validated. When organising the validation results we noticed that the biggest synsets were the ones with more problems. So, besides the complete validation results, Table 3 also contains the results considering only synsets of ten or less words, when a ' is after the name of the thesaurus. The presented numbers are the average between the classifications given by the two reviewers and the agreement rate corresponds to the number of times both reviewers agreed on the classification.

Even though these results might be subjective, since they are based on the reviewers criteria and on the dictionaries they used, they can give an insight on the quality of the synsets. The precision results are acceptable and are improved if the automatically created thesaurus is merged with the ones created manually, and also when bigger synsets are ignored. Most of the times, big synsets are confusing because they bring together more than one concept that share at least one term. For instance, take the synset: *insobriedade, desmedida, imoderação, excesso, nimiedade, desmando, desbragamento, troco, descontrolo, superabundância, desbunda, desregramento, demasia, incontinência, imodicidade, superação, intemperança, descomedimento, superfluidade, sobejidão, acrasia*, where there is a mix of the concepts: (a) insobriety, not following all the rules, heedless of the consequences and, (b) surplus. Both of these concepts can be referred to as an *excess* (*excesso*).

6.2 Automatic validation of triples

The automatic validation of the triples attached to our wordnet consisted of using Google web search engine to look for evidence on their truth. This procedure started by removing terms whose occurrences in Google were less than 5,000. Synsets that became empty were not considered and, from the rest, a sample was selected for each one of the three types of relation.

Following the idea in (Gonçalo Oliveira et al., 2009), a set of natural language generic patterns, indicative of each relation, was defined having in mind their input to Google[8]. Then, for each triple $(A\ R\ B)$, the patterns were used to search for ev-

[8]Hypernymy patterns included: [hypo] *é um|uma (tipo|forma|variedade|...)* de* [hyper], [hypo] *e outros|outras* [hyper] or [hyper] *tais como* [hypo]. Patterns for part-of and member-of were the same because these relations can be expressed in very similar ways, and included: [part/member] *é (parte|membro|porção) do|da* [whole/group], [part/member] *(faz parte)* do|da* [whole/group] or [whole/group] *é um (grupo|conjunto|...) de* [part/member].

	Sample	Correct	Incorrect	N/A	Agreement
CLIP	519 sets	65.8%	31.7%	2.5%	76.1%
CLIP'	310 sets	81.1%	16.9%	2.0%	84.2%
TOP	480 sets	83.2%	15.8%	1.0%	82.3%
TOP'	448 sets	86.8%	12.3%	0.9%	83.0%

Table 3: Results of manual synset validation.

Relation	**Sample size**	**Validation**
Hypernymy_of	419 synsets	44,1%
Member_of	379 synsets	24,3%
Part_of	290 synsets	24,8%

Table 4: Automatic validation of triples

idence on each combination of terms $a \in A$ and $b \in B$ connected by a pattern indicative of R. The triple validation score was then calculated by expression 1, where $found(A, B, R) = 1$ if evidence is found for the triple or 0 otherwise.

$$score = \frac{\sum_{i=1}^{|A|} \sum_{j=1}^{|B|} found(A, B, R)}{|A| * |B|} \quad (1)$$

Table 4 shows the results obtained for each validated sample. Pantel and Pennacchiotti (2008) perform a similar task and present precision results for part-of (40.7%-57.4%) and causation (40.0%-45%) relations. It is however not possible to make a straight comparison. For their experimentation, they selected only correct term-based triples extracted from text and their results were manually validated by human judges. On the other hand, we have used term-based triples extracted automatically from a dictionary, with high but not 100% precision, from where we did not choose only the correct ones, and we have used synsets obtained from our clustering procedure which, once again, have lower precision. Moreover, we validated our results with Google where, despite its huge dimension, there are plenty of ways to denote a semantic relation, when we had just a small set textual patterns. Also, despite occurring more than 5,000 times in Google, some terms correctly included in a synset were conveying less common meanings.

Nevertheless, we could not agree more with Pantel and Pennacchiotti (2008) who state that attaching term-based triples to an ontology is not an easy task. Therefore, we believe our results to be promising and, if more refined rules are added to our set, which is still very simple, they will surely be improved.

7 Concluding remarks

We have presented our first approach on two crucial steps on the automatic creation of a wordnet lexical ontology. Clustering proved to be a good alternative to create a thesaurus from a dictionary's synonymy network, while a few rules can be defined to attach a substantial number of term-based triples to a synset based resource.

Despite interesting results, in the future we will work on refining the attachment rules and start integrating other relations such as causation or purpose. Furthermore, we are devising new methods for attaching terms to synsets. For instance, we have recently started to do some experiences with an attaching method which uses the lexical network's adjacency matrix to find the most similar pair of synsets, each of them containing one of the arguments of a term-based triple.

References

Tim Berners-Lee, James Hendler, and Ora Lassila. 2001. The Semantic Web. *Scientific American*, May.

Nicoletta Calzolari, Laura Pecchia, and Antonio Zampolli. 1973. Working on the italian machine dictionary: a semantic approach. In *Proc. 5th Conference on Computational Linguistics*, pages 49–52, Morristown, NJ, USA. Association for Computational Linguistics.

Gerard de Melo and Gerhard Weikum. 2008. On the utility of automatically generated wordnets. In *Proc. 4th Global WordNet Conf. (GWC)*, pages 147–161, Szeged, Hungary. University of Szeged.

Bento Carlos Dias-Da-Silva and Helio Roberto de Moraes. 2003. A construção de um thesaurus eletrônico para o português do Brasil. *ALFA*, 47(2):101–115.

Beate Dorow. 2006. *A Graph Model for Words and their Meanings*. Ph.D. thesis, Institut fur Maschinelle Sprachverarbeitung der Universitat Stuttgart.

Christiane Fellbaum, editor. 1998. *WordNet: An Electronic Lexical Database (Language, Speech, and Communication)*. The MIT Press.

David Gfeller, Jean-Cédric Chappelier, and Paulo De Los Rios. 2005. Synonym Dictionary Improvement through Markov Clustering and Clustering Stability. In *Proc. of International Symposium on Applied Stochastic Models and Data Analysis (ASMDA)*, pages 106–113.

Roxana Girju, Adriana Badulescu, and Dan Moldovan. 2006. Automatic discovery of part-whole relations. *Computational Linguistics*, 32(1):83–135.

Hugo Gonçalo Oliveira, Diana Santos, and Paulo Gomes. 2009. Relations extracted from a portuguese dictionary: results and first evaluation. In *Local Proc. 14th Portuguese Conf. on Artificial Intelligence (EPIA)*.

Thomas R. Gruber. 1993. A translation approach to portable ontology specifications. *Knowledge Acquisition*, 5(2):199–220.

Sanda M. Harabagiu and Dan I. Moldovan. 2000. Enriching the wordnet taxonomy with contextual knowledge acquired from text. In *Natural language processing and knowledge representation: language for knowledge and knowledge for language*, pages 301–333. MIT Press, Cambridge, MA, USA.

Marti A. Hearst. 1992. Automatic acquisition of hyponyms from large text corpora. In *Proc. 14th Conf. on Computational Linguistics*, pages 539–545, Morristown, NJ, USA. Association for Computational Linguistics.

Graeme Hirst. 2004. Ontology and the lexicon. In Steffen Staab and Rudi Studer, editors, *Handbook on Ontologies*, International Handbooks on Information Systems, pages 209–230. Springer.

Adam Kilgarriff. 1997. "I don't believe in word senses". *Computing and the Humanities*, 31(2):91–113.

Dekang Lin and Patrick Pantel. 2002. Concept discovery from text. In *Proc. 19th Intl. Conf. on Computational Linguistics (COLING)*, pages 577–583.

Palmira Marrafa. 2002. Portuguese Wordnet: general architecture and internal semantic relations. *DELTA*, 18:131–146.

Emmanuel Navarro, Franck Sajous, Bruno Gaume, Laurent Prévot, ShuKai Hsieh, Tzu Y. Kuo, Pierre Magistry, and Chu R. Huang. 2009. Wiktionary and nlp: Improving synonymy networks. In *Proc. Workshop on The People's Web Meets NLP: Collaboratively Constructed Semantic Resources*, pages 19–27, Suntec, Singapore. Association for Computational Linguistics.

Roberto Navigli, Paola Velardi, Alessandro Cucchiarelli, and Francesca Neri. 2004. Extending and enriching wordnet with ontolearn. In *Proc. 2nd Global WordNet Conf. (GWC)*, pages 279–284, Brno, Czech Republic. Masaryk University.

Patrick Pantel and Marco Pennacchiotti. 2008. Automatically harvesting and ontologizing semantic relations. In Paul Buitelaar and Phillip Cimmiano, editors, *Ontology Learning and Population: Bridging the Gap between Text and Knowledge*. IOS Press.

J. Raman and Pushpak Bhattacharyya. 2008. Towards automatic evaluation of wordnet synsets. In *Proc. 4th Global WordNet Conf. (GWC)*, pages 360–374, Szeged, Hungary. University of Szeged.

Stephen D. Richardson, William B. Dolan, and Lucy Vanderwende. 1998. Mindnet: Acquiring and structuring semantic information from text. In *Proc. 17th Intl. Conf. on Computational Linguistics (COLING)*, pages 1098–1102.

Maria Ruiz-Casado, Enrique Alfonseca, and Pablo Castells. 2005. Automatic assignment of wikipedia encyclopedic entries to wordnet synsets. In *Proc. Advances in Web Intelligence Third Intl. Atlantic Web Intelligence Conf. (AWIC)*, pages 380–386. Springer.

Diana Santos, Anabela Barreiro, Luís Costa, Cláudia Freitas, Paulo Gomes, Hugo Gonçalo Oliveira, José Carlos Medeiros, and Rosário Silva. 2009. O papel das relações semânticas em português: Comparando o TeP, o MWN.PT e o PAPEL. In *Actas do XXV Encontro Nacional da Associação Portuguesa de Linguística (APL)*. forthcomming.

Stephen Soderland and Bhushan Mandhani. 2007. Moving from textual relations to ontologized relations. In *Proc. AAAI Spring Symposium on Machine Reading*.

Jorge Teixeira, Luís Sarmento, and Eugénio C. Oliveira. 2010. Comparing verb synonym resources for portuguese. In *Computational Processing of the Portuguese Language, 9th Intl. Conference, Proc. (PROPOR)*, pages 100–109.

Peter D. Turney. 2001. Mining the web for synonyms: PMI–IR versus LSA on TOEFL. In *Proc. 12th European Conf. on Machine Learning (ECML)*, volume 2167, pages 491–502. Springer.

S. M. van Dongen. 2000. *Graph Clustering by Flow Simulation*. Ph.D. thesis, University of Utrecht.

Piek Vossen. 1997. Eurowordnet: a multilingual database for information retrieval. In *Proc. DELOS workshop on Cross-Language Information Retrieval*, Zurich.

Tonio Wandmacher, Ekaterina Ovchinnikova, Ulf Krumnack, and Henrik Dittmann. 2007. Extraction, evaluation and integration of lexical-semantic relations for the automated construction of a lexical ontology. In *Third Australasian Ontology Workshop (AOW)*, volume 85 of *CRPIT*, pages 61–69, Gold Coast, Australia. ACS.

Torsten Zesch, Christof Müller, and Iryna Gurevych. 2008. Extracting lexical semantic knowledge from Wikipedia and Wiktionary. In *Proc. 6th Intl. Language Resources and Evaluation (LREC)*, Marrakech, Morocco.

An Investigation on the Influence of Frequency on the Lexical Organization of Verbs

Daniel Cerato Germann[1] **Aline Villavicencio**[2] **Maity Siqueira**[3]
[1]Institute of Informatics, Federal University of Rio Grande do Sul (Brazil)
[2]Department of Computer Sciences, Bath University (UK)
[3]Institute of Language Studies, Federal University of Rio Grande do Sul (Brazil)
{dcgermann,avillavicencio}@inf.ufrgs.br, maitysiqueira@hotmail.com

Abstract

This work extends the study of Germann et al. (2010) in investigating the lexical organization of verbs. Particularly, we look at the influence of frequency on the process of lexical acquisition and use. We examine data obtained from psycholinguistic action naming tasks performed by children and adults (speakers of Brazilian Portuguese), and analyze some characteristics of the verbs used by each group in terms of similarity of content, using Jaccard's coefficient, and of topology, using graph theory. The experiments suggest that younger children tend to use more frequent verbs than adults to describe events in the world.

1 Introduction

The cognitive influence of frequency has been proven strong in the learning process of both sense and nonsense words (Howes and Solomon, 1951; Solomon and Postman, 1952). Frequency has also been shown to highly correlate with semantic factors, endorsing its importance, through the so called "light verbs" (Goldberg, 1999).

In this study, we investigate whether words that are more frequent have a higher chance of earlier acquisition. For this purpose, we compare data from children and adults, native speakers of Brazilian Portuguese, on an action naming task, looking at lexical evolution, using statistical and topological analysis of the data modeled as graphs. Our approach innovates in the sense that it directly simulates the influence of a linguistic factor over the process of lexical evolution.

This paper is structured as follows. Section 2 describes related work. Section 3 presents the materials and methods employed. Section 4 presents the results and section 5 concludes.

2 Related Work

Steyvers and Tenenbaum (2005), use some properties of language networks to propose a model of semantic growth, which is compatible with the effects of age of acquisition and frequency, in semantic processing tasks. The approach proposed in this paper follows Steyvers and Tenenbaum in the sense of iterative modifications of graphs, but differs in method (we use involutions instead of evolutions) and objective: modifications are motivated by the study of frequency instead of production of a topological arrangement. It also follows Deyne and Storms (2008), in directly relating linguistic factors and graph theory metrics, and Coronges et al. (2007), in comparing networks of different populations.

This study also follows Tonietto et al. (2008) in using data from a psycholinguistic action naming task. However, the analysis is done in terms of graph manipulation, instead of pure statistics.

3 Materials and Methods

3.1 The Data

The action naming task was performed by different age groups: 55 children and 55 young adults. Children's data are longitudinal; participants of the first data collection (G1) aged between 2;0 and 3;11 (average 3;1), and in the second collection (G2), between 4;1 and 6;6 (average 5;5) as described by Tonietto et al. (2008). The adult group is unrelated to the children, and aged between 17;0 and 34;0 (average 21;8). Participants were shown 17 actions of destruction or division (Tonietto et al, 2008) and asked to describe it.

Proceedings of the 2010 Workshop on Graph-based Methods for Natural Language Processing, ACL 2010, pages 19–23,
Uppsala, Sweden, 16 July 2010.

Data processing and justification of the chosen domain are described in Germann et al. (2010).

The answers given by each participant were collected and annotated with two frequency scores, each calculated from a different source. The first, Fscore, is the number of occurrences of the verb in the “Florianópolis” corpus (Scliar-Cabral, 1993; MacWhinney, 2000). The second, Yscore, is the number of given results searching for the infinitive form of the verb in the “Yahoo!" Searcher (http://br.yahoo.com). In the advanced settings, “Brazil” was selected as country and “Portuguese” as language. Information about these two scores for each group is shown in Table 1.

	G1	G2	G3
Average type Fscore	44.05	35.92	17.84
Average token Fscore	43.44	35.71	21.22
Average type Yscore	15441904	18443193	10419263
Average token Yscore	10788194	9277047	8927866

Table 1: Type and token scores[1].

All scores but type Yscore, decrease as age increases, which is compatible with the hypothesis investigated.

3.2 Simulation Dynamics

Linguistic production of each group was expressed in terms of graphs, whose nodes represent the mentioned verbs. All verbs uttered for the same video were assumed share semantic information, and then linked together, forming a (clique) subgraph. The subgraphs were then connected in a merging step, through the words uttered for more than one video.

To investigate the influence of frequency on the language acquisition process, we used it to change the network over time. Network involution, the strategy adopted, works in the opposite way than network growth (Albert and Barabási, 2002). Instead of adding nodes, it takes an older group graph as the source and decides on the nodes to iteratively remove (taking the younger group graph only as a reference for comparison).

Verbs were ranked in increasing order of frequency. At each step of graph involution, the less frequent verb was selected to be removed, and the resulting graph was measured. Results are reported in terms of the averages of 10-fold cross-validation (because ties imply in random selection).

Graph theory metrics were used to measure structural similarity: average minimal path length (*L*), density (*D*), average node connectivity (*k*) and average clustering coefficient (*C/s*)[2]. In the involution, *k* and *D*, measure semantic share, since that is what relations among nodes are supposed to mean (see above). *L* and *C/s* are intended to measure vocabulary uniformity, since greater distances and lower clusterization are related to the presence of subcenters of meaning.

In order to compare the contents of each graph as well, we employed a measure of set similarity: Jaccard's similarity coefficient (Jaccard, 1901). Given two sets *A* and *B*, the Jaccard's coefficient *J* can be calculated as follows:

$$J(A, B) = \frac{x}{(x+y+z)} ,$$

where “*x*” is the number of elements in both *A* and *B*, “*y*” is the number of elements only in *A*, and “*z*” is the number of elements only in *B*.

4 Simulation Results

As we remove the verbs with lower frequency from the graph of an older group, the overall structure should approximate to that of a younger group, and both should get more similar concerning content. Therefore, the most relevant part of each chart is the begging: the first removed verbs are expected to be those that differentiate graphs.

4.1 Network Involution Topology

The graph theory metrics are shown in Figures 1 and 2 in terms of 2 lines: network involution (a) by using the selected criterion, and (b) by using random selection (10-fold cross validation). In addition, each figure also shows the measure for the younger group as reference (a dashed, straight, thick line).

In Figure 1, columns represent a graph theory metric, and rows represent the use of a different score. Each legend refers to all charts.

The results for the simulations from G2 to G1, (Figure 1) show that the four metrics are clearly distinct from random elimination from the beginning, indicating that frequency plays a role in the process. *C/s* is particularly distinct from ran-

[1] Given the measure magnitude, values of Yscore were presented without the decimal fraction.

[2] We adopted the local clustering coefficient of Watts and Strogatz (1998), but as the graphs may become disconnected during network modification, this value is further divided by the number of disconnected subgraphs.

dom: while the former remains constant almost to the end, indicating a highly structured (clustered) graph, the later shows effects of graph partitioning. The remaining metrics presented their greatest approximations to the reference line before the middle of the chart, suggesting that the initial verbs were actually the ones differentiating both graphs. These results suggest an initial increase in semantic share, as *k* and *D* increase, and in uniformity, as nodes get closer to one another (*L*) and remain clustered (*C/s*). In Figure 2, the same tendencies are maintained, although not as clearly as the previous results. The greatest approximations of *k* and *D* happen in the first half of the chart, but in a smoother way. *C/s* still behaves steadily, remaining stable during most of the simulation. Yscore resembles Fscore (the same way as in Figure 1), and was not presented due to space restrictions.

4.2 Network Involution Set Similarity

In the Jaccard's coefficient charts, a rise or stabilization means that "different verbs" (present only in the older graph) were eliminated (increasing set similarity), and a descent means that "common verbs" (present in both graphs) were eliminated instead.

Charts for "excluded different" and "excluded common" verbs (and their random counterparts) are presented in percentage. By doing so, it is possible to measure the exact evolution of both, despite the proportion between them (there are much more "common" than "different" verbs). A rise in the "Excluded Different" line means that sets are getting similar, while stabilization (descents are not possible) means that they are getting different. The opposite applies to the "Excluded Common" line.

In the figures, charts are arranged in columns (the score being used) and rows (the parameter being measured). Each legend is particular to each row (one to Jaccard's coefficient and another to the excluded verbs).

Both simulation sets (Figures 3 and 4) confirm the expected pattern in general: an initial increase in the proportion between "different" and "common" verbs. In Figure 3, Yscore presents an unexpected descent just before the middle, followed by a sharp rise. Since the greatest descent happens just in the end, we interpret this middle descent as data noise. In Figure 4, Fscore presents an almost random result, indicating that the score had low impact in content similarity for this simulation. Fscore in Figure 3 and Yscore in Figure 4 behaved as expected, with most "differ-

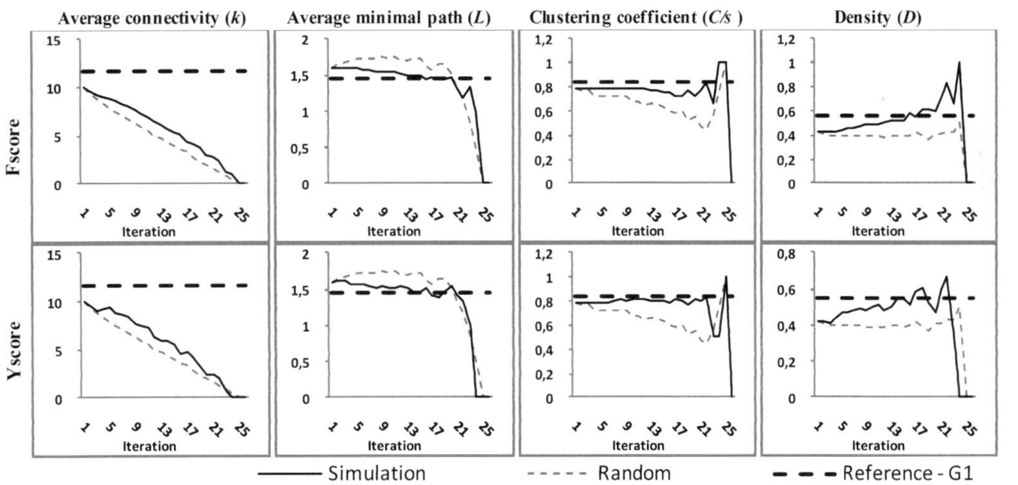

Figure 1. Involution from G2 to G1 using three scores for node removal: graph theory metrics.

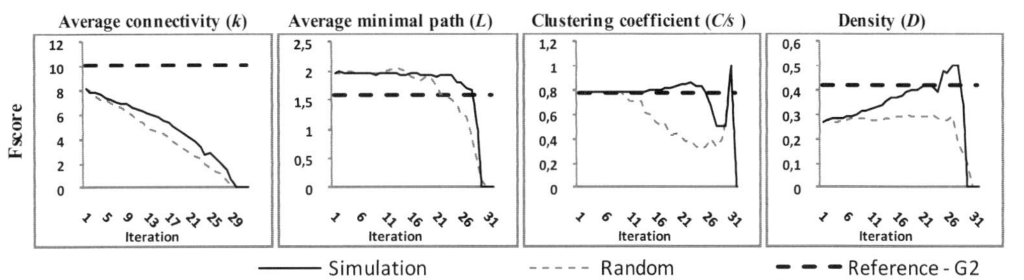

Figure 2. Involution from G3 to G2 using three scores for node removal: graph theory metrics.

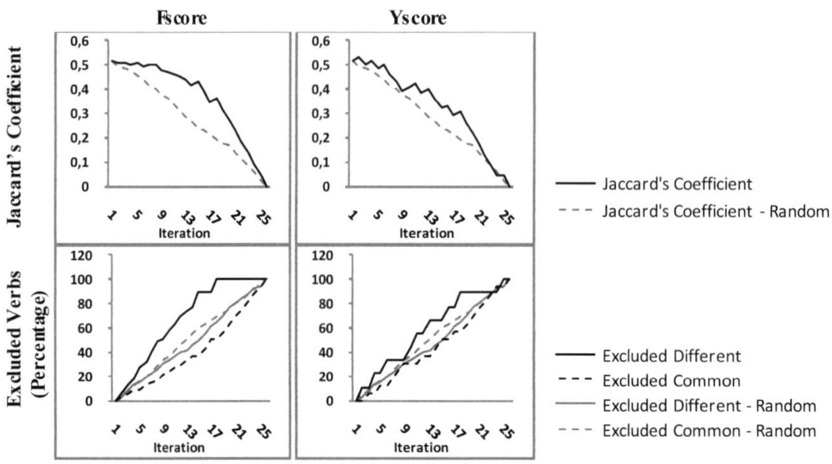

Figure 3. Involution from G2 to G1 using three scores for node removal: set theory metrics.

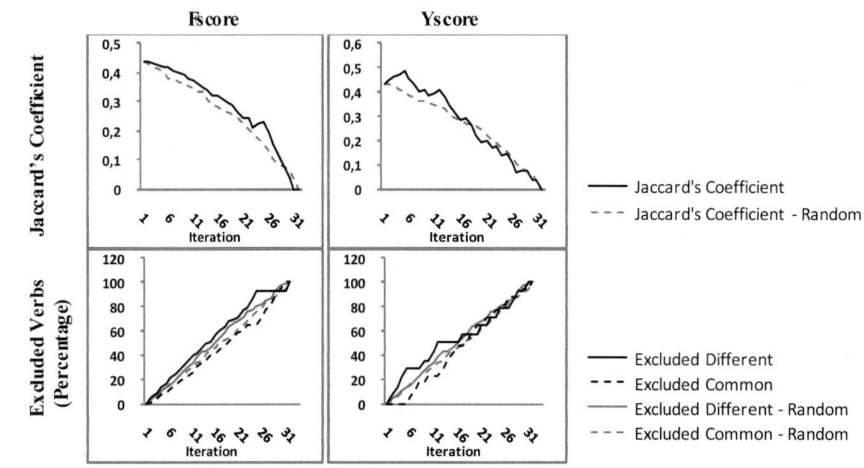

Figure 4. Involution from G3 to G2 using three scores for node removal: set theory metrics.

ent" verbs being excluded before the middle of the chart. Jaccard's coefficient follows the same pattern.

5 Conclusions and Future Work

This study has investigated the influence of frequency on verb acquisition and organization using both graph and set theory metrics. In general, results from the topological analysis showed a tendency towards the reference value, and the greatest similarities were mostly collected in the beginning, pointing for a preference of children to use verbs more frequently perceived in the language. So we conclude that both the model of involution and the given analysis are appropriate for linguistic studies concerning vocabulary evolution[3].

For future work, we intend to apply the same approach to other parameters, such as concreteness, and syntactic complexity (and combinations, and to investigate lexical dissolution in the context of pathologies, such as Alzheimer's disease, and in larger data sets, in order to further confirm the results obtained so far.

Acknowledgments

This research was partly supported by CNPq (Projects 479824/2009-6 and 309569/2009-5), FINEP and SEBRAE (COMUNICA project FINEP/SEBRAE 1194/07). We would also like to thank Maria Alice Parente, Lauren Tonietto, Bruno Menegola and Gustavo Valdez for providing the data.

[3] Since the measures were taken from the whole graph, it is not possible to determine a measure of significance. However, the comparisons with random elimination can be seen as a tendency. Additionally, the experiments consist of two simulations, over three different data sets, using two different sets of frequency (and a combination with polysemy) and two kinds of metrics, which provide robustness to the results.

References

Réka Albert and Albert-László Barabási. 2002. Statistical mechanics of complex networks. *Reviews of modern physics*, 74(1):47-97.

Kathryn A. Coronges, Alan W. Stacy and Thomas W. Valente. 2007. Structural Comparison of Cognitive Associative Networks in Two Populations. *Journal of Applied Social Psychology*, 37(9): 2097-2129.

Simon de Deyne and Gert Storms. 2008. Word associations: Network and semantic properties. *Behavior Research Methods*, 40(1): 213-231.

Daniel Cerato Germann, Aline Villavicencio and Maity Siqueira. In press. An Investigation on Polysemy and Lexical Organization of Verbs. In *Proceedings of the NAALHT - Workshop on Computacional Linguistics 2010*.

Adele E. Goldberg. The Emergence of the Semantics of Argument Structure Constructions. 1999. In *Emergence of Language*. Lawrence Erlbaum Associates , Mahwah, NJ.

Davis H. Howes and Richard L. Solomon. 1952. Visual duration threshold as a function of word-probability. *Journal of Experimental Psychology*, 41(6): 401-410.

Paul Jaccard. 1901. Distribution de la flore alpine dans le Bassin des Drouces et dans quelques regions voisines. *Bulletin de la Société Vaudoise des Sciences Naturelles*, 37(140): 241–272.

B. MacWhinney. 2000. *The CHILDES project: Tools for analyzing talk*. Lawrence Erlbaum Associates, Mahwah, NJ.

Scliar-Cabral . 1993. *Corpus Florianópolis*. Retrieved January 10, 2009, from http://childes.psy.cmu.edu/data/Romance/Portuguese/Florianopolis.zip

Richard L. Solomon and Leo Postman. 1952. Frequency of usage as a determinant of recognition thresholds for words. *Journal of Experimental Psychology*, 43(3): 195-201.

Mark Steyvers and Joshua B. Tenenbaum. 2005. The Large-Scale Structure of Semantic Networks: Statistical Analyses and a Model of Semantic Growth. *Cognitive Science: A Multidisciplinary Journal*, 29(1): 41-78.

Lauren Tonietto et al. 2008. A especificidade semântica como fator determinante na aquisição de verbos. *Psico*, 39(3): 343-351.

Duncan J. Watts and Steven H. Strogatz. 1998. Collective dynamics of 'small-world' networks. *Nature*, 6684(393):440-442.

Robust and Efficient Page Rank for Word Sense Disambiguation

Diego De Cao, Roberto Basili, Matteo Luciani, Francesco Mesiano, Riccardo Rossi
Dept. of Computer Science,
University of Roma Tor Vergata, Roma, Italy
{decao,basili}@info.uniroma2.it
{matteo.lcn,fra.mesiano,ricc.rossi}@gmail.com

Abstract

Graph-based methods that are *en vogue* in the social network analysis area, such as centrality models, have been recently applied to linguistic knowledge bases, including unsupervised Word Sense Disambiguation. Although the achievable accuracy is rather high, the main drawback of these methods is the high computational demanding whenever applied to the large scale sense repositories. In this paper an adaptation of the PageRank algorithm recently proposed for Word Sense Disambiguation is presented that preserves the reachable accuracy while significantly reducing the requested processing time. Experimental analysis over well-known benchmarks will be presented in the paper and the results confirm our hypothesis.

1 Introduction

Lexical ambiguity is a fundamental aspect of natural language. Word Sense Disambiguation (WSD) investigates methods to automatically determine the intended sense of a word in a given context according to a predefined set of sense definitions, provided by a semantic lexicon. Intuitively, WSD can be usefully exploited in a variety of NLP (e.g. Machine Translation (Chan et al., 2007; Carpuat and Wu, 2007)) and Information Retrieval tasks such as *ad hoc retrieval* (Krovetz, 1997; Kim et al., 2004) or Question Answering (Beale et al., 2004). However controversial results have been often obtained, as for example the study on text classification reported in (Moschitti and Basili, 2004). The impact of WSD on IR tasks is still an open issue and large scale assessment is needed. For this reason, unsupervised approaches to inductive WSD are appealing. In contrast with supervised methods that strongly rely on manually labeled data sets, those methods do not require annotated examples for all words and can thus support realistic (large scale) benchmarks, as needed in IR research.

In recent years different approaches to Word Sense Disambiguation task have been evaluated through comparative campaigns, such as the earlier Senseval evaluation exercises. (Palmer et al., 2001; Snyder and Palmer, 2004) or the most recent (Pradhan et al., 2007).

The best accuracy is reached by WSD based on supervised methods that exploit large amounts of hand-tagged data to train discriminative or generative disambiguation models. The common alternative to supervised systems are knowledge-based WSD systems that try to exploit information made available by large Lexical Knowledge Bases (LKB). They enable the definition of several metrics to estimate semantic similarity (e.g. (Lesk, 1986) or (Agirre and Rigau, 1996), (Basili et al., 2004) methods) and then use it to rank the alternative senses according to the incoming context. Moreover they make available large relationship sets between pairs of lexical meaning units, such as synonymy, hyponymy or meronymy. The resulting networks represent at various grains and degrees of approximation models of the mental lexicons. It is not by chance that early research on WSD based on semantic dictionaries were applying models of network activation processes (in particular simulated annealing as in (Cowie et al., 1992)) for precise and fast disambiguation.

It has been more recently that graph-based methods for knowledge-based WSD have gained much attention in the NLP community ((Sinha and Mihalcea, 2007), (Navigli and Lapata, 2007), (Agirre and Soroa, 2008), (Agirre and Soroa, 2009)). In these methods a graph representation for senses (nodes) and relation (edges) is first built. Then graph-based techniques that are sensible to the structural properties of the graph are used to find the best senses for words in the incoming contexts. The relation employed by the different methods are of several types such as synonymy, antonymy but also co-occurrence based lexical similarity computed externally over a corpus. These give rise to real-valued weights that determine large weighted directed graphs. Usu-

Proceedings of the 2010 Workshop on Graph-based Methods for Natural Language Processing, ACL 2010, pages 24–32,
Uppsala, Sweden, 16 July 2010.

ally, the employed disambiguation is carried out by ranking the graph nodes. Thus the concepts with highest ranks are assigned to the corresponding words. In (Agirre and Soroa, 2009), a comparative analysis of different graph-based models over two well known WSD benchmarks is reported. In the paper two variants of the random surfer model as defined by PageRank model (Brin and Page, 1998) are analyzed. A special emphasis for the resulting computational efficiency is also posed there. In particular, a variant called *Personalized PageRank* (PPR) is proposed (Agirre and Soroa, 2009) that tries to trade-off between the amount of the employed lexical information and the overall efficiency. In synthesis, along the ideas of the Topic sensitive PageRank (Haveliwala, 2002), PPR suggests that a proper initialization of the teleporting vector $\vec{p}$ suitably captures the context information useful to drive the random surfer PageRank model over the graph to converge towards the proper senses in fewer steps. The basic idea behind the adoption of PPR is to impose a personalized vector that expresses the contexts of all words targeted by the disambiguation. This method improves on the complexity of the previously presented methods (e.g. (Agirre and Soroa, 2008)) as it allows to contextualize the behaviors of PageRank over a sentence, without asking for a different graph: in this way the WordNet graph is always adopted, in a word or sentence oriented fashion. Moreover, it is possible to avoid to rebuild a graph for each target word, as the entire sentence can be coded into the personalization vector. In (Agirre and Soroa, 2009), a possible, and more accurate alternative, is also presented called PPR word2word ($PPRw2w$) where a different personalization vector is used for each word in a sentence. Although clearly less efficient in terms of time complexity, this approach guarantees the best accuracy, so that it can be considered the state-of-the art in unsupervised WSD.

In this paper a different approach to personalization of the PageRank is presented, aiming at preserving the suitable efficiency of the sentence oriented *PPR* algorithm for WSD but achieving an accuracy at least as high as the $PPRw2w$ one. We propose to use distributional evidence that can be automatically acquired from a corpus to define the topical information encoded by the personalization vector, in order to amplify the bias on the resulting PPR and improve the performance of the sentence oriented version. The intuition is that distributional evidence is able to cover the gap between word oriented usages of the PPR as for the $PPRw2w$ defined in (Agirre and Soroa, 2009), and its sentence oriented counterpart. In this way we can preserve higher accuracy levels while limiting the number of PageRank runs, i.e. increasing efficiency.

The paper is structured as follows. We first give a more detailed overview of the *PageRank* and *Personalized PageRank* algorithms in Section 2. In Section, 3 a description of our distributional approach to the personalized PageRank is provided. A comparative evaluation with respect to previous works is then reported in Section 4 while section 5 is left for conclusions.

2 Graph-based methods for Word Sense Disambiguation

Word sense disambiguation algorithms in the class of graph-based method are unsupervised approaches to WSD that rely almost exclusively on the lexical KB graph structure for inferring the relevance of word senses for a given context. Much current work in WSD assume that meaning distinctions are provided by a reference lexicon (the LKB), which encodes a discrete set of senses for each individual word. Although the largely adopted reference resource is WordNet (Miller et al., 1990), the graph-based algorithms are not limited to this particular lexicon. In these methods, nodes are derived from the sense units, i.e. the synsets, and edges are derived from semantic relations established between synsets. We will hereafter use WordNet to discuss the details of the different steps. Every algorithm can be decomposed in a set of general steps:

Building the graph. The first step proceeds to the definition of the graph structure. As introduced before, WordNet is mapped into a graph whose nodes are concepts (represented by *synsets* (i.e., synonym sets)) and whose edges are semantic relations between concepts (e.g., *hyperonymy*, *meronymy*). For each sentence, a graph $G = (V, E)$ is built, which is derived from the entire graph of the reference lexicon. More formally, given a sentence $\sigma = w_1, w_2, \ldots, w_n$, where w_i is a word, the following steps are executed to build G: (1) the sense vocabulary V_σ is derived as $V_\sigma := \bigcup_{i=1}^{n} Senses(w_i)$, where $Senses(w_i)$ is the set of senses of any of the w_i of the sentence. (2) For each node $v \in V_\sigma$, a visit of the WordNet graph is performed: every time a node $v' \in V_\sigma(v' \neq v)$ is encountered along a path $v \rightarrow v_1 \rightarrow \ldots \rightarrow v_k \rightarrow v'$ all intermediate nodes and edges on the path from v to v' are added to the graph: $V := V \bigcup \{v_1, \ldots, v_k\}$ and $E := E \bigcup \{(v, v_1), \ldots, (v_k, v')\}$. The constructed graph is the subgraph covering the nodes and relations of all the relevant vocabulary in the sentence.

Sense Ranking. The derived graph is then used with different ranking models to find the correct senses of words into the sentence σ. A suitable interpretation of the source sentence can be in fact obtained by ranking each vertex in the graph G according its centrality. In (Navigli and Lapata, 2007) different ranking models are described. The specific algorithm presented in (Agirre and Soroa, 2008) is the major inspiration of the present paper, and makes use of PageRank (Brin and Page, 1998) to rank edges in the graph G. PageRank tries to separate these nodes from the other candidate synsets of words in σ, which are expected to activate less relations on average and remain isolated. Let the vector $\vec{Rank}$ express the probability to reach any of the vertices V_σ, and let M represent the edge information. The expected rank between senses satisfies:

$$\vec{Rank} = (1 - \alpha) M \times \vec{Rank} + \alpha \vec{p} \quad (1)$$

whereas $0 \leq \alpha \leq 1$. α is called the *damping factor*. It models the amount of likelihood that a generic Web surfer, standing at a vertex, randomly follows a link from this vertex toward any other vertex in the graph: the uniform probability $p_i = \frac{1}{N} \quad \forall i$, is assigned to each one of the N vertices in G. While it guarantees the convergence of the algorithm, it expresses the trade-off between the probability of following links provided by the Web graph and the freedom to violate them. An interesting aspect of the ranking process is the initial state. Many algorithms (as well as the one proposed by (Agirre and Soroa, 2009)) initialize the ranks of the vertex at a uniform value (usually $1/N$ for a graph with N vertices). Then Equation 1 is iterated until convergence is achieved or a maximum fix number of iterations has been reached.

Disambiguation. Finally, the disambiguation step is performed by assigning to each word w_i in the source sentence σ, the associated j-th concept $sense_{ij}$ (i.e. the j-th valid interpretation for w_i) associated to the maximum resulting rank. In case of ties all the concepts with maximum rank are assigned to $w_i \in \sigma$.

The above process has several sources of complexity, but the major burden is related to the *Sense ranking* step. While complex methods have been proposed (as discussed in (Navigli and Lapata, 2007)), sentence oriented algorithms, that build the graph G once per each sentence σ, whatever the number of $w_i \in \sigma$ is, are much more efficient. The problem is twofold:

- How different sentences can be targeted without major changes in the graph G? How the matrix M can be made as much reusable as possible?
- How to encode in Eq. 1 the incoming context in order to properly address the different words in the sentence σ?

In order to address the above problems, in line with the notion of topic-sensitive PageRank, a personalized PageRank approach has been recently devised (Agirre and Soroa, 2009) as discussed in the next section.

2.1 Personalizing PageRank for WSD

In (Agirre and Soroa, 2009), a novel use of PageRank for word sense disambiguation is presented. It aims to present an optimized version of the algorithm previously discussed in (Agirre and Soroa, 2008). The main difference concerns the method used to initialize and use the graph G for disambiguating a sentence with respect to the overall graph (hereafter GKB) that represents the complete lexicon.

Previous methods (such as (Agirre and Soroa, 2008)) derive G as the subgraph of GKB whose vertices and edges are particularly relevant for the given input sentence σ. Such a subgraph is often called the *disambiguation subgraph* σ, $GD(\sigma)$. GD is a subgraph of the original GKB, obtained by computing the shortest paths between the concepts of the words co-occurring in the context. These are expected to capture most of the information relevant to the disambiguation (i.e. sense ranking) step.

The alternative proposed in (Agirre and Soroa, 2009) allows a more static use of the full LKB. Context words are newly introduced into the graph G as nodes, and linked with directed edges (i.e. the lexical relations) to their respective concepts (i.e. synsets). Topic-sensitive PageRank over the graph G (Haveliwala, 2002) is then applied: the initial probability mass is concentrated uniformly over the newly introduced word nodes through the setting of the personalization vector $\vec{p}$ in Eq. 1 (Haveliwala, 2002). Words are linked to the concepts by directed edges that act as sources to propagate probability into the GKB concepts they are associated with. A personalized PageRank vector is finally produced that defines a measure of the (topological) relevance of the GKB nodes (concepts) activated by the input context. The overall time complexity is limited by the above sketched *Personalized PageRank* approach (PPR) as a single initialization of the graph GKB is requested for an entire target sentence. This *sentence oriented* method reuses the GKB of the entire lexicon, while the second step runs the sense ranking once for all the words. This method reduces the number of invocations of PageRank thus lowering the average disambiguation time.

A *word oriented* version of the algorithm is also proposed in (Agirre and Soroa, 2009). It defines different initializations for the different words $w_i \in \sigma$: these are obtained by setting the initial probability mass in $\vec{p}$ to 0 for all the senses $Sense(w_i)$ of the targeted w_i. In this way, only the context words and not the target are used for the personalization step[1]. This approach to the personalized PageRank is termed word-by-word or $PPRw2w$ version in (Agirre and Soroa, 2009). $PPRw2w$ is run on the same graph but with n different initializations where n is the number of words in σ. Although less efficient, $PPRw2w$ is shown to outperform the sentence oriented PPR model.

3 A distributional extension of PageRank

The key idea in (Agirre and Soroa, 2009) is to adapt the matrix initialization step in order to exploit the available contextual evidence. Notice that personalization in Word Sense Disambiguation is inspired by the topic-sensitive PageRank approach, proposed in (Haveliwala, 2002), for Web search tasks. It exploits a context dependent definition of the vector $\vec{p}$ in Eq. 1 to influence the link-based sense ranking achievable over a sentence. Context is used as only words of the sentence (or words co-occurring with the target w_i in the $w2w$ method) are given non zero probability mass in $\vec{p}$: this provides a *topical* bias to PageRank. A variety of models of topical information have been proposed in IR (e.g. (Landauer and Dumais, 1997)) to generalize documents or shorter texts (e.g. query). They can be acquired through large scale corpus analysis in the so called distributional approaches to language modeling. While *contexts* can be defined in different ways (e.g as the set of words surrounding a target word), their analysis over large corpora has been shown to effectively capture topical and paradigmatic relations (Sahlgren, 2006). We propose to use the topical information about a sentence σ, acquired through Latent Semantic Analysis (Landauer and Dumais, 1997), as a source information for the initialization of the vector $\vec{p}$ in the PPR (or $PPRw2w$) disambiguation methods.

SVD usually improves the word similarity computation for three different reasons. First, SVD tends to remove the random noise present in the source matrix. Second, it allows to discover the latent meanings of a target word through the corpus, and to compute second-order relations among targets, thus improving the similarity computation. Third, similarities are computed in a lower dimensional space, thus speeding up the computation. For the above reasons by mapping a word, or a sentence, in the corresponding Latent Semantic Space, we can estimate the set of its similar words according to implicit semantic relations acquired in an unsupervised fashion. This can be profitably used as a personalization model for PPR.

For the WSD task, our aim is to exploit an externally acquired semantic space to expand the incoming sentence σ into a set of *novel* terms, different but *semantically related* with the words in σ. In analogy with topic-driven PageRank, the use of these words as a seed for the iterative algorithm is expected to amplify the effect of local information (i.e. σ) onto the recursive propagation across the lexical network: the interplay of the global information provided by the whole lexical network with the local information characterizing the initialization lexicon is expected to maximize their independent effect.

More formally, let the matrix $W_k := U_k S_k$ be the matrix that represents the lexicon in the k-dimensional LSA space. Given an input sentence σ, a vector representation $\vec{w_i}$ for each term w_i in σ is made available. The corresponding representation of the sentence can be thus computed as the

[1]This seems to let the algorithm to avoid strong biases toward pairs of senses of a given word that may appear in some semantic relations (thus connected in the graph), that would be wrongly emphasized by the PPR method.

linear combination through the original $tf \cdot idf$ scores of the corresponding $\vec{w_i}$: this provides always an unique representation $\vec{\sigma}$ for the sentence. $\vec{\sigma}$ locates the sentence in the LSA space and the set of terms that are *semantically related* to the sentence σ can be easily found in the neighborhood. A lower bound can be imposed on the cosine similarity scores over the vocabulary to compute the lexical expansion of σ, i.e. the set of terms that are enough similar to $\vec{\sigma}$ in the k dimensional space. Let D be the vocabulary of all terms, we define as the lexical expansion $T(\sigma) \subset D$ of $\vec{\sigma}$ as follows:

$$T(\sigma) = \{w_j \in D : sim(\vec{w_j}, \vec{\sigma}) > \tau\} \quad (2)$$

where τ represents a real-valued threshold in the set $[0, 1)$. In order to improve precision it is also possible to impose a limit on the cardinality of $T(\sigma)$ and discard terms characterized by lower similarity factors.

Let the $t = |T(\sigma)|$ be the number of terms in the expansion, we extend the original set σ of terms in the sentence, so that the new seed vocabulary is $\sigma \cup T(\sigma) = \{w_1, w_2, \ldots, w_n, w_{n+1}, \ldots, w_{n+t}\}$. The nodes in the graph G will be thus computed as $Vext_\sigma := \bigcup_{i=1}^{n+t} Senses(w_i)$ and a new personalization vector $\vec{p_{ext}}$ will then replace $\vec{p}$ in Eq. 1: it will assign a probability mass to the words $w_1, ..., w_{n+t}$ proportional to their similarity to $\vec{\sigma}$, i.e.

$$p_{k_i} = \frac{sim(\vec{w_i}, \vec{\sigma})}{\sum_{j=1}^{n+t} sim(\vec{w_j}, \vec{\sigma})} \quad \forall i = 1, ..., n+t \quad (3)$$

whereas k_i is the index of the node corresponding to the word w_i in the graph. Finally, the later steps of the PPR methods remain unchanged, and the PageRank works over the corresponding graph G are carried out as described in Section 2.

4 Empirical Evaluation

The evaluation of the proposed model was focused on two main aspects. First we want to measure the impact of the topical expansion at sentence level on the accuracy reachable by the personalized PageRank PPR. This will be done also comparatively with the state of the art of unsupervised systems over a consolidated benchmark, i.e. Semeval 2007. In Table 1 a comparison between the official Semeval 2007 results for unsupervised methods is reported. Table 1 shows also the results of the standard PPR methods over the Semeval 2007 dataset. Second, we want to analyze the efficiency of the algorithm and its impact in a sentence (i.e. PPR) or word oriented (i.e. $w2w$) perspective. This will allow to asses its applicability to realistic tasks, such as query processing or document indexing.

Experimental Set-up In order to measure accuracy, the Senseval 2007 coarse WSD dataset[2] (Navigli et al., 2007) has been employed. It includes 245 sentences for a total number of 2,269 ambiguous words. In line with the results reported in (Agirre and Soroa, 2009), experiments against two different WordNet versions, 1.7 and 3.0, have been carried out. Notice that the best results in (Agirre and Soroa, 2009) were obtained over the enriched version of the LKB, i.e. the combination of WordNet and extra information supplied by *extended WordNet* (Harabagiu and Moldovan, 1999).

The adopted vector space has been acquired over a significant subset of the BNC 2.0 corpus, made of 923k sentences. The most frequent 200k words (i.e. the contextual features) were acquired through LSA. The corpus has been processed with the LTH parser (Johansson and Nugues, 2007) to obtain POS tags for every token. Moreover, a dimensionality reduction factor of $k = 100$ was applied.

In subsection 4.1, a comparative analysis of the accuracy achieved in the disambiguation task is discussed. Subsection 4.2 presents a corresponding study of the execution times aiming to compare the relative efficiency of the methods and their application into a document semantic tagging task.

4.1 Comparative evaluation: accuracy on the Semeval '07 data

The approaches proposed in Semeval 2007 can be partitioned into two major types. The supervised or semi-supervised approaches and the unsupervised ones that rely usually on WordNet. As the basic *Page Rank* as well as our LSA extension makes no use of sense labeled data, we will mainly focus on the comparative evaluation among unsupervised WSD systems. In order to compare the quality of the proposed approach, the results of the personalized PageRank proposed in (Agirre and Soroa, 2009) over the same dataset are reported in Table 1 (The * systems, denoted by UKB). As also suggested in (Agirre and Soroa, 2009) the best per-

[2]The dataset is publicly available from http://nlp.cs.swarthmore.edu/semeval/tasks/task07/data.shtml

System	P	R	F1
LSA_UKB_1.7x	71.66	71.53	**71.59**
UKB_1.7x *	71.38	71.13	71.26
TKB-UO	70.21	70.21	70.21
UKB_3.0g *	68.47	68.05	68.26
LSA_UKB_3.0g	67.02	66.73	66.87
LSA_UKB_1.7	66.96	65.66	66.31
LSA_UKB_3.0	66.60	65.31	65.95
RACAI-SYNWSD	65.71	65.71	65.71
UKB_3.0 *	63.29	61.92	62.60
SUSSX-FR	71.73	52.23	60.44
UKB_1.7 *	59.30	57.99	58.64
UOFL	52.59	48.74	50.60
SUSSX-C-WD	54.54	39.71	45.96
SUSSX-CR	54.30	39.53	45.75

Table 1: Official Results over the Semeval'07 dataset. The * systems was presented in (Agirre and Soroa, 2009). The *LSA_UKB_1.7* and *LSA_UKB_3.0* show the rank of the model proposed in this paper.

Model	Iter.	PPR			w2w		
		Prec	Rec	F1	Prec	Rec	F1
17_LSA100	5	65.8	64.5	**65.2**	65.7	64.4	**65.1**
	15	65.6	64.3	**65.0**	66.3	65.0	**65.7**
17_UKB	5	60.9	59.7	60.3	65.3	63.8	64.5
	15	61.3	60.1	60.7	61.6	60.2	60.9
17x_LSA100	5	71.5	71.4	**71.5**	71.1	71.0	**71.1**
	15	71.5	71.4	**71.4**	71.6	71.5	**71.5**
17x_UKB	5	67.4	67.3	67.4	70.9	70.6	70.7
	15	67.5	67.4	67.5	71.3	71.1	71.2
30_LSA100	5	66.5	65.2	**65.8**	65.7	64.4	**65.1**
	15	66.9	65.6	**66.2**	66.6	65.3	**65.9**
30_UKB	5	61.7	60.5	61.1	64.7	63.3	64.0
	15	63.5	62.2	62.8	63.2	61.9	62.6
30g_LSA100	5	66.6	66.3	**66.4**	66.6	66.3	66.5
	15	66.7	66.4	**66.5**	67.0	66.7	66.8
30g_UKB	5	60.8	60.5	60.6	68.1	67.7	**67.9**
	15	60.7	60.5	60.6	68.4	68.0	**68.2**

Table 2: Accuracy of the LSA-based sentence expansion PageRank model, as compared with the sentence (PPR) and word oriented ($w2w$) versions of the personalized PageRank over the Semeval 2007 datasets. 17x and 30g refer to the extended resources of WordNet 1.7 and 3.0, respectively.

formances are obtained according to the *PPRw2w* word oriented approach.

For sake of comparison we applied the LSA-based expansion to the Personalized Page Rank in a sentence oriented fashion (i.e., only one PageRank is run for all the target words of a sentence, PPR). Notice that PPR models the context of the sentence with a single iterative run of PageRank, while $PPRw2w$ disambiguates each word with a dedicated PageRank. In line with (Agirre and Soroa, 2009), different types of WordNet graphs are employed in our experiments:

WN17 all hyponymy links between synsets of the WN1.7 dictionary are considered;

WN17x all hyponymy links as well as the extended 1.7 version of WordNet, whereas the syntactically parsed glosses, are semantically disambiguated and connected to the corresponding synsets;

WN3.0 all hyponymy links between synsets of the WN3.0 dictionary are considered;

WN30g all hyponymy links as well as the extended 3.0 version of WordNet, whereas the syntactically parsed glosses, are semantically disambiguated and connected to the corresponding synsets;

The impact of the LSA sentence expansion technique proposed in this paper on the different involved resources, i.e. WN1.7 to WN30g, has been measured. The 1.7 configuration provides the most efficient one as it runs the original PPR against a graph built around the only hyponymy relations among synsets. We used the Senseval'02 and Senseval'03 datasets to fine tune parameters of our LSA model, that are: (1) the dimensionality cut k to derive the LSA space; (2) the threshold τ to determine the expansion dictionary in the LSA space for every POS tag (e.g. noun or adjectives), that may require different values; (3) the damping factor α and (4) the number of iteration over the graph. In (Agirre and Soroa, 2009) the suggested parameters are $\alpha = 0.85$ as the damping factor and 30 as the upper limit to the PageRank iterations. We always adopted this setting to estimate the performances of the standard PPR and $PPRw2w$ algorithms referred through UKB. Due the novel configuration of the graph that in our model also includes many other similar terms, the damping factor and the number of iterations have been re-estimated. k has been set to 100 as different values did not seem to influence accuracy. We adopted fixed limits for sentence expansion where values from 20 up to 150 terms have been tested. The good scores obtained on the development set suggested that a number of iterations lower than 30 is in general enough to get good accuracy levels: 15 iterations, instead of 30, have been judged adequate. Finally, on average, the total number of lexical items in the expanded sentence $T(\sigma)$ includes about 40% of nouns, 30% of verbs, 20% of adjectives and 10% of adverbs.

Finally, a damping factor $\alpha = 0.98$ has been used.

Table 2 reports Precision, Recall and F1 scores of the different models as obtained over the test SemEval '07 data. Every row pair compares the LSA model with the original corresponding UKB version over a given graph (from WN1.7 to WN30g). For each model the accuracy corresponding to two iterations (5 and 15) is reported to analyze also the overall trend during PageRank. The best F1 scores between any pair are emphasized in bold, to comparatively asses the results. As a confirmation of the outcome in (Agirre and Soroa, 2009), different lexical resources achieve different results. In general by adopting the graph derived from WN3.0 (i.e. WN30 and WN30g) lower performance can be achieved. Moreover, the word-by-word model (last three columns for the w2w side of the Table) is evidently superior. Interestingly, almost on every type of graph and for every approach (sentence or word oriented) the LSA-based method outperforms the original UKB PPR. This confirms that the impact of the topical information provided by the LSA expansion of the sentence is beneficial for a better use of the lexical graph. An even more interesting outcome is that the improvement implied by the proposed LSA method on the sentence oriented model (i.e. the standard PPR method of (Agirre and Soroa, 2009)) is higher, so that the difference between the performances of the $PPRw2w$ model are no longer strikingly better than the PPR one. For example, on the simple WN1.7 hyponymy network the $PPR - LSA100$ [3] method abolishes the gap of about 4% previously observed for the PPR-UKB model. When LSA is used, it seems that the word-by-word approach is no longer required. On the contrary, in the WN17x case the best figure after 5 iterations is obtained by the PPR-LSA100 method instead of the w2w-LSA100 one (71.5% vs. 71.1%). The good accuracy reachable by the sentence oriented strategy (i.e. LSA100 and w2w) is also very interesting as for the higher efficiency of the PPR approach with respect to the word-by-word $PPRw2w$ one.

4.2 Time Efficiency

In the attempt to validate the hypothesis that LSA is helpful to improve time complexity of the WSD, we analyzed the processing times of the different data sets, in order to cross compare methods and resources[4]. The aim of the evaluation is to study the contribution of the sentence expansion using Latent Semantic Analysis and the Page Rank algorithm. Tests were performed comparing different parameter values (e.g. cardinality t of the sentence expansion, different values for the acceptability threshold) as well as several settings of the damping factor for the personalized PageRank algorithm (Eq 1) and the number of iterations over the KB Graph. In figure 1, the processing speed, measured as seconds per sentence, has been plot for different graphs and configurations. Notice that one sentence is equivalent on average to 9,6 target words. As clearly shown in the figure, the processing times for the word-by-word method over the extended WN 1.7 (i.e. WN17x) are not acceptable for IR tasks such as query processing, or document indexing. For an entire document of about 20 sentences the overall amount of processing required by the w2w_17x_UKB method is about 45 minutes. Word-by-word methods are just slightly more efficient whenever applied to graphs with lower connectivity (e.g. WN17 vs. WN17x as in Fig. 1 left plot). The same tasks with PPR methods are solved in a quite faster way, with a general ratio of 1:14 with the extended versions and 1:6 with the hyponymy graphs. The processing time of the proposed LSA method is thus at least 6 times faster than the UKB method with the comparable accuracy level. Moreover, as accuracy between PPR and w2w is comparable when LSA is adopted, this efficiency can be guaranteed at no loss in accuracy. By integrating the evidence of Figure 1 with the ones of Table 1, we observe that accuracy reachable by LSA-UKB is independent by the standard or word-by-word configuration so that the overall process can be made about 10 times faster. Notice that the representation in the LSA space that is projected for a target sentence can be easily obtained also for longer text fragments. Moreover, as for the *one sense per discourse* hypothesis it is possible that every word can be processed once in an entire text. This suggests that a document oriented usage of the personalized PageRank based on LSA can be designed achieving the maximal efficiency. In order to evaluate the corresponding impact on accuracy a dedicated dataset has been defined and more tests have been run, as discussed hereafter.

[3] 100 refers to the dimension k of the LSA space

[4] Tests were carried out on a 32-bit machine with a 3.2 Ghz CPU and 2 Gbyte Memory. Gnu/Linux operative system is installed on it, with the kernel 2.6.28-16-generic.

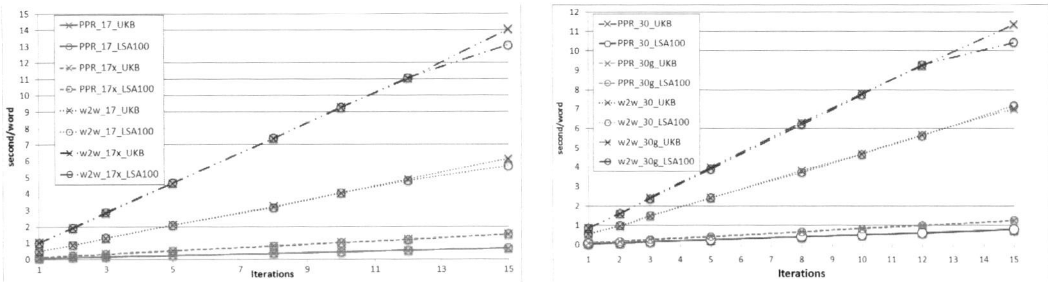

Figure 1: Processing Times for the PPR, $w2w$ and LSA methods as applied on the WN 1.7 (left plot) and WN 3.0 (right plot) resources, respectively: 17x and 30g refer to test over the extended resources.

4.3 Document oriented PPR

While the LSA model has been actually applied to determine an expansion for the entire target sentence, nothing prevents to apply it to larger text units, in order to bias the PageRank for all words in a document. In order to verify if such a process disambiguation could preserve the same accuracy, we measured the accuracy reachable over the same Semeval'07 data organized in documents. The sentences have been grouped in 5 documents, made of about about 250 sentences: during the tagging process, the system generates a lexical expansion for an entire document, about 450 target words on average. Then PageRank is carried out and the resulting ranking is projected to the senses of all the targeted words in the document. Due to the much wider locality managed in this process, a larger cardinality for the expansion is used and the most similar 400 words are collected as a bias for the PageRank. The accuracy reachable is reported in Table 4.3. As expected, the same trends as for the sentence based approach are observed: the best resource is still the WN17x for which the best results is obtained. However, the crucial result here is that no drop in performance is also observed. This implies that the much more efficient document oriented strategy can be always applied through LSA without major changes in accuracy. Also results related to the processing time follow the trends of the sentence based method. Accordingly 28 seconds required to process a document in the worst case is an impressive achievement because the same accuracy was obtained, without LSA, in 2 orders of magnitude more time.

Model	Iter.	Prec	Rec	F1
PPR_17_LSA400	5	0.6670	0.6540	**0.6604**
	15	0.6800	0.6668	**0.6733**
PPR_17_UKB	5	0.6440	0.6316	0.6377
	15	0.6360	0.6236	0.6297
PPR_17x_LSA400	5	0.7130	0.7118	**0.7124**
	15	0.7152	0.7140	**0.7146**
PPR_17x_UKB	5	0.7108	0.7096	0.7102
	15	0.7073	0.7060	0.7067
PPR_30_LSA400	5	0.6593	0.6465	**0.6529**
	15	0.6688	0.6558	0.6622
PPR_30_UKB	5	0.6445	0.6320	0.6382
	15	0.6724	0.6593	**0.6658**
PPR_30g_LSA400	5	0.6636	0.6606	**0.6621**
	15	0.6653	0.6624	**0.6639**
PPR_30g_UKB	5	0.6543	0.6514	0.6528
	15	0.6565	0.6536	0.6550

Table 3: Accuracy of the LSA-based PPR model when applied in a document oriented fashion on the Semeval '07 dataset. LSA400 stands for the size t of the applied sentence expansion $T(\sigma)$.

5 Conclusions

In this paper an extension of a PageRank-based algorithm for Word Sense Disambiguation has been presented. It suggests a kind of personalization based on sentence expansion, obtained as a side effect of Latent Semantic Analysis. The major results achieved are in terms of improved efficiency that allows to use smaller resources or less iterations with similar accuracy results. The resulting speed-up can be also improved when the disambiguation is run in a document oriented fashion, and the PageRank is run once per each document. The overall results can achieve a speed-up of two order of magnitude at no cost in accuracy. Moreover the presented approach constitutes the state-of-the-art among the unsupervised WSD algorithms over the Semeval'07 datasets, while improving the efficiency of the PPR method by a factor 10 in the worst case. This work opens perspectives towards more sophisticated distributional models (such as syntax-driven ones) as well as cross-linguistic applications supported by multilingual lexical sense repositories.

References

E. Agirre and G. Rigau. 1996. Word sense disambiguation using conceptual density. In *Proceedings of COLING-96*, Copenhagen, Denmark.

Eneko Agirre and Aitor Soroa. 2008. Using the multilingual central repository for graph-based word sense disambiguation. In *Proceedings of the LREC'08*, Marrakech, Morocco, May.

E. Agirre and A. Soroa. 2009. Personalizing pagerank for word sense disambiguation. In *Proceedings of the 12th conference of EACL '09*, Athens, Greece, March 30 - April 3.

R. Basili, M. Cammisa, and F.M. Zanzotto. 2004. A semantic similarity measure for unsupervised semantic disambiguation. In *Proceedings of LREC-04*, Lisbon, Portugal.

Stephen Beale, Benoit Lavoie, Marjorie McShane, Sergei Nirenburg, and Tanya Korelsky. 2004. Question answering using ontological semantics. In *TextMean '04: Proceedings of the 2nd Workshop on Text Meaning and Interpretation*, pages 41–48, Morristown, NJ, USA. Association for Computational Linguistics.

Sergey Brin and Lawrence Page. 1998. The anatomy of a large-scale hypertextual web search engine. *Computer Networks and ISDN Systems*, 30(1–7):107–117.

M. Carpuat and D. Wu. 2007. Improving statistical machine translation using word sense disambiguation. In *Proceedings of the Joint Conference EMNLP-CoNLL '09*, Prague, Czech Republic.

Y. Chan, H. Ng, and D. Chiang. 2007. Word sense disambiguation improves statistical machine translation. In *Proceedings of the ACL '09*, Prague, Czech Republic.

Jim Cowie, Louise Guthrie, and Joe Guthrie. 1992. Lexical disambiguation using simulated annealing. In *Proc. of 14th Int. Conf. COLING '92*, pages 359–365, Nantes, France.

Sanda M. Harabagiu and Dan I. Moldovan. 1999. Enriching the wordnet taxonomy with contextual knowledge acquired from text. In *in Iwanska, L.M., and Shapiro, S.C. eds 2000. Natural Language Processing and Knowledge Representation: Language*, pages 301–334. AAAI/MIT Press.

T. H. Haveliwala. 2002. Topic-sensitive pagerank. In *Proc. of 11th Int. Conf. on World Wide Web*, page 517526, New York, USA. ACM.

Richard Johansson and Pierre Nugues. 2007. Semantic structure extraction using nonprojective dependency trees. In *Proceedings of SemEval-2007*, Prague, Czech Republic, June 23-24.

S. B. Kim, H. Seo, and H. Rim. 2004. Information retrieval using word senses: root sense tagging approach. In *Proceedings of the International ACM-SIGIR Conference '09*, Sheffield, UK, July.

H. Krovetz. 1997. Homonymy and polysemy in information retrieval. In *Proceedings of the 35th ACL '09*.

Tom Landauer and Sue Dumais. 1997. A solution to plato's problem: The latent semantic analysis theory of acquisition, induction and representation of knowledge. *Psychological Review*, 104:211–240.

M. Lesk. 1986. Automatic sense disambiguation using machine readable dictionaries: how to tell a pine cone from an ice cream cone. In *SIGDOC '86: Proceedings of the 5th annual international conference on Systems documentation*, New York, NY, USA.

G. Miller, R. Beckwith, C. Fellbaum, D. Gross, and K. Miller. 1990. An on-line lexical database. *International Journal of Lexicography*, 13(4):235–312.

Alessandro Moschitti and Roberto Basili. 2004. Complex linguistic features for text classification: A comprehensive study. In *Proc. of the European Conf. on IR, ECIR*, pages 181–196, New York, USA.

Roberto Navigli and Mirella Lapata. 2007. Graph connectivity measures for unsupervised word sense disambiguation. In *Proceedings of IJCAI'07*, pages 1683–1688, San Francisco, CA, USA. Morgan Kaufmann Publishers Inc.

Roberto Navigli, Kenneth C. Litkowski, and Orin Hargraves. 2007. Semeval-2007 task 07: coarse-grained english all-words task. In *SemEval '07*, pages 30–35, Morristown, NJ, USA. Association for Computational Linguistics.

M. Palmer, C. Fellbaum, S. Cotton, L. Delfs, and H.T. Dang. 2001. English tasks: All-words and verb lexical sample. In *Proceedings of SENSEVAL-2*, Tolouse, France, July.

S. Pradhan, E. Loper, D. Dligach, and M. Palmer. 2007. Semeval-2007 task-17: English lexical sample srl and all words. In *Proceedings of SemEval-2007*, Prague, Czech Republic, June.

Magnus Sahlgren. 2006. *The Word-Space Model*. Department of Linguistics, Stockholm University.

Ravi Sinha and Rada Mihalcea. 2007. Unsupervised graph-based word sense disambiguation using measures of word semantic similarity. In *IEEE ICSC 2007*.

B. Snyder and M. Palmer. 2004. The english all-words task. In *Proceeding of ACL 2004 Senseval-3 Workshop*, Barcelona, Spain, July.

Hierarchical spectral partitioning of bipartite graphs to cluster dialects and identify distinguishing features

Martijn Wieling
University of Groningen
The Netherlands
m.b.wieling@rug.nl

John Nerbonne
University of Groningen
The Netherlands
j.nerbonne@rug.nl

Abstract

In this study we apply hierarchical spectral partitioning of bipartite graphs to a Dutch dialect dataset to cluster dialect varieties and determine the concomitant sound correspondences. An important advantage of this clustering method over other dialectometric methods is that the linguistic basis is *simultaneously* determined, bridging the gap between traditional and quantitative dialectology. Besides showing that the results of the hierarchical clustering improve over the flat spectral clustering method used in an earlier study (Wieling and Nerbonne, 2009), the values of the second singular vector used to generate the two-way clustering can be used to identify the most important sound correspondences for each cluster. This is an important advantage of the hierarchical method as it obviates the need for external methods to determine the most important sound correspondences for a geographical cluster.

1 Introduction

For almost forty years quantitative methods have been applied to the analysis of dialect variation (Séguy, 1973; Goebl, 1982; Nerbonne et al., 1999). Until recently, these methods focused mostly on identifying the most important dialectal groups using an aggregate analysis of the linguistic data.

One of these quantitative methods, clustering, has been applied frequently to dialect data, especially in an effort to compare computational analyses to traditional views on dialect areas (Davis and Houck, 1995; Clopper and Pisoni, 2004; Heeringa, 2004; Moisl and Jones, 2005; Mucha and Haimerl, 2005; Prokić and Nerbonne, 2009).

While viewing dialect differences at an aggregate level certainly gives a more comprehensive view than the analysis of a single subjectively selected feature, the aggregate approach has never fully convinced traditional linguists of its use as it fails to identify the linguistic distinctions among the identified groups. Recently, however, Wieling and Nerbonne (2009; 2010) answered this criticism by applying a promising graph-theoretic method, the spectral partitioning of bipartite graphs, to cluster varieties and simultaneously determine the linguistic basis of the clusters.

The spectral partitioning of bipartite graphs has been a popular method for the task of co-clustering since its introduction by Dhillon in 2001. Besides being used in the field of information retrieval for co-clustering words and documents (Dhillon, 2001), this method has also proven useful in the field of bioinformatics, successfully co-clustering genes and conditions (Kluger et al., 2003).

Wieling and Nerbonne (2009) used spectral partitioning of bipartite graphs to co-cluster dialect varieties and sound correspondences with respect to a set of reference pronunciations. They reported a fair geographical clustering of the varieties in addition to sensible sound correspondences. In a follow-up study, Wieling and Nerbonne (2010) developed an external method to rank the sound correspondences for each geographic cluster, which also conformed largely to the subjectively selected "interesting" sound correspondences in their earlier study (Wieling and Nerbonne, 2009).

In all the aforementioned studies, the spectral graph partitioning method was used to generate a flat clustering. However, Shi and Malik (2000) indicated that a hierarchical clustering obtained by repeatedly grouping in two clusters should be preferred over the flat clustering approach as approximation errors are reduced. More importantly, genealogical relationships between languages (or dialects) are generally expected to have a hierarchical structure due to the dynamics of language

Proceedings of the 2010 Workshop on Graph-based Methods for Natural Language Processing, ACL 2010, pages 33–41,
Uppsala, Sweden, 16 July 2010.

Figure 1: Distribution of GTRP varieties including province names

change in which early changes result in separate varieties which then undergo subsequent changes independently (Jeffers and Lehiste, 1979).

In this study, we will apply the hierarchical spectral graph partitioning method to a Dutch dialect dataset. Besides comparing the results to the flat clustering obtained by Wieling and Nerbonne (2009), we will also show that identifying the most important sound correspondences is inherent to the method, alleviating the need for an external ranking method (e.g., see Wieling and Nerbonne, 2010).

While the current study applies the hierarchical clustering and (novel) ranking method to pronunciation data, we would also like to point out that these methods are not restricted to this type of data and can readily be applied to other domains such as information retrieval and bioinformatics where other spectral methods (e.g., principal component analysis) have already been applied successfully (e.g., see Furnas et al., 1988 and Jolicoeur and Mosimann, 1960).

2 Material

In this study, we use the same dataset as discussed by Wieling and Nerbonne (2009). In short, the Goeman-Taeldeman-Van Reenen-project data (GTRP; Goeman and Taeldeman, 1996; Van den

[redacted]

Figure 2: Example of a bipartite graph of varieties and sound correspondences

Berg, 2003) is the most recent Dutch dialect dataset digitally available consisting of 1876 phonetically transcribed items for 613 dialect varieties in the Netherlands and Flanders. We focus on a subset of 562 words selected by Wieling et al. (2007) for all 424 Netherlandic varieties. We do not include the Belgian varieties, as the transcriptions did not use the same number of tokens as used for the Netherlandic transcriptions. The geographic distribution of the GTRP varieties including province names is shown in Figure 1.

3 Methods

The spectral graph partitioning method we apply requires as input an undirected bipartite graph. A bipartite graph is a graph consisting of two sets of vertices where each edge connects a vertex from one set to a vertex in the other set. Vertices within a set are not connected. An example of a bipartite graph is shown in Figure 2. The vertices on the left side represent the varieties, while the vertices on the right side represent the sound correspondences (each individual sound is surrounded by a set of square brackets). An edge between a variety and a sound correspondence indicates that the sound correspondence occurs in that variety with respect to a specific reference variety.

As we are interested in clustering dialect varieties and detecting their underlying linguistic basis, our bipartite graph consists of dialect varieties and for each variety the presence of sound correspondences compared to a reference variety (indicated by an edge; see Figure 2). Because we do not have pronunciations of standard (or historical) Dutch, we use the pronunciations of the city Delft as our reference, since they are close to standard

Dutch (Wieling and Nerbonne, 2009) and allow a more straightforward interpretation of the sound correspondences than those of other varieties.

3.1 Obtaining sound correspondences

We obtain the sound correspondences by aligning the pronunciations of Delft against the pronunciations of all other dialect varieties using the Levenshtein algorithm (Levenshtein, 1965). The Levenshtein algorithm generates an alignment by minimizing the number of edit operations (insertions, deletions and substitutions) needed to transform one string into the other. For example, the Levenshtein distance between [bɪndən] and [bɛində], two Dutch dialect pronunciations of the word 'to bind', is 3:

bɪndən	insert ɛ	1
bɛɪndən	subst. i/ɪ	1
bɛindən	delete n	1
bɛində		
		3

The corresponding alignment is:

b		ɪ	n	d	ə	n
b	ɛ	i	n	d	ə	
	1	1				1

When all edit operations have the same cost, it is clear that the vowel [ɪ] in the alignment above can be aligned with either the vowel [ɛ] or the vowel [i]. To improve the initial alignments, we use an empirically derived segment distance table obtained by using the pointwise mutual information (PMI) procedure as introduced by Wieling et al. (2009).[1] They showed that applying the PMI procedure resulted in much better alignments than using several other alignment procedures.

The initial step of the PMI procedure consists of obtaining a starting set of alignments. In our case we obtain these by using the Levenshtein algorithm with a syllabicity constraint: vowels may only align with (semi-)vowels, and consonants only with consonants, except for syllabic consonants which may also be aligned with vowels. Subsequently, the substitution cost of every segment pair (a segment can also be a gap, representing an insertion or a deletion) can be calculated according to a pointwise mutual information procedure assessing the statistical dependence between the two segments:

$$\text{PMI}(x, y) = \log_2 \left(\frac{p(x, y)}{p(x)\, p(y)} \right)$$

Where:

- $p(x, y)$ is estimated by calculating the number of times x and y occur at the same position in two aligned strings X and Y, divided by the total number of aligned segments (i.e. the relative occurrence of the aligned segments x and y in the whole data set). Note that either x or y can be a gap in the case of insertion or deletion.

- $p(x)$ and $p(y)$ are estimated as the number of times x (or y) occurs, divided by the total number of segment occurrences (i.e. the relative occurrence of x or y in the whole data set). Dividing by this term normalizes the co-occurrence frequency with respect to the frequency expected if x and y are statistically independent.

In short, this procedure adapts the distance between two sound segments based on how likely it is that they are paired in the alignments. If two sounds are seen more (less) often together than we would expect based on their relative frequency in the dataset, their PMI score will be positive (negative). Higher scores indicate that segments tend to co-occur in correspondences more often, while lower scores indicate the opposite. New segment distances (i.e. segment substitution costs) are obtained by subtracting the PMI score from 0 and adding the maximum PMI score (to enforce that the minimum distance is 0). Based on the adapted segment distances we generate new alignments and we repeat this procedure until the alignments remain constant.

We extract the sound correspondences from the final alignments and represent the bipartite graph by a matrix $\boldsymbol{A}$ having 423 rows (all varieties, except Delft) and 957 columns (all occurring sound correspondences). We do not include frequency information in this matrix, but use binary values to indicate the presence (1) or absence (0) of a sound correspondence with respect to the reference pronunciation.[2] To reduce the effect of noise, we only

[1] The PMI procedure is implemented in the dialectometry package RUG/L04 which can be downloaded from http://www.let.rug.nl/ kleiweg/L04.

[2] We decided against using (the log) of the frequencies, as results showed that this approach gave too much weight to uninformative high-frequent substitutions of two identical sounds.

regard a sound correspondence as present in a variety when it occurs in at least three aligned pronunciations. Consequently, we reduce the number of sound correspondences (columns of $\boldsymbol{A}$) by more than half to 477.

3.2 Hierarchical spectral partitioning of bipartite graphs

Spectral graph theory is used to find the principal properties and structure of a graph from its graph spectrum (Chung, 1997). Wieling and Nerbonne (2009) used spectral partitioning of bipartite graphs as introduced by Dhillon (2001) to co-cluster varieties and sound correspondences, enabling them to obtain a geographical clustering with a simultaneously derived linguistic basis (i.e. the clustered sound correspondences). While Wieling and Nerbonne (2009) focused on the flat clustering approach, we will use the hierarchical approach by iteratively clustering in two groups. This approach is preferred by Shi and Malik (2000), because approximation errors are reduced compared to the flat clustering approach.

The hierarchical spectral partitioning algorithm, following Dhillon (2001), proceeds as follows:

1. Given the 423×477 variety-by-segment-correspondence matrix $\boldsymbol{A}$ as discussed previously, form

$$\boldsymbol{A_n} = \boldsymbol{D_1}^{-1/2}\boldsymbol{A}\boldsymbol{D_2}^{-1/2}$$

   with $\boldsymbol{D_1}$ and $\boldsymbol{D_2}$ diagonal matrices such that $D_1(i,i) = \Sigma_j A_{ij}$ and $D_2(j,j) = \Sigma_i A_{ij}$

2. Calculate the singular value decomposition (*SVD*) of the normalized matrix $\boldsymbol{A_n}$

$$SVD(\boldsymbol{A_n}) = \boldsymbol{U}\boldsymbol{\Lambda}\boldsymbol{V}^{\mathsf{T}}$$

   and take the singular vectors $\boldsymbol{u_2}$ and $\boldsymbol{v_2}$

3. Compute $\boldsymbol{z_2} = \begin{bmatrix} \boldsymbol{D_1}^{-1/2}\boldsymbol{u_2} \\ \boldsymbol{D_2}^{-1/2}\boldsymbol{v_2} \end{bmatrix}$

4. Run the k-means algorithm on $\boldsymbol{z_2}$ to obtain the bipartitioning

5. Repeat steps 1 to 4 on both clusters separately to create the hierarchical clustering

The following example (taken from Wieling and Nerbonne, 2010) shows how we can co-cluster the graph of Figure 2 in two groups. The matrix representation of this graph is as follows:

	[ʌ]:[ɪ]	[-]:[ə]	[d]:[w]
Appelscha (Friesland)	1	1	0
Oudega (Friesland)	1	1	0
Vaals (Limburg)	0	1	1
Sittard (Limburg)	0	1	1

The first step is to construct matrices $\boldsymbol{D_1}$ and $\boldsymbol{D_2}$ which contain the total number of edges from every variety ($\boldsymbol{D_1}$) and every sound correspondence ($\boldsymbol{D_2}$) on the diagonal. Both matrices are shown below.

$$\boldsymbol{D_1} = \begin{bmatrix} 2 & 0 & 0 & 0 \\ 0 & 2 & 0 & 0 \\ 0 & 0 & 2 & 0 \\ 0 & 0 & 0 & 2 \end{bmatrix} \qquad \boldsymbol{D_2} = \begin{bmatrix} 2 & 0 & 0 \\ 0 & 4 & 0 \\ 0 & 0 & 2 \end{bmatrix}$$

The normalized matrix $\boldsymbol{A_n}$ can be calculated using the formula displayed in step 1 of the hierarchical bipartitioning algorithm:

$$\boldsymbol{A_n} = \begin{bmatrix} .5 & .35 & 0 \\ .5 & .35 & 0 \\ 0 & .35 & .5 \\ 0 & .35 & .5 \end{bmatrix}$$

Applying the singular value decomposition to $\boldsymbol{A_n}$ yields:

$$\boldsymbol{U} = \begin{bmatrix} -.5 & .5 & .71 & 0 \\ -.5 & .5 & -.71 & 0 \\ -.5 & -.5 & 0 & -.71 \\ -.5 & -.5 & 0 & .71 \end{bmatrix}$$

$$\boldsymbol{\Lambda} = \begin{bmatrix} 1 & 0 & 0 \\ 0 & .71 & 0 \\ 0 & 0 & 0 \\ 0 & 0 & 0 \end{bmatrix}$$

$$\boldsymbol{V}^{\mathsf{T}} = \begin{bmatrix} -.5 & -.71 & -.5 \\ .71 & 0 & -.71 \\ -.5 & .71 & -.5 \end{bmatrix}$$

Finally, we look at the second singular vector of $\boldsymbol{U}$ (second column) and $\boldsymbol{V}^{\mathsf{T}}$ (second row; i.e. second column of $\boldsymbol{V}$) and compute the 1-dimensional vector $\boldsymbol{z_2}$:

$$\boldsymbol{z_2} = \begin{bmatrix} .35 & .35 & -.35 & -.35 & .5 & 0 & -.5 \end{bmatrix}^T$$

The first four values correspond with the places Appelscha, Oudega, Vaals and Sittard, while the last three values correspond to the segment substitutions [ʌ]:[ɪ], [-]:[ə] and [d]:[w].

After running the k-means algorithm (with random initialization) on $\boldsymbol{z_2}$, the items are assigned to one of two clusters as follows:

$$\begin{bmatrix}1 & 1 & 2 & 2 & 1 & 1 & 2\end{bmatrix}^T$$

This clustering shows that Appelscha and Oudega are grouped together (corresponding to the first and second item of the vector, above) and linked to the clustered segment substitutions of [ʌ]:[ɪ] and [-]:[ə] (cluster 1). Also, Vaals and Sittard are clustered together and linked to the clustered segment substitution [d]:[w] (cluster 2). The segment substitution [-]:[ə] (an insertion of [ə]) is actually not meaningful for the clustering of the varieties (as can be seen in $\boldsymbol{A}$), because the middle value of $\boldsymbol{V}^{\mathrm{T}}$ corresponding to this segment substitution equals 0. It could therefore just as likely be grouped cluster 2. Nevertheless, the k-means algorithm always assigns every item to one cluster.[3]

3.3 Determining the importance of sound correspondences

Wieling and Nerbonne (2010) introduced a *post hoc* method to rank each sound correspondence [a]:[b] based on the representativeness R in a cluster c_i (i.e. the proportion of varieties v in cluster c_i containing the sound correspondence):

$$R(\mathrm{a}, \mathrm{b}, c_i) = \frac{|v \text{ in } c_i \text{ containing [a]:[b]}|}{|v \text{ in } c_i|}$$

and the distinctiveness D (i.e. the number of varieties v within as opposed to outside cluster c_i containing the sound correspondence normalized by the relative size of the cluster):

$$D(\mathrm{a}, \mathrm{b}, c_i) = \frac{O(\mathrm{a}, \mathrm{b}, c_i) - S(c_i)}{1 - S(c_i)}$$

Where the relative occurrence O and the relative size S are given by:

$$O(\mathrm{a}, \mathrm{b}, c_i) = \frac{|v \text{ in } c_i \text{ containing [a]:[b]}|}{|v \text{ containing [a]:[b]}|}$$

$$S(c_i) = \frac{|v \text{ in } c_i|}{|\text{all } v\text{'s}|}$$

[3]Note that we could also have decided to drop this sound correspondence. However using our ranking approach (see Secion 3.3) already ensures that the uninformative sound correspondences are ranked very low.

The importance I is then calculated by averaging the distinctiveness and representativeness:

$$I(\mathrm{a}, \mathrm{b}, c_i) = \frac{R(\mathrm{a}, \mathrm{b}, c_i) + D(\mathrm{a}, \mathrm{b}, c_i)}{2}$$

An extensive explanation of this method can be found in Wieling and Nerbonne (2010).

As we now only use a single singular vector to determine the partitioning (in contrast to the study of Wieling and Nerbonne, 2010 where they used multiple singular vectors to determine the flat clustering), we will investigate if the values of the singular vector $\boldsymbol{v_2}$ reveal information about the importance (as defined above) of the individual sound correspondences. We will evaluate these values by comparing them to the importance values on the basis of the representativeness and distinctiveness (Wieling and Nerbonne, 2010).

4 Results

In this section, we will report the results of applying the hierarchical spectral partitioning method to our Dutch dialect dataset. In addition, we will also compare the geographical clustering to the results obtained by Wieling and Nerbonne (2009).

We will only focus on the four main clusters each consisting of at least 10 varieties. While our method is able to detect smaller clusters in the data, we do not believe these to be stable. We confirmed this by applying three well-known distance-based clustering algorithms (i.e. UPGMA, WPGMA and Ward's Method; Prokić and Nerbonne, 2009) to our data which also only agreed on four main clusters. In addition, Wieling and Nerbonne (2009) reported reliable results on a maximum of 4 clusters.

4.1 Geographical results

Figure 3 shows a dendrogram visualizing the obtained hierarchy as well as a geographic visualization of the clustering. For comparison, Figure 4 shows the visualization of four clusters based on the flat clustering approach of Wieling and Nerbonne (2009).

It is clear that the geographical results of the hierarchical approach (Figure 3) are comparable to the results of the flat clustering approach (Figure 4) of Wieling and Nerbonne (2009).[4] How-

[4]Note that the results of the flat clustering approach were based on all 957 sound correspondences. No noise-reducing frequency threshold was applied there, as this was reported to lead to poorer results (Wieling and Nerbonne, 2009).

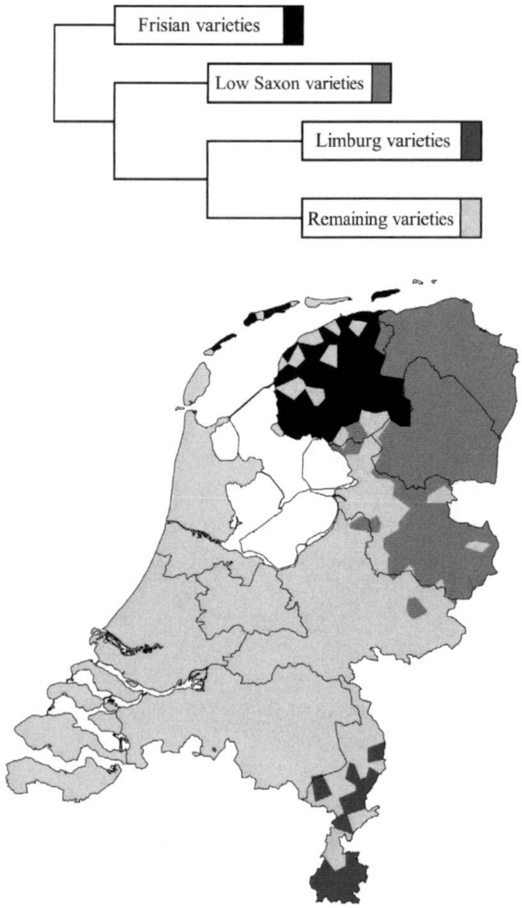

Figure 3: Geographic visualization of the clustering including dendrogram. The shades of grey in the dendrogram correspond with the map (e.g., the Limburg varieties can be found at the bottom-right).

ever, despite the Frisian area (top-left) being identical, we clearly observe that both the Low Saxon area (top-right) and the Limburg area (bottom-right) are larger in the map based on the hierarchical approach. As this better reflects the traditional Dutch dialect landscape (Heeringa, 2004), the hierarchical clustering method seems to be an improvement over the flat clustering method. Also the hierarchy corresponds largely with the one found by Heeringa (2004, Chapter 9), identifying Frisian, Limburg and Low Saxon as separate groups.

4.2 Most important sound correspondences

To see whether the values of the singular vector $\boldsymbol{v}_2$ can be used as a substitute for the external ranking method, we correlated the absolute values of the

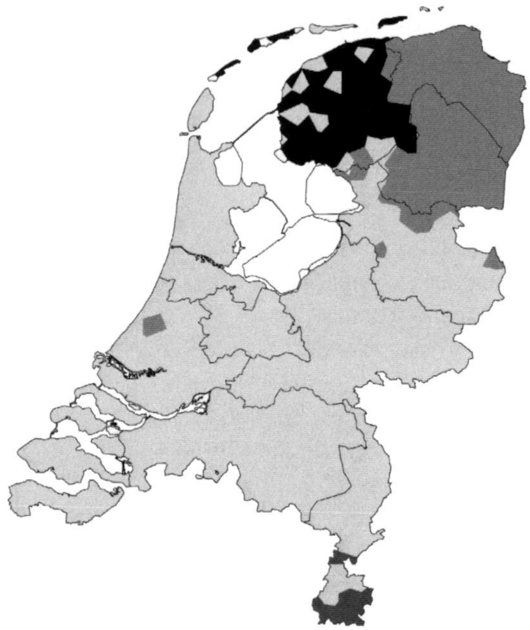

Figure 4: Geographic visualization of the flat clustering reported in Wieling and Nerbonne (2009). The shades of grey are identical to the shades of grey in Figure 3.

singular vector with the importance values based on the distinctiveness and representativeness. For the sound correspondences of the Frisian area we obtained a high Spearman's rank correlation coefficient ρ of .92 ($p < .001$). For the Low Saxon area and the Limburg area we obtained similar values ($\rho = .87, p < .001$ and $\rho = .88, p < .001$, respectively). These results clearly show that the values of the second singular vector $\boldsymbol{v}_2$ can be used as a good substitute for the external ranking method.

Frisian area

The following table shows the five most important sound correspondences for the Frisian area.

Rank	1	2	3	4	5
Reference	-	[x]	[f]	[x]	[a]
Frisian	[ʃ]	[j]	-	[z]	[i]

While we have limited overlap (only [x]:[z]; occuring in e.g. *zeggen* 'say' Dutch [zɛxə], Frisian [sizə]) with the sound correspondences selected and discussed by Wieling and Nerbonne (2010) who used the flat clustering method without a frequency threshold (also causing some of the differences), we observe more overlap with the subjectively selected sound correspondences in Wieling and Nerbonne (2009; [x]:[j] in e.g. *geld* 'money' Dutch [xɛlt], Frisian [jɪlt]; and [a]:[i] in e.g. *kaas* 'cheese' Dutch [kas], Frisian [tsis]). In addition, we detected two novel sound correspondences ([f]:[-] and [-]:[ʃ]).

We commonly find the correspondence [-]:[ʃ] in the infinitive form of verbs such as *wachten* 'wait' Dutch [waxtə], Frisian [waxtʃə]; *vechten* 'fight' Dutch [vɛxtə], Frisian [vɛxtʃə]; or *spuiten* 'spray' Dutch [spœʏtə], Frisian [spoʏtʃə], but it also appears e.g. in Dutch *tegen* 'against' [teixə], Frisian [tʃɪn]. The [f]:[-] correspondence is found in words like *sterven* 'die' standard Dutch [stɛrfə], Frisian [stɛrə].

Low Saxon area

The most important sound correspondences of the Low Saxon area are shown in the table below.

Rank	1	2	3	4	5
Reference	[k]	[v]	[ə]	[f]	[p]
Low Saxon	[ʔ]	[b]	[m]	[b]	[ʔ]

These sound correspondences overlap to a large extent with the most important sound correspondences identified and discussed by Wieling and Nerbonne (2010). The correspondence [k]:[ʔ] can be found in words like *planken* 'boards', Dutch [plɑŋkə], Low Saxon [plɑŋʔŋ̍], while the correspondence [v]:[b] is found in words like *bleven* 'remain' Dutch [blɛvən], Low Saxon [blibm̩]. The final overlapping correspondence [f]:[b] can be observed in words like *proeven* 'test' Dutch [prufə], Low Saxon [proybm̩].

The sound correspondence [ə]:[m] was discussed and selected by Wieling and Nerbonne (2009) as an interesting sound correspondence, occurring in words like *strepen* 'stripes' Dutch [strepə], Low Saxon [strepm̩].

The new correspondence [p]:[ʔ] occurs in words such as *lampen* 'lamps' standard Dutch [lampə], Aduard (Low Saxon) [lamʔm̩], but also postvocalically, as in *gapen* 'yawn', standard Dutch [xapə], Aduard (Low Saxon) [xoʔm̩]. It is obviously related to the [k]:[ʔ] correspondence discussed above.

Limburg area

The most important sound correspondences for the Limburg area are displayed in the table below.

Rank	1	2	3	4	5
Reference	[r]	[s]	[o]	[n]	[r]
Limburg	[x]	[ʒ]	-	[x]	[ʀ]

For this area, we observe limited overlap with the most important sound correspondences based on distinctiveness and representativeness (Wieling and Nerbonne, 2010; only [n]:[x] overlaps, occuring in words like *kleden* 'cloths' Dutch [kledən], Limburg [klɛɪdəx]), as well as with the subjectively selected interesting sound correspondences (Wieling and Nerbonne, 2009; only [r]:[ʀ] overlaps, which occurs in words like *breken* 'to break' Dutch [brekə], Limburg [bʀɛkə]).

The sound correspondence [o]:[-] can be found in *wonen* 'living', pronounced [wounə] in our reference variety Delft and [wunə] in Limburg. As the standard Dutch pronunciation is actually [wonə], this correspondence is caused by the choice of our reference variety, which is unfortunately not identical to standard Dutch.

The other two sound correspondences are more informative. The sound correspondence [r]:[x] can be found in words like *vuur* 'fire' Dutch [fyr], Limburg [vyəx] and is similar to the sound correspondence [r]:[ʀ] discussed above. The other correspondence [s]:[ʒ] occurs when comparing the standard-like Delft variety to Limburg varietes in words such as *zwijgen* 'to be silent' [sweixə], Limburg [ʒwiɣə]; or *zwemmen* 'swim' [swɛmə], Limburg [ʒwəmə].

Hierarchical versus flat clustering

In general, then, the sound correspondences uncovered by the hierarchical version of the spectral clustering technique turn out to be at least as interesting as those uncovered by the flat clustering, which leads us to regard the hierarchical clustering technique as defensible in this respect. Since dialectologists are convinced that dialect areas are organized hierarchically, we are naturally inclined toward hierarchical clustering techniques as well. We note additionally that the using the values of the second singular vector is an adequate substitution of the external ranking method based on distinctiveness and representativeness, which means that the present paper also marks a step forward in simplifying the methodology.

5 Discussion

In this study we showed that using hierarchical spectral partitioning of bipartite graphs results in an improved geographical clustering over the flat partitioning method and also results in sensible concomitant sound correspondences. One of the reasons for the improvement of the geographical clustering could be the approximation errors which arise when going from the real valued solution to the discrete valued solution, and which increase with every additional singular vector used (Shi and Malik, 2000).

In addition, we showed that using the values of the second singular vector obviates the need for an external ranking method (e.g., see Wieling and Nerbonne, 2010) to identify the most important sound correspondences.

Since the spectral partitioning of bipartite graphs appears to be identifying significant (representative and distinctive) correspondences well – both in the flat clustering design and in the (present) hierarchical scheme, several further opportunities become worthy of exploration. First, we might ask if we can automatically identify a threshold of significance for such correspondences, as to-date we have only sought to verify significance, not to exclude marginally significant elements. Second, while we have applied the technique exclusively to data for which the correspondence consists of a comparison of dialect data to (near) standard data, the analysis of historical data, in which varieties are compared to an earlier form, is within reach. As the first step, we should wish to compare data to a well-established historical predecessor as further steps might require genuine reconstruction, still beyond anyone's reach (as far as we know). Third, the technique would be more generally applicable if it did not require agreeing on a standard, or pole of comparison. This sounds difficult, but multi-alignment techniques might bring it within reach (Prokić et al., 2009).

It is intriguing to note that Nerbonne (in press) found only sporadic correspondences using factor analysis on data which incorporated frequency of correspondence, and we have likewise found frequency-weighted data less successful as a basis for spectral bipartite clustering. Shackleton (2007), Wieling and Nerbonne (2010) and the current paper are more successful using data which lacks information about the frequency of occurrence of sounds and/or sound correspondences. The question arises as to whether this is general and why this is so. Is it due to the skewness of frequency distributions, in which a suitable normalization might be attempted? Or is it simply more straightforward to focus on the absolute presence or absence of a sound or sound correspondence?

While sound correspondences function well as a linguistic basis, it might also be interesting to investigate morphological distinctions present in the GTRP corpus. This would enable us to compare the similarity of the geographic distributions of pronunciation variation and morphological variation.

Finally, while we only tested this method on a single dataset, it would be interesting to see if our results and conclusions also hold when applied to more and different datasets. We also realize that the evaluation in this study is rather qualitative, but we intend to develop more quantitative evaluation methods for future studies.

Acknowledgements

We thank Gertjan van Noord and Tim Van de Cruys for their comments during a presentation about the flat spectral graph partitioning method, which instigated the search for an inherent ranking method.

References

Fan Chung. 1997. *Spectral graph theory*. American Mathematical Society.

Cynthia G. Clopper and David B. Pisoni. 2004. Some acoustic cues for the perceptual categorization of American English regional dialects. *Journal of Phonetics*, 32(1):111–140.

L.M. Davis and C.L. Houck. 1995. What Determines a Dialect Area? Evidence from the Linguistic Atlas of the Upper Midwest. *American Speech*, 70(4):371–386.

Inderjit Dhillon. 2001. Co-clustering documents and words using bipartite spectral graph partitioning. In *Proceedings of the seventh ACM SIGKDD international conference on Knowledge discovery and data mining*, pages 269–274. ACM New York, NY, USA.

George Furnas, Scott Deerwester, Susan Dumais, Thomas Landauer, Richard Harshman, Lynn Streeter, and Karen Lochbaum. 1988. Information retrieval using a singular value decomposition model of latent semantic structure. In *Proceedings of the 11th annual international ACM SIGIR conference on Research and development in information retrieval*, pages 465–480. ACM.

Hans Goebl. 1982. *Dialektometrie: Prinzipien und Methoden des Einsatzes der Numerischen Taxonomie im Bereich der Dialektgeographie*.

Österreichische Akademie der Wissenschaften, Wien.

Ton Goeman and Johan Taeldeman. 1996. Fonologie en morfologie van de Nederlandse dialecten. Een nieuwe materiaalverzameling en twee nieuwe atlasprojecten. *Taal en Tongval*, 48:38–59.

Wilbert Heeringa. 2004. *Measuring Dialect Pronunciation Differences using Levenshtein Distance*. Ph.D. thesis, Rijksuniversiteit Groningen.

Robert Jeffers and Ilse Lehiste. 1979. *Principles and methods for historical linguistics*. MIT Press, Cambridge.

Pierre Jolicoeur and James E. Mosimann. 1960. Size and shape variation in the painted turtle. A principal component analysis. *Growth*, 24:339–354.

Yuval Kluger, Ronen Basri, Joseph Chang, and Mark Gerstein. 2003. Spectral biclustering of microarray data: Coclustering genes and conditions. *Genome Research*, 13(4):703–716.

Vladimir Levenshtein. 1965. Binary codes capable of correcting deletions, insertions and reversals. *Doklady Akademii Nauk SSSR*, 163:845–848.

Hermann Moisl and Val Jones. 2005. Cluster analysis of the newcastle electronic corpus of tyneside english: A comparison of methods. *Literary and Linguistic Computing*, 20(supp.):125–146.

Hans-Joachim Mucha and Edgard Haimerl. 2005. Automatic validation of hierarchical cluster analysis with application in dialectometry. In Claus Weihs and Wolgang Gaul, editors, *Classification—the Ubiquitous Challenge. Proc. of the 28th Meeting of the Gesellschaft für Klassifikation, Dortmund, March 9–11, 2004*, pages 513–520, Berlin. Springer.

John Nerbonne, Wilbert Heeringa, and Peter Kleiweg. 1999. Edit distance and dialect proximity. In David Sankoff and Joseph Kruskal, editors, *Time Warps, String Edits and Macromolecules: The Theory and Practice of Sequence Comparison, 2nd ed.*, pages v–xv. CSLI, Stanford, CA.

John Nerbonne. in press. Various Variation Aggregates in the LAMSAS South. In C. Davis and M. Picone, editors, *Language Variety in the South III*. University of Alabama Press, Tuscaloosa.

Jelena Prokić and John Nerbonne. 2009. Recognizing groups among dialects. In John Nerbonne, Charlotte Gooskens, Sebastian Kurschner, and Rene van Bezooijen, editors, *International Journal of Humanities and Arts Computing, special issue on Language Variation*.

Jelena Prokić, Martijn Wieling, and John Nerbonne. 2009. Multiple sequence alignments in linguistics. In Lars Borin and Piroska Lendvai, editors, *Language Technology and Resources for Cultural Heritage, Social Sciences, Humanities, and Education*, pages 18–25.

Jean Séguy. 1973. La dialectométrie dans l'atlas linguistique de gascogne. *Revue de Linguistique Romane*, 37(145):1–24.

Robert G. Shackleton, Jr. 2007. Phonetic variation in the traditional english dialects. *Journal of English Linguistics*, 35(1):30–102.

Jianbo Shi and Jitendra Malik. 2000. Normalized cuts and image segmentation. *IEEE Transactions on pattern analysis and machine intelligence*, 22(8):888–905.

Boudewijn van den Berg. 2003. *Phonology & Morphology of Dutch & Frisian Dialects in 1.1 million transcriptions*. Goeman-Taeldeman-Van Reenen project 1980-1995, Meertens Instituut Electronic Publications in Linguistics 3. Meertens Instituut (CD-ROM), Amsterdam.

Martijn Wieling and John Nerbonne. 2009. Bipartite spectral graph partitioning to co-cluster varieties and sound correspondences in dialectology. In Monojit Choudhury, Samer Hassan, Animesh Mukherjee, and Smaranda Muresan, editors, *Proc. of the 2009 Workshop on Graph-based Methods for Natural Language Processing*, pages 26–34.

Martijn Wieling and John Nerbonne. 2010. Bipartite spectral graph partitioning for clustering dialect varieties and detecting their linguistic features. *Computer Speech and Language*. Accepted to appear in a special issue on network models of social and cognitive dynamics of language.

Martijn Wieling, Wilbert Heeringa, and John Nerbonne. 2007. An aggregate analysis of pronunciation in the Goeman-Taeldeman-Van Reenen-Project data. *Taal en Tongval*, 59:84–116.

Martijn Wieling, Jelena Prokić, and John Nerbonne. 2009. Evaluating the pairwise alignment of pronunciations. In Lars Borin and Piroska Lendvai, editors, *Language Technology and Resources for Cultural Heritage, Social Sciences, Humanities, and Education*, pages 26–34.

A Character-Based Intersection Graph Approach to Linguistic Phylogeny

Jessica Enright
University of Alberta
Edmonton, Alberta, Canada
enright@cs.ualberta.ca

Abstract

Linguists use phylogenetic methods to build evolutionary trees of languages given lexical, phonological, and morphological data. Perfect phylogeny is too restrictive to explain most data sets. Conservative Dollo phylogeny is more permissive, and has been used in biological applications. We propose the use of conservative Dollo phylogeny as an alternative or complementary approach for linguistic phylogenetics. We test this approach on an Indo-European dataset.

1 Introduction

1.1 Language Phylogeny

A linguistic phylogenetic tree is a tree describing the evolution of some set of languages. Usually, we build such a tree using information given by a set of characters associated with those languages.

We say that a character *back-mutated* if after evolving from 0 state to 1 state, it subsequently is lost and switches back on the tree from 1 state to 0 state. We say that a character has *parallel evolution* if it evolves twice on the tree from state 0 to state 1 independently. We say that a character is *borrowed* if, on the true evolutionary tree, it has been transfered from one branch to another by contact between linguistic groups. Loanwords are an example of this.

1.2 Perfect phylogeny

Given a set of binary characters $\mathcal{C} = \{c_1...c_j\}$, we say that a rooted tree $T = (r, V_T, E_T)$ with languages $\mathcal{L} = l_1...l_k$ as the leaf nodes of T is a *perfect phylogeny* if there is a binary labeling of each character at each node such that the root node is labeled with a zero for each character, and for each character both the subtree induced by the nodes labeled 1 at that character, and the subtree induced by the nodes labeled 0 at that character are connected.

This means that each character evolves exactly once, and that there is no back-mutation or borrowing.

We can recognize whether a set of characters admits a perfect phylogeny in polynomial time (Felsenstein, 2004). Unfortunately, often character data does not admit a perfect phylogeny.

Usually the question given character data is: How far away is this data from admitting a perfect phylogeny? What is the minimum level of borrowing, back mutation or parallel evolution that we must allow to produce a tree that describes this data? Answering this question is NP-Hard (Day et al., 1986).

Many approaches describe and formalize this question. Nakhleh et al. (2005b) provide an excellent survey of linguistic phylogenetic methods.

Nakhleh et al. (2005a) proposed perfect phylogeny networks as a way of considering the phylogeny problem. A perfect phylogeny network is a graph that is not required to be a tree such that every character exhibits a perfect phylogeny on at least one of the subtrees of that graph.

Unfortunately, even given a phylogenetic tree and character data, determining the minimum number of edges one must add to produce a perfect phylogeny network is NP-Hard (Day et al., 1986). Nakhleh et al. (2005a) mention that applying the perfect phylogeny network approach to their Indo-European language dataset is tractable only because one need only add very few edges to their tree to produce a perfect phylogeny network.

1.3 Dollo Phylogenies

In contrast to a perfect phylogeny, a Dollo phylogeny allows an arbitrary number of back mutations.

Given a set of binary characters $\mathcal{C} = \{c_1...c_j\}$, we say that a rooted tree $T = (r, V_T, E_T)$ with

Proceedings of the 2010 Workshop on Graph-based Methods for Natural Language Processing, ACL 2010, pages 42–46,
Uppsala, Sweden, 16 July 2010. ©2010 Association for Computational Linguistics

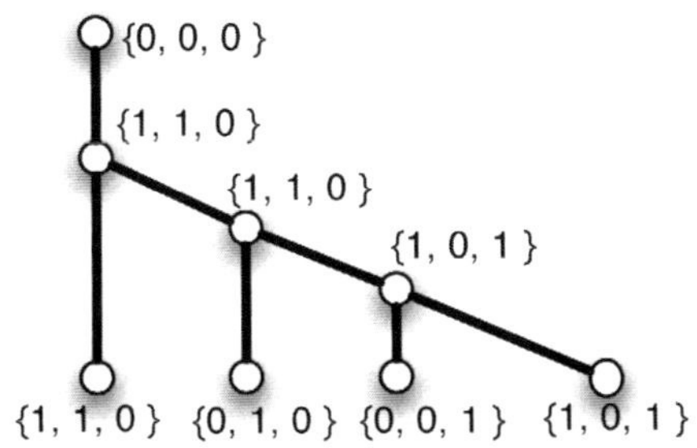

Figure 1: A tree that is a conservative Dollo phylogeny, but not a perfect phylogeny, as characters one and two back-mutate. The lists at each node contain the state of characters one, two, and three in that order.

languages $\mathcal{L} = l_1 ... l_k$ as the leaf nodes of T is a *Dollo phylogeny* if there is a binary labeling of each character at each node such that the root node is labeled with a zero for each character, and for each character the subtree induced by the nodes labeled 1 is connected.

This means that each character evolves exactly once but an arbitrary number of back-mutations are allowed. Unfortunately, every set of character data admits a Dollo phylogeny. Clearly Dollo phylogeny is too permissive to be a useful notion in linguistic phylogenetics.

Przytycka et al. (2006) discussed the idea of a *conservative Dollo phylogeny*.

Given a set of binary characters $\mathcal{C} = \{c_1 ... c_j\}$, we say that a rooted tree $T = (r, V_T, E_T)$ with languages $\mathcal{L} = l_1 ... l_k$ as the leaf nodes of T is a *conservative Dollo phylogeny* (CDP) if there is a binary labeling of each character at each node such that the root node is labeled with a zero for each character, for each character the subtree induced by the nodes labeled 1 is connected, and if two characters appear together in their 1 states in the tree at an internal node, they also occur together in their 1 states in the tree at a leaf node. Recall that the leaves in this tree are the languages for which we have data. For an example, see Figure 1.

If two characters existed together in some ancestral language, they must also exist together in at least one leaf language. That is, if they have ever existed together in the same language, we have evidence of it in the form of a known language that possessed both of those characters. Is this a reasonable assumption? We have no evidence that it is. However, it's certainly a more reasonable assumption than that required for a perfect phylogeny. We expect that often, data sets will not admit a CDP, and that, like for perfect phylogeny, the question will be: How far away are the data from admitting a CDP?

Przytycka et al. (2006) prove that a set of characters admit a CDP if and only if their intersection graph is chordal. Chordal graphs are graphs with no induced cycles longer than three vertices. Rose et al. (1976) provide a linear-time recognition algorithm for chordal graphs.

Graph $G = (V, E)$ is an intersection graph of a family of sets $\mathcal{S}$ if there is a bijection $\mathcal{F}$ between V and $\mathcal{S}$ such that for every two sets $s, t \in \mathcal{S}$ $\mathcal{F}(s)$ is adjacent to $\mathcal{F}(t)$ if and only if s intersects t. Set s intersects set t if they share at least one element. Given sets, we can compute their intersection graph in linear time. For an example of an intersection graph derived from a family of sets, see Figure 2.

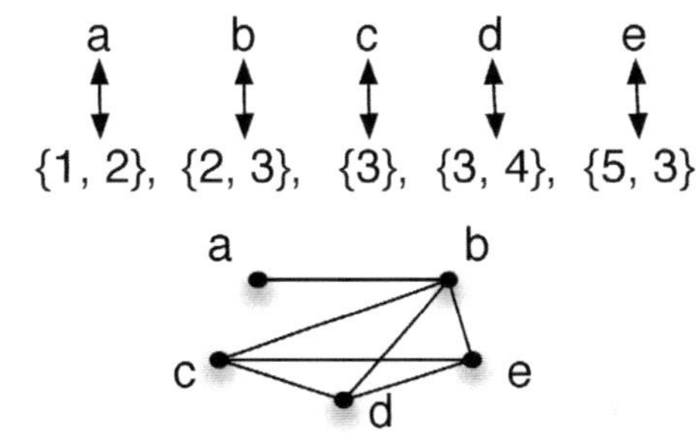

Figure 2: An example of a family of sets labeled a, b, c, d, e on the top and the intersection graph of those sets on the bottom.

We can then determine if a set of characters admits a CDP in linear time. This approach to phylogeny was used by Przytycka et al. (2006) in a biological phylogenetic application. Here, we use it for linguistic phylogeny.

2 Methodology

We implemented an algorithm to, given a character dataset, compute the intersection graph of those characters, and determine whether the resulting graph is chordal as given by Rose et al. (1976). This tells us whether or not the dataset admits a CDP. We also implemented an exhaustive search that computes the minimum number of characters that must be borrowed to otherwise admit a CDP.

We ran our program on the Indo-European character dataset used by Nakhleh et al. (2005a), and available online at http://www.cs.rice.edu/ nakhleh/CPHL/.

2.1 Language Family Grouping

Nakhleh et al. (2005a) combined established language groups into a single language during computation to decrease computation time. We use the same families as they do, and do the same in two of our experiments.

For example, we consider the Tocharian language family, consisting of Tocharian A and Tocharian B to be a single language when building our intersection graph. This language grouping is done as a preprocessing step to the construction of the intersection graph of the characters.

We expect this transformation to be particularly useful in the CDP setting, beyond just decreasing computation time. We expect it will make our data closer to admitting a CDP in a way consistent with true evolutionary history.

Consider the difference between the intersection graph of a set of characters with family grouping and without. Let s and t be two characters that, are considered to intersect with family grouping, but not without. Then s and t are not present in any of the same languages, but there are two languages l_i, l_j such that l_i has character s but not t and language l_j has character t but not s, and l_i and l_j are in the same family L.

We use the language family definitions given by Nakhleh et al. (2005a), where these language families are identified as consistent with all characters, and it is argued that it is very unlikely there is any borrowing between a portion of the tree inside the family, and a portion of the tree outside the family.

Therefore, if s and t are both present within leaves in the language family L, and neither is borrowed from outside the family, then each of s, t is either present only within language family L, or is present in at least one internal node ancestral to language family L. If s and t are only present within the language family, they are not informative when language family grouping is used.

However, if both s and t are present at an internal node ancestral to language family L, then this is important information that we have derived by applying family language grouping, and will make the data closer to admitting a CDP in terms of number of borrowings required.

2.2 Binary Data

We made the data binary by separating states of a given character as best indicated by notes provided by Nakhleh et al. (2005a) on their coding of the characters. In making the data binary, we have likely lost some constraining information. When a language (or language family, when that grouping was used) has a unique state at a character, we coded this as having all possible non-ancestral states. The basis for this is that some of these codes indicate that there is no data for that character at that language, or that if that language actually does have a unique state at that character, it is uninformative, but could have evolved from any other state. Data processing by someone more highly trained in linguistics would either confirm this decision or provide an alternative approach. We have tried to remain as close as possible to how the data is used in Nakhleh et al. (2005a).

3 Experiments

We ran four experiments to investigate the usefulness of the conservative Dollo parsimony approach. We ran our implementation on:

1. All characters without language family grouping
2. All characters with language family grouping
3. Phonological and morphological characters only without language family grouping
4. Phonological and morphological characters only with language family grouping

4 Results

We give our results in Table 4

For the morphological and phonological dataset, both grouped and ungrouped, we extracted a phylogenetic tree from our program's output. These trees were consistent with Tree A in (Nakhleh et al., 2005a). The fact that we managed to build a tree consistent with expectations without any input tree is very encouraging.

Recall that when we use language grouping we combine all languages identified as being from an established family by Nakhleh et al. (2005a) into a single language. For example, instead of considering both Tocharian A and Tocharian B, in our experiments with language grouping we consider a single language, Tocharian, that has all characteristics of Tocharian A and all characteristics of Tocharian B.

Table 1: The results of conservative Dollo phylogeny checking algorithm on modified versions of the Indo-European character dataset as used in (Nakhleh et al., 2005a). We ran each program for at most 1 hour. Entries of "Too slow" indicate that we did not allow the program to halt.

Dataset	Admits a CDP?		Minimum number of languages that must borrow	
	Answer	Time	Answer	Time
Phonological, Morphological Data without Language Grouping	Yes	<1 s	0	<1 s
Phonological, Morphological Data with Language Grouping	Yes	<1 s	0	<1 s
All Data without Language Grouping	No	<1 s	-	Too slow
All Data with Language Grouping	No	<1 s	2	< 1 s

In our experiments without language grouping, we do not combine languages in this way, and instead consider all 24 languages separately.

5 Discussion

When is the CDP approach useful for linguistic phylogenetics?

Because a CDP allows back-mutation, it is likely most useful for datasets that exhibit a lot of back mutation, and not a lot of borrowing. Phonological and morphological characters are more likely to fit this requirement than lexical data. This is reflected in our positive results on the phonological and morphological characters alone.

In contrast, when we included the lexical data, the dataset did not admit a conservative Dollo parsimony, whether or not we used language family grouping. We expect this is due to borrowing of lexical characters.

The full dataset with language family grouping was much closer to admitting a conservative Dollo parsimony than the full dataset without language family grouping. As explained in our Methodology section, this was expected and reinforces our position that language family grouping is extremely useful when computing conservative Dollo phylogenies.

Our experiments ran in either negligible time, or were not allowed to halt. The speed of the fast experiments suggests that computing conservative Dollo phylogenies might be useful in constructing a tree when no tree is known, and the amount of character data causes computing other types of phylogenies to be intractable.

6 Future Work

We are currently pursuing several extensions to this work.

First, we are developing an improved heuristic search for the minimum number of edges that need to be removed from or added to a graph to make the resulting graph chordal. This will enable us to use the Dollo phylogeny approach outlined here on character data sets that require more borrowing to fully explain them.

Using this improved search, we will run experiments on other sets of character data.

Nakhleh et al. (2005a) started with several proposed trees in their work on perfect phylogenetic networks. We plan to implement a version of our CDP approach that takes as input a proposed tree. This version will calculate the minimum number of edges that must be added to create a Dollo phylogeny network, as analogous to Nakhleh et al.'s perfect phylogenetic network. This minimum number of edges would be useful as a lower bound for the required number of edges one must add to produce a perfect phylogeny network.

7 Conclusion

We have presented an alternative phylogeny that may be of use in linguistic phylogenetics, particularly on phonological or morphological data. We have proposed a number of future extensions based on our experiments that we hope will improve the performance of this approach.

Acknowledgments

The author would like to acknowledge the helpful input of reviewers, as well as Dr. Gzegorz Kondrak and Dr. Lorna Stewart.

References

William Day, David Johnson, and David Sankoff. 1986. The computational complexity of inferring rooted phylogenies by parsimony. *Mathematical Biosciences*, 81:33–42.

Joseph Felsenstein. 2004. *Inferring Phylogenies*. Number 1. Sinauer Associates, Massachusetts, USA.

Luay Nakhleh, Don Ringe, and Tandy Warnow. 2005a. Perfect phylogenetic networks: A new methodology for reconstructing the evolutionary history of natural languages. *Language (Journal of the Linguistic Society of America)*, 81(2):382–420.

Luay Nakhleh, Tandy Warnow, Don Ringe, and Steven N. Evans. 2005b. A comparison of phylogenetic reconstruction methods on an ie dataset. *The Transactions of the Philological Society*, 3(2):171 – 192.

Teresa Przytycka, George Davis, Nan Song, and Dannie Durand. 2006. Graph theoretical insights into evolution of multidomain proteins. *Journal of computational biology : a journal of computational molecular cell biology*, 13(2):351–363.

Donald J. Rose, R. Endre Tarjan, and George S. Leuker. 1976. Algorithmic aspects of vertex elimination on graphs. *SIAM Journal of Computing*, 5(2):266–283.

Spectral Approaches to Learning in the Graph Domain

Edwin Hancock
Department of Computer Science
University of York
York YO10 5DD, UK
erh@cs.york.ac.uk

Abstract

The talk will commence by discussing some of the problems that arise when machine learning is applied to graph structures. A taxonomy of different methods organised around a) clustering b) characterisation and c) constructing generative models in the graph domain will be introduced. With this taxonomy in hand, Dr. Hancock will then describe a number of graph-spectral algorithms that can be applied to solve the many different problems inherent to graphs, drawing examples from computer vision research.

Proceedings of the 2010 Workshop on Graph-based Methods for Natural Language Processing, ACL 2010, page 47,
Uppsala, Sweden, 16 July 2010.

Cross-lingual comparison between distributionally determined word similarity networks

Olof Görnerup
Swedish Institute of Computer Science
(SICS)
164 29 Kista, Sweden
olofg@sics.se

Jussi Karlgren
Swedish Institute of Computer Science
(SICS)
164 29 Kista, Sweden
jussi@sics.se

Abstract

As an initial effort to identify universal and language-specific factors that influence the behavior of distributional models, we have formulated a distributionally determined word similarity network model, implemented it for eleven different languages, and compared the resulting networks. In the model, vertices constitute words and two words are linked if they occur in similar contexts. The model is found to capture clear isomorphisms across languages in terms of syntactic and semantic classes, as well as functional categories of abstract discourse markers. Language specific morphology is found to be a dominating factor for the accuracy of the model.

1 Introduction

This work takes as its point of departure the fact that most studies of the distributional character of terms in language are language specific. A model or technique—either geometric (Deerwester et al., 1990; Finch and Chater, 1992; Lund and Burgess, 1996; Letsche and Berry, 1997; Kanerva et al., 2000) or graph based (i Cancho and Solé, 2001; Widdows and Dorow, 2002; Biemann, 2006)—that works quite well for one language may not be suitable for other languages. A general question of interest is then: What strengths and weaknesses of distributional models are universal and what are language specific?

In this paper we approach this question by formulating a distributionally based network model, apply the model on eleven different languages, and then compare the resulting networks. We compare the networks both in terms of global statistical properties and local structures of word-to-word relations of linguistic relevance. More specifically, the generated networks constitute words (vertices) that are connected with edges if they are observed to occur in similar contexts. The networks are derived from the Europarl corpus (Koehn, 2005)—the annotated proceedings of the European parliament during 1996-2006. This is a parallel corpus that covers Danish, Dutch, English, Finnish, French, German, Greek, Italian, Portuguese, Spanish and Swedish.

The objective of this paper is not to provide a extensive comparison of how distributional network models perform in specific applications for specific languages, for instance in terms of benchmark performance, but rather to, firstly, demonstrate the expressive strength of distributionally based network models and, secondly, to highlight fundamental similarities and differences between languages that these models are capable of capturing (and fail in capturing).

2 Methods

We consider a base case where a context is defined as the preceding and subsequent words of a focus word. Word order matters and so a context forms a word pair. Consider for instance the following sentence[1]:

> *Ladies and gentlemen, once again, we see it is essential for Members to bring their voting cards along on a Monday.*

Here the focus word *essential* occurs in the context *is* $*$ *for*, the word *bring* in the context *to* $*$ *their* etcetera (the asterisk $*$ denotes an intermediate focus word). Since a context occurs with a word with a certain probability, each word w_i is associated with a probability distribution of contexts:

$$P_i = \{\Pr[w_p w_i w_s | w_i]\}_{w_p, w_s \in \mathcal{W}}, \qquad (1)$$

[1] Quoting Nicole Fontaine, president of the European Parliament 1999-2001, from the first session of year 2000.

Proceedings of the 2010 Workshop on Graph-based Methods for Natural Language Processing, ACL 2010, pages 48–54, Uppsala, Sweden, 16 July 2010. ©2010 Association for Computational Linguistics

where $\mathcal{W}$ denotes the set of all words and $\Pr[w_p w_i w_s | w_i]$ is the conditional probability that context $w_p * w_s$ occurrs, given that the focus word is w_i. In practice, we estimate P_i by counting the occurring contexts of w_i and then normalizing the counts. Context counts, in turn, were derived from trigram counts. No pre-processing, such as stemming, was performed prior to collecting the trigrams.

2.1 Similarity measure

If two words have similar context distributions, they are assumed to have a similar function in the language. For instance, it is reasonable to assume that the word "salt" to a higher degree occurs in similar contexts as "pepper" compared to, say, "friendly". One could imagine that a narrow 1+1 neighborhood only captures fundamental syntactic agreement between words, which has also been argued in the literature (Sahlgren, 2006). However, as we will see below, the intermediate two-word context also captures richer word relationships.

We measure the degree of similarity by comparing the respective context distributions. This can be done in a number of ways. For example, as the Euclidian distance (also known as L_2 divergence), the Harmonic mean, Spearman's rank correlation coefficient and the Jensen-Shannon divergence (information radius). Here we quantify the difference between two words w_i and w_j, denoted d_{ij}, by the variational distance (or L_1 divergence) between their corresponding context distributions P_i and P_j:

$$d_{ij} = \sum_{c \in \mathcal{C}} |P_i(X = c) - P_j(X = c)|, \quad (2)$$

where X is a stochastic variable drawn from $\mathcal{C}$, which is the set of contexts that either w_i or w_j occur in. $0 \leq d_{ij} \leq 2$, where $d_{ij} = 0$ if the two distributions are identical and $d_{ij} = 2$ if the words do not share any contexts at all. It is not obvious that the variational distance is the best choice of measure. However, we chose to employ it since it is a well-established and well-understood statistical measure; since it is straightforward and fast to calculate; and since it appears to be robust. To compare, we have also tested to employ the Jensen-Shannon divergence (a symmetrized and smoothed version of Kullback information) and acquire very similar results as those presented here. In fact, this is expected since the two measures are found to be approximately linearly related in this context. However, for the two first reasons listed above, the variational distance is our divergence measure of choice in this study.

2.2 Network representation

A set of words and their similarity relations are naturally interpreted as a weighted and undirected network. The vertices then constitute words and two vertices are linked by an edge if their corresponding words w_i and w_j have overlapping context sets. The strength of the links vary depending on the respective degrees of word similarities. Here the edge between two words w_i and w_j's is weighted with $w_{ij} = 2 - d_{ij}$ (note again that $\max_{ij} d_{ij} = 2$) since a large word difference implies a weak link and vice versa.

In our experiment we consider the 3000 most common words, excluding the 19 first ones, in each language. To keep the data more manageable during analysis we employ various thresholds. Firstly, we only consider context words that occur five times or more. As formed by the remaining context words, we then only consider trigrams that occur three times or more. This allows us to cut away a large chunk of the data. We have tested to vary these thresholds and the resulting networks are found to have very similar statistical properties, even though the networks differ by a large number of very weak edges.

3 Results

3.1 Degree distributions

The degree g_i of a vertex i is defined as the sum of weights of the edges of the vertex: $g_i = \sum w_{ij}$. The degree distribution of a network may provide valuable statistical information about the networks structure. For the word networks, Figure 1, the degree distributions are all found to be highly right-skewed and have longer tails than expected from random graphs (Erdős and Rényi, 1959). This characteristics is often observed in complex networks, which typically also are scale-free (Newman, 2003). Interestingly, the word similarity networks are not scale-free as their degree distributions do no obey power-laws: $\Pr(g) \sim g^{-\alpha}$ for some exponent α. Instead, the degree distributions of each word network appears to lay somewhere between a power-law distribution and an exponential distribution ($\Pr(g) \sim e^{-g/\kappa}$). However, due to quite noisy statistics it is difficult to reliably measure and characterize the tails in the word networks. Note that there appears to be a bump in the distributions for some languages at around degree 60, but again, this may be due to noise and more data is required before we can draw any conclusions. Note also that the degree distribution of Finnish stands out: Finnish words typically have less or weaker links than words in the other languages. This is reasonably in view of the special morphological character of Finnish compared to Indo-European languages (see below).

3.2 Community structures

The acquired networks display interesting global structures that emerge from the local and pairwise word to word relations. Each network form a single strongly connected component. In other words, any vertex can be reached by any other vertex and so there is always a path of "associations" between any two words. Furthermore, all word networks have significant community structures; vertices are organized into groups, where there are higher densities of edges within groups than between them. The strength of community structure can be quantified as follows (Newman and Girvan, 2004): Let $\{v_i\}_{i=1}^{n}$ be a partition of the set of vertices into n groups, r_i the fraction of edge weights that are internal to v_i (i.e. the sum of internal weights over the sum of all weights in the network), and s_i the fraction of edge weights of the edges starting in v_i. The modularity strength is then defined as

$$Q = \sum_{i=1}^{n}(r_i - s_i^2). \qquad (3)$$

Q constitutes the fraction of edge weights given by edges in the network that link vertices within the same communities, minus the expected value of the same quantity in a random network with the same community assignments (i.e. the same vertex set partition). There are several algorithms that aim to find the community structure of a network by maximizing Q. Here we use an agglomerative clustering method by Clauset (2005), which works as follows: Initialize by assigning each vertex to its own cluster. Then successively merge clusters such that the positive change of Q is maximized. The procedure is repeated as long as Q increases.

Typically Q is close to 0 for random partitions and indicates strong community structure when approaching its maximum 1. In practice Q is typically within the range 0.3 to 0.7, also for highly modular networks (Newman and Girvan, 2004). As can be seen in Table 1, all networks are highly modular, although the degree of modularity varies between languages. Greek in particular stands out. However, the reason for this remains an open question that requires further investigations.

Dutch	0.43	Swedish	0.58
German	0.43	French	0.63
Spanish	0.48	Finnish	0.68
Portuguese	0.51	Italian	0.68
English	0.53	Greek	0.78
Danish	0.55		

Table 1: Community modularity.

Communities become more apparent when edges are pruned by a threshold as they crystalize into isolated subgraphs. This is exemplified for English in Figure 2.

4 Discussion

We examine the resulting graphs and show in this section through some example subgraphs how features of human language emerge as charactersitics of the model.

4.1 Morphology matters

Morphology is a determining and observable characteristic of several languages. For the purposes of distributional study of linguistic items, morphological variation is problematic, since it splits one lexical item into several surface realisations, requiring more data to perform reliable and robust statistical analysis. Of the languages studied in this experiment, Finnish stands out atypical through its morphological characteristics. In theory, Finnish nouns can take more than 2 000 surface forms, through more than 12 cases in singular and plural as well as possessive suffixes and clitic particles (Linden and Pirinen, 2009), and while in practice something between six and twelve forms suffice to cover about 80 per cent of the variation (Kettunen, 2007) this is still an order of magnitude more variation than in typical Indo-European languages such as the others in this sample. This variation is evident in Figure 1—Finnish behaves differently than the Indo-European languages in the sample: as each word is split in several other surface forms, its links to other forms will be weaker. Morphological analysis, transforming surface forms to base forms

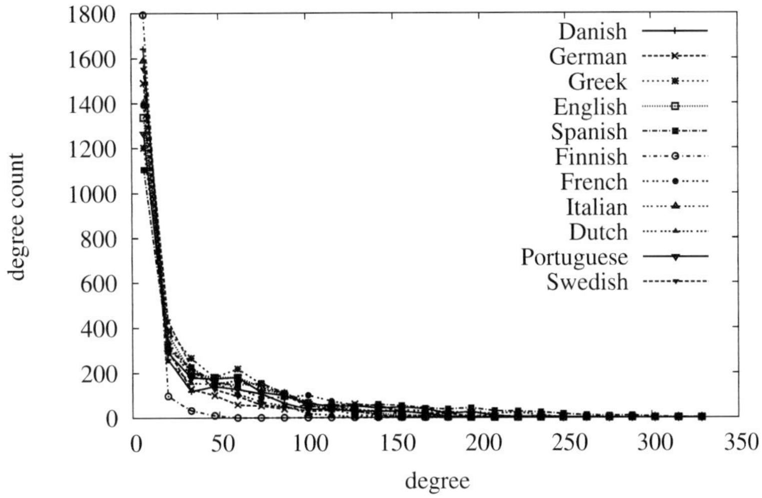

Figure 1: Degree histograms of word similarity networks.

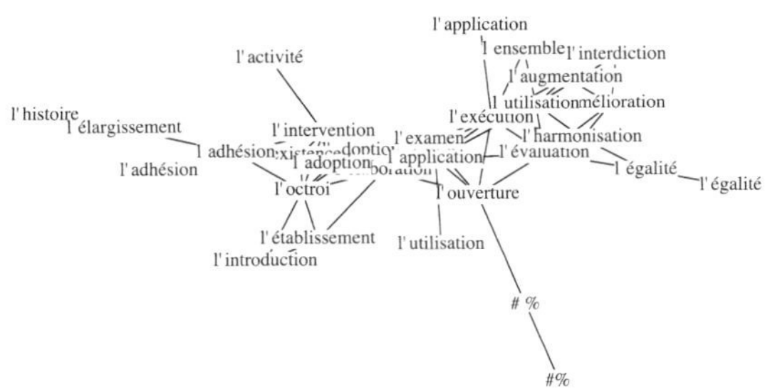

Figure 3: French definite nouns clustered.

would strengthen those links.

In practice, the data sparsity caused by morphological variation causes semantically homogenous classes to be split. Even for languages such as English and French, with very little data variation we find examples where morphological variation causes divergence as seen in Figure 3, where French nouns in definite form are clustered. It is not surprising that certain nouns in definite form assume similar roles in text, but the neatness of the graph is a striking exposition of this fact.

These problems could have been avoided with better preprocessing—simple such processing in the case of English and French, and considerably more complex but feasible in the case of Finnish—but are retained in the present example as proxies for the difficulties typical of processing unknown languages. Our methodology is robust even in face of shoddy preprocessing and no knowledge of the morphological basis of the target language. In general, as a typological fact, it is reasonable to assume that morphological variation is offset for the language user in a greater freedom in choice of word order. This would seem to cause a great deal of problems for an approach such as the present one, since it relies on the sequential organisation of symbols in the signal. However, it is observable that languages with free word order have preferred unmarked arrangements for their sentence structure, and thus we find stable relationships in the data even for Finnish, although weaker than for the other languages examined.

4.2 Syntactic classes

Previous studies have shown that a narrow context window of one neighbour to the left and one neighbour to the right such as the one used in the present experiments retrieves syntactic relationships (Sahlgren, 2006). We find several such examples in the graphs. In Figure 2 we can see subgraphs with past participles, auxiliary verbs, progressive verbs, person names.

4.3 Semantic classes

Some of the subgraphs we find are models of clear semantic family resemblance as shown in Figure 4. This provides us with a good argument for blurring the artificial distinction between syntax and semantics. Word classes are defined by their meaning and usage alike; the *a priori* distinction between classification by function such as auxiliary verbs given above and classification by meaning such months and places given here is not fruitful. We expect to be able to provide much more in-

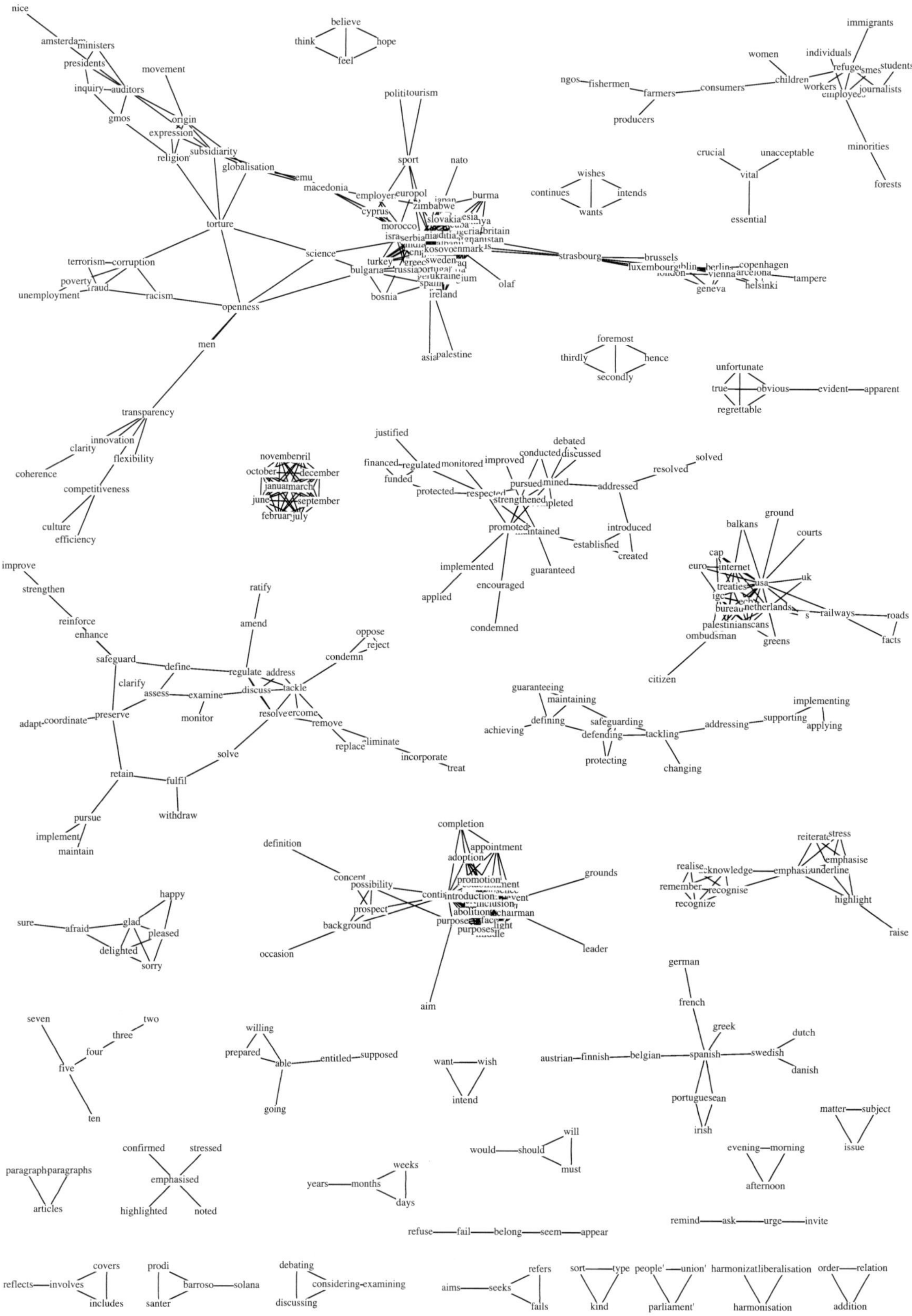

Figure 2: English. Network involving edges with weights $w \geq 0.85$. For sake of clarity, only subgraphs with three or more words are shown. Note that the threshold 0.85 is used only for the visualization. The full network consists of the 3000 most common words in English, excluding the 19 most common ones.

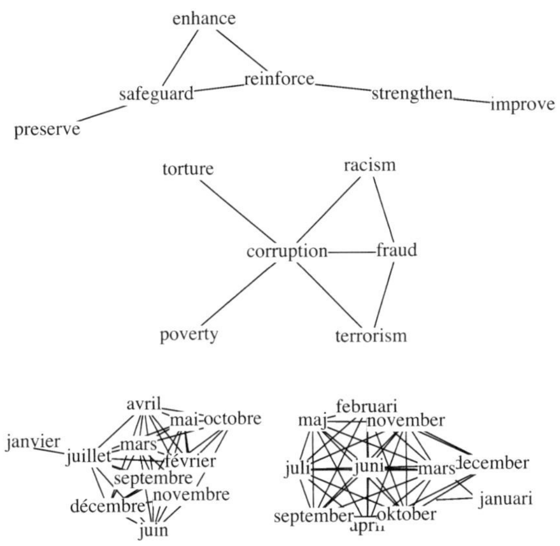

Figure 4: Examples of semantically homogenous classes in English, French and Swedish.

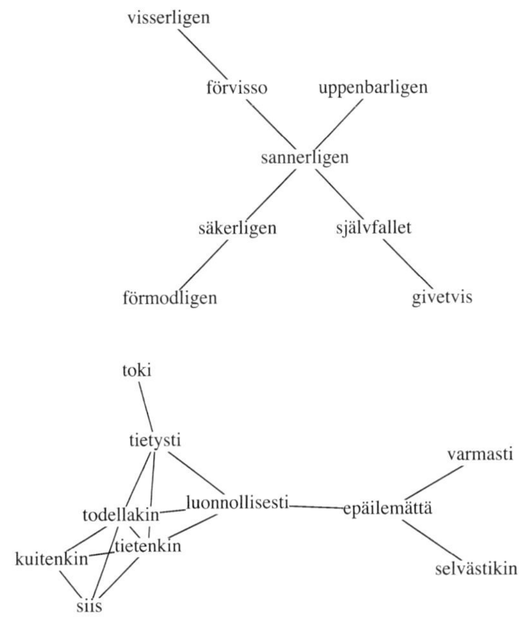

Figure 5: Examples of discourse functional classes in Swedish and Finnish. The terms in the two subgraphs are discourse markers and correspond to English "certainly", "possibly", "evidently", "naturally", "absolutely", "hence" and similar terms.

formed classification schemes than the traditional "parts of speech" if we define classes by their distributional qualities rather than by the "content" they "represent", schemes which will cut across the function-topic distinction.

4.4 Abstract discourse markers are a functional category

Further, several subgraphs have clear collections of discourse markers of various types where the terms are markers of informational organisation in the text, as exemplified in Figure 5.

5 Conclusions

This preliminary experiment supports future studies to build knowledge structures across languages, using distributional isomorphism between linguistic material in translated or even comparable corpora, on several levels of abstraction, from function words, to semantic classes, to discourse markers. The isomorphism across the languages is clear and incontrovertible; this will allow us to continue experiments using collections of multilingual materials, even for languages with relatively little technological support. Previous studies show that knowledge structures of this type that are created in one language show considerable isomorphism to knowledge structures created in another language if the corpora are comparable (Holmlund et al., 2005). Holmlund et al show how translation equivalences can be established using two semantic networks automatically created in two languages by providing a relatively limited set of equivalence relations in a translation lexicon. This study supports those findings.

The results presented here display the potential of distributionally derived network representations of word similarities. Although geometric (vector based) and probabilistic models have proven viable in various applications, they are limited by the fact that word or term relations are constrained by the geometric (often Euclidian) space in which they live. Network representations are richer in the sense that they are not bound by the same constraints. For instance, a polyseme word ("may" for example) can have strong links to two other words ("might" and "September" for example), where the two other words are completely unrelated. In an Euclidean space this relation is not possible due to the triangle inequality. It is possible to embed a network in a geometric space, but this requires a very high dimensionality which makes the representation both cumbersome and inefficient in terms of computation and memory. This has been addressed by coarse graining or dimension reduction, for example by means of singular value decomposition (Deerwester et al., 1990; Letsche and Berry, 1997; Kanerva et al., 2000), which results in information loss. This can be problematic, in particular since distributional models often face data sparsity due to the curse of dimensionality. In a network representation, such dimension reduction is not necessary and so potentially important information about word or term relations is retained.

The experiments presented here also show the potential of moving from a purely probabilistic model of term occurrence, or a bare distributional model such as those typically presented using a geometric metaphor, in that it affords the possibility of abstract categories inferred from the primary distributional data. This will give the possibility of further utilising the results in studies, e.g. for learning syntactic or functional categories in more complex constructional models of linguistic form. Automatically establishing lexically and functionally coherent classes in this manner will have bearing on future project goals of automatically learning syntactic and semantic roles of words in language. This target is today typically pursued relying on traditional lexical categories which are not necessarily the most salient ones in view of actual distributional characteristics of words.

Acknowledgments: OG was supported by Johan and Jacob Söderberg's Foundation. JK was supported by the Swedish Research Council.

References

Chris. Biemann. 2006. Chinese whispers - an efficient graph clustering algorithm and its application to natural language processing problems. In *Proceedings of the HLT-NAACL-06 Workshop on Textgraphs-06*, New York, USA.

Aaron Clauset. 2005. Finding local community structure in networks. *Physical Review E*, 72:026132.

Scott Deerwester, Susan T. Dumais, George W. Furnas, Thomas K. Landauer, and Richard Harshman. 1990. Indexing by latent semantic analysis. *Journal of the American Society for Information Science*, 41:391–407.

Pal Erdős and Alfréd Rényi. 1959. On random graphs. *Publications Mathematicae*, 6:290.

Steven Finch and Nick Chater. 1992. Bootstrapping syntactic categories. In *Proceedings of the Fourteenth Annual Conference of the Cognitive Science Society*, pages 820–825, Bloomington, IN. Lawrence Erlbaum.

Jon Holmlund, Magnus Sahlgren, and Jussi Karlgren. 2005. Creating bilingual lexica using reference wordlists for alignment of monolingual semantic vector spaces. In *Proceedings of 15th Nordic Conference of Computational Linguistics*.

Ramon Ferrer i Cancho and Ricard V. Solé. 2001. The small world of human language. *Proceedings of the Royal Society of London. Series B, Biological Sciences*, 268:2261–2266.

Pentti Kanerva, Jan Kristoferson, and Anders Holst. 2000. Random indexing of text samples for latent semantic analysis. In *Proceedings of the 22nd Annual Conference of the Cognitive Science Society*, pages 103–6.

Kimmo Kettunen. 2007. Management of keyword variation with frequency based generation of word forms in ir. In *Proceedings of SIGIR 2007*.

Philipp Koehn. 2005. Europarl: A parallel corpus for statistical machine translation. In *MT Summit*.

Todd Letsche and Michael Berry. 1997. Large-scale information retrieval with latent semantic indexing. *Information Sciences*, 100(1-4):105–137.

Krister Linden and Tommi Pirinen. 2009. Weighting finite-state morphological analyzers using hfst tools. In *Proceedings of the Finite-State Methods and Natural Language Processing*. Pretoria, South Africa.

Kevin Lund and Curt Burgess. 1996. Producing high-dimensional semantic spaces from lexical co-occurrence. *Behavior Research Methods, Instruments, and Computers*, 28(2):203–208.

Mark Newman and Michelle Girvan. 2004. Finding and evaluating community structure in networks. *Physical Review E*, 69(2).

Mark E. J. Newman. 2003. The structure and function of complex networks. *SIAM Review*, 45(2):167–256.

Magnus Sahlgren. 2006. *The Word-Space Model: Using distributional analysis to represent syntagmatic and paradigmatic relations between words in high-dimensional vector spaces*. PhD Dissertation, Department of Linguistics, Stockholm University.

Dominic Widdows and Beate Dorow. 2002. A graph model for unsupervised lexical acquisition. In *In 19th International Conference on Computational Linguistics*, pages 1093–1099.

Co-occurrence Cluster Features for Lexical Substitutions in Context

Chris Biemann
Powerset (a Microsoft company)
475 Brannan St Ste. 330
San Francisco, CA 94107, USA
cbiemann@microsoft.com

Abstract

This paper examines the influence of features based on clusters of co-occurrences for supervised Word Sense Disambiguation and Lexical Substitution. Co-occurrence cluster features are derived from clustering the local neighborhood of a target word in a co-occurrence graph based on a corpus in a completely unsupervised fashion. Clusters can be assigned in context and are used as features in a supervised WSD system. Experiments fitting a strong baseline system with these additional features are conducted on two datasets, showing improvements. Co-occurrence features are a simple way to mimic Topic Signatures (Martínez et al., 2008) without needing to construct resources manually. Further, a system is described that produces lexical substitutions in context with very high precision.

1 Introduction

Word Sense Disambiguation (WSD, see (Agirre and Edmonds, 2006) for an extensive overview) is commonly seen as an enabling technology for applications like semantic parsing, semantic role labeling and semantic retrieval. Throughout recent years, the Senseval and Semeval competitions have shown that a) WordNet as-is is not an adequate semantic resource for reaching high precision and b) supervised WSD approaches outperform unsupervised (i.e. not using sense-annotated examples) approaches. Due to the manual effort involved in creating more adequate word sense inventories and sense-annotated training data, WSD has yet to see its prime-time in real world applications.

Since WordNet's sense distinctions are often too fine-grained for allowing reliable distinctions by machines and humans, the OntoNotes project (Hovy et al., 2006) conflated similar WordNet senses until 90% inter-annotator agreement on sense-labelling was reached. The SemEval 2007 lexical sample task employs this "coarse-grained" inventory, which allows for higher system performance.

To alleviate the bottleneck of sense-labelled sentences, (Biemann and Nygaard, 2010) present an approach for acquiring a sense inventory along with sense-annotated example usages using crowdsourcing, which makes the acquisition process cheaper and potentially quicker.

Trying to do away with manual resources entirely, the field of Word Sense Induction aims at inducing the inventory from text corpora by clustering occurrences or senses according to distributional similarity, e.g. (Veronis, 2004). While such unsupervised and knowledge-free systems are capable of discriminating well between different usages, it is not trivial to link their distinctions to existing semantic resources, which is often necessary in applications.

Topic Signatures (Martínez et al., 2008) is an attempt to account for differences in relevant topics per target word. Here, a large number of contexts for a given sense inventory are collected automatically using relations from a semantic resource, sense by sense. The most discriminating content words per sense are used to identify a sense in an unseen context. This approach is amongst the most successful methods in the field. It requires, however, a semantic resource of sufficient detail and size and a sense-labeled corpus to estimate priors from the sense distribution. Here, a similar approach is described that uses an unlabeled

Proceedings of the 2010 Workshop on Graph-based Methods for Natural Language Processing, ACL 2010, pages 55–59,
Uppsala, Sweden, 16 July 2010.

corpus alone for unsupervised topic signature acquisition using graph clustering, not relying on the existence of a WordNet. Unlike in previous evaluations like (Agirre et al., 2006), parameters for word sense induction are not optimized globally, but instead several parameter settings are offered as features to a Machine Learning setup.

Experimental results are provided for two datasets: the Semeval-2007 lexical sample task (Pradhan et al., 2007) and the Turk bootstrap Word Sense Inventory (TWSI[1], (Biemann and Nygaard, 2010)).

2 Cluster Co-occurrence Features

2.1 Graph Preperation and Parameterization

Similar to the approach in (Widdows and Dorow, 2002), a word graph around each target word is constructed. In this work, sentence-based co-occurrence statistics from a large corpus are used as a basis to to construct several word graphs for different parameterizations. Significant co-occurrences between all content words (nouns, verbs, adjectives as identified by POS tagging) are computed from a large corpus using the tinyCC[2] tool. The full word graph for a target word is defined as all words significantly co-occurring with the target as nodes, with edge weights set to the log-likelihood significance of the co-occurrence between the words corresponding to nodes. Edges between words that co-occur only once or with significance smaller than 6.63 (1% confidence level) are omitted.

Aiming at different granularities of usage clusters, the graph is parameterized by a size parameter t and a density parameter n: Only the most significant t co-occurrences of the target enter the graph as nodes, and an edge between nodes is drawn only if one of the corresponding words is contained in the most significant n co-occurrences of the other.

2.2 Graph Clustering Parameterization

As described in (Biemann, 2006), the neighborhood graph is clustered with Chinese Whispers. This efficient graph clustering algorithm finds the numbers of clusters automatically and returns a partition of the nodes. It is initialized by assigning different classes to all nodes in the graph. Then, a number of local update steps are performed, in which a node inherits the predominant class in its neighborhood. At this, classes of adjacent nodes are weighted by edge weight and downweighted by the degree (number of adjacent nodes) of the neighboring node. This results in hard clusters of words per target, which represent different target usages.

Downweighting nodes by degree is done according to the following intuition: nodes with high degrees are probably very universally used words and should be less influential for clustering. Three ways of node weighting are used: (a) dividing the influence of a node in the update step by the degree of the node, (b) dividing by the natural logarithm of the degree + 1 and (c) not doing node weighting. The more aggressive the downweighting, the higher granularity is expected for the clustering.

It is emphasized that no tuning techniques are applied to arrive at the 'best' clustering. Rather, several clusterings of different granularities as *features* are made available to a supervised system. Note that this is different from (Agirre et al., 2006), where a single global clustering was used *directly* in a greedy mapping to senses.

2.3 Feature Assignment in Context

For a given occurrence of a target word, the overlap in words between the textual context and all clusters from the neighborhood graph is measured. The cluster ID of the cluster with the highest overlap is assigned as a feature. This can be viewed as a word sense induction system in its own right.

At this, several clusterings from different parameterizations are used to form distinct features, which enables the machine learning algorithm to pick the most suitable cluster features per target word when building the classification model.

2.4 Corpora for Cluster Features

When incorporating features that are induced using large unlabeled corpora, it is important to ensure that the corpus for feature induction and the word sense labeled corpus are from the same domain, ideally from the same source.

Since TWSI has been created from Wikipedia, an English Wikipedia dump from January 2008 is used for feature induction, comprising a total of 60 million sentences. The source for the lexical sample task is the Wall Street Journal, and since the

[1]full dataset available for download at http://aclweb.org/aclwiki/index.php?title=Image:TWSI397.zip

[2]http://beam.to/biem/software/TinyCC2.html

76,400 sentences from the WSJ Penn Treebank are rather small for co-occurrence analysis, a 20 Million sentence New York Times corpus was used instead.
For each corpus, a total of 45 different clusterings were prepared for all combinations of t={50,100,150,200,250}, n={50,100,200} and node degree weighting options (a), (b) and (c).

3 Experimental Setup

3.1 Machine Learning Setup

The classification algorithm used throughout this work is the AODE (Webb et al., 2005) classifier as provided by the WEKA Machine Learning software (Hall et al., 2009). This algorithm is similar to a Naïve Bayes classifier. As opposed to the latter, AODE does not assume mutual independence of features but models correlations between them explicitly, which is highly desirable here since both baseline and co-occurrence cluster features are expected to be highly correlated. Further, AODE handles nominal features, so it is directly possible to use lexical features and cluster IDs in the classifier. AODE showed superior performance to other classifiers handling nominal features in preliminary experiments.

3.2 Baseline System

The baseline system relies on 15 lexical and POS-based nominal features: word forms left and right from target, POS sequences left and right bigram around target, POS tags of left and right word from target, and POS tag of target, two left and two right nouns from target, left and right verbs from target and left and right adjectives from target.

3.3 Feature Selection

To determine the most useful cluster co-occurrence features, they were added to the baseline features one at the time, measuring the contribution using 10-fold cross validation on the training set. Then, the best k single cluster features for k={2,3,5,10} were added together to account for a range of different granularities. The best performing system on the lexical sample training data resulted in a 10-fold accuracy of 88.5% (baseline: 87.1%) for k=3. On the 204 ambiguous words (595 total senses with 46 sentences per sense on average) of the TWSI only, the best system was found at k=5 with a 10-fold accuracy of 83.0% (baseline: 80.7%, MFS: 71.5%). Across the board, all single co-occurrence features improve over the baseline, most of them significantly.

System	F1
NUS-ML	88.7% ± 1.2
top3 cluster, optimal F1	88.0% ± 1.2
top3 cluster, max recall	87.8% ± 1.2
baseline, optimal F1	87.5% ± 1.2
baseline, max recall	87.3% ± 1.2
UBC-ALM	86.9% ± 1.2

Table 1: Cluster co-occurrence features and baseline in comparison to the best two systems in the SemEval 2007 Task 17 Lexical Sample evaluation (Pradhan et al., 2007). Error margins provided by the task organizers.

4 Results

4.1 SemEval 2007 lexical sample task

The system in the configuration determined above was trained on the full training set and applied it to the test data provided bt the task organizers.
Since the AODE classifier reports a confidence score (corresponding to the class probability for the winning class at classification time), it is possible to investigate a tradeoff between precision and recall to optimize the F1-value[3] used for scoring in the lexical sample task.

It is surprising that the baseline system outperforms the second-best system in the 2007 evaluation, see Table 1. This might be attributed to the AODE classifier used, but also hints at the power of nominal lexical features in general.
The co-occurrence cluster system outperforms the baseline, but does not reach the performance of the winning system. However, all reported systems fall into each other's error margins, unlike when evaluating on training data splits. In conclusion, the WSD setup is competitive to other WSD systems in the literature, while using only minimal linguistic preprocessing and no word sense inventory information beyond what is provided by training examples.

[3] $F1 = (2 \cdot precision \cdot recall)/(precision + recall)$

	Substitutions		
	Gold	**System**	**Random**
YES	469 (93.8%)	456 (91.2%)	12 (2.4%)
NO	14 (2.8%)	27 (5.4%)	485 (97.0%)
SOMEWHAT	17 (3.4%)	17 (3.4%)	3 (0.6%)

Table 2: Substitution acceptability as measured by crowdsourcing for TWSI gold assignments, system assignments and random assignments.

coverage	YES	NO
100%	91.2%	5.4%
95%	91.8%	3.4%
90%	93.8%	2.9%
80%	94.8%	2.0%
70%	95.7%	0.9%

Table 3: Substitution acceptability in reduced coverage settings. SOMEWHAT class accounts for percentage points missing to 100%.

4.2 Substitution Acceptability

For evaluating substitution acceptability, 500 labeled sentences from the overall data (for all 397 nouns, not just the ambiguous nouns used in the experiments above) were randomly selected. The 10-fold test classifications as described above were used for system word sense assignment. The three highest ranked substitutions per sense from the TWSI are supplied as substitutions.

In a crowdsourcing task, workers had to state whether the substitutions provided for a target word in context do not change the meaning of the sentence. Each assignment was given to three workers.

Since this measures both substitution quality of the TWSI and the system's capability of assigning the right sense, workers were also asked to score the substitutions for the gold standard assignments of this data set. For control, random substitution quality for all sentences is measured.

Table 2 shows the results for averaging over the worker's responses. For being counted as belonging to the YES or NO class, the majority of workers had to choose this option, otherwise the item was counted into the SOMEWHAT class.

The substitution quality of the gold standard is somewhat noisy, containing 2.8% errors and 3.4% questionable cases. Despite this, the system is able to assign acceptable substitutions in over 91% of cases, questionable substitutions for 3.4% at an error rate of only 5.4%. Checking the positively judged random assignments, an acceptable substitution was found in about half of the cases by the author, which allows to estimate the worker noise at about 1%.

When using confidence values of the AODE classifier to control recall as reported in Table 3, it is possible to further reduce error rates, which might e.g. improve retrieval applications.

5 Conclusion

A way to improve WSD accuracy using a family of co-occurrence cluster features was demonstrated on two data sets. Instead of optimizing parameters globally, features corresponding to different granularities of induced word usages are made available in parallel as features in a supervised Machine Learning setting.

Whereas the contribution of co-occurrence features is significant on the TWSI, it is not significantly improving results on the SemEval 2007 data. This might be attributed to a larger number of average training examples in the latter, making smoothing over clusters less necessary due to less lexical sparsity.

We measured performance of our lexical substitution system by having the acceptability of the system-provided substitutions in context manually judged. With error rates in the single figures and the possibility to reduce error further by sacrificing recall, we provide a firm enabling technology for semantic search.

For future work, it would be interesting to evaluate the full substitution system based on the TWSI in a semantic retrieval application.

References

Eneko Agirre and Philip Edmonds, editors. 2006. *Word Sense Disambiguation: Algorithms and Applications*, volume 33 of *Text, Speech and Language Technology*. Springer, July.

Eneko Agirre, David Martínez, Oier L. de Lacalle, and Aitor Soroa. 2006. Evaluating and optimizing the parameters of an unsupervised graph-based wsd algorithm. In *Proceedings of TextGraphs: the Second Workshop on Graph Based Methods for Natural Language Processing*, pages 89–96, New York City. Association for Computational Linguistics.

Chris Biemann and Valerie Nygaard. 2010. Crowdsourcing WordNet. In *Proceedings of the 5th Global WordNet conference*, Mumbai, India. ACL Data and Code Repository, ADCR2010T005.

Chris Biemann. 2006. Chinese whispers - an efficient graph clustering algorithm and its application to natural language processing problems. In *Proceedings of the HLT-NAACL-06 Workshop on Textgraphs-06*, New York, USA.

Mark Hall, Eibe Frank, Geoffrey Holmes, Bernhard Pfahringer, Peter Reutemann, and Ian H. Witten. 2009. The WEKA data mining software: An update. *SIGKDD Explorations*, 11(1).

Eduard Hovy, Mitchell Marcus, Martha Palmer, Lance Ramshaw, and Ralph Weischedel. 2006. OntoNotes: The 90% solution. In *Proceedings of HLT-NAACL 2006*, pages 57–60.

David Martínez, Oier Lopez de Lacalle, and Eneko Agirre. 2008. On the use of automatically acquired examples for all-nouns word sense disambiguation. *J. Artif. Intell. Res. (JAIR)*, 33:79–107.

Sameer Pradhan, Edward Loper, Dmitriy Dligach, and Martha Palmer. 2007. SemEval-2007 Task-17: English Lexical Sample, SRL and All Words. In *Proceedings of the Fourth International Workshop on Semantic Evaluations (SemEval-2007)*, pages 87–92, Prague, Czech Republic, June. Association for Computational Linguistics.

Jean Veronis. 2004. Hyperlex: lexical cartography for information retrieval. *Computer Speech & Language*, 18(3):223–252.

G. Webb, J. Boughton, and Z. Wang. 2005. Not so Naive Bayes: Aggregating one-dependence estimators. *Machine Learning*, 58(1):5–24.

Dominic Widdows and Beate Dorow. 2002. A graph model for unsupervised lexical acquisition. In *Proceedings of the 19th international conference on Computational linguistics*, pages 1–7, Morristown, NJ, USA. Association for Computational Linguistics.

Contextually–Mediated Semantic Similarity Graphs for Topic Segmentation

Geetu Ambwani
StreamSage/Comcast
Washington, DC, USA
ambwani@streamsage.com

Anthony R. Davis
StreamSage/Comcast
Washington, DC, USA
davis@streamsage.com

Abstract

We present a representation of documents as directed, weighted graphs, modeling the range of influence of terms within the document as well as contextually determined semantic relatedness among terms. We then show the usefulness of this kind of representation in topic segmentation. Our boundary detection algorithm uses this graph to determine topical coherence and potential topic shifts, and does not require labeled data or training of parameters. We show that this method yields improved results on both concatenated pseudo-documents and on closed-captions for television programs.

1 Introduction

We present in this paper a graph-based representation of documents that models both the long-range scope "influence" of terms and the semantic relatedness of terms in a local context. In these graphs, each term is represented by a series of nodes. Each node in the series corresponds to a sentence within the span of that term's influence, and the weights of the edges are proportional to the semantic relatedness among terms in the context. Semantic relatedness between terms is reinforced by the presence of nearby, closely related terms, reflected in increased connection strength between their nodes.

We demonstrate the usefulness of our representation by applying it to partitioning of documents into topically coherent segments. Our segmentation method finds locations in the graph of a document where one group of strongly connected nodes ends and another begins, signaling a shift in topicality. We test this method both on concatenated news articles, and on a more realistic segmentation task, closed-captions from commercial television programs, in which topic transitions are more subjective and less distinct. Our methods are unsupervised and require no training; thus they do not require any labeled instances of segment boundaries. Our method attains results significantly superior to that of Choi (2000), and approaches human performance on segmentation of television closed-captions, where inter-annotator disagreement is high.

2 Graphs of lexical influence

2.1 Summary of the approach

Successful topic segmentation requires some representation of semantic and discourse cohesion, and the ability to detect where such cohesion is weakest. The underlying assumption of segmentation algorithms based on lexical chains or other term similarity measures between portions of a document is that continuity in vocabulary reflects topic continuity. Two short examples illustrating topic shifts in television news programs, with accompanying shift in vocabulary, appear in Figure 1.

We model this continuity by first modeling what the extent of a term's influence is. This differs from a lexical chain approach in that we do not model text cohesion through recurrence of terms. Rather, we determine, for each occurrence of a term in the document (excluding terms generally treated as stopwords), what interval of sentences surrounding that occurrence is the best estimate of the extent of its relevance. This idea stems from work in Davis, et al. (2004), who describe the use of *relevance intervals* in multimedia information retrieval. We summarize their procedure for constructing relevance intervals in

Proceedings of the 2010 Workshop on Graph-based Methods for Natural Language Processing, ACL 2010, pages 60–68,
Uppsala, Sweden, 16 July 2010.

section 2.2. Next, we calculate the relatedness of these terms to one another. We use pointwise mutual information (PMI) as a similarity measure between terms, but other measures, such as WordNet-based similarity or Wikipedia Miner similarity (Milne and Witten, 2009), could augment or replace it.

S_44 Gatorade has discontinued a drink with his image but that was planned before the company has said and they have issued a statement in support of tiger woods.
S_45 And at t says that while it supports tiger woods personally, it is evaluating their ongoing business relationship.
S_46 I'm sure, alex, in the near future we're going to see more of this as companies weigh the short term difficulties of staying with tiger woods versus the long term gains of supporting him fully.
S_47 Okay.
S_48 Mark potter, miami.
S_49 Thanks for the wrapup of that.
S_50 We'll go now to deep freeze that's blanketing the great lakes all the way to right here on the east coast.

S_190 We've got to get this addressed and hold down health care costs.
S_191 Senator ron wyden the optimist from oregon, we appreciate your time tonight.
S_192 Thank you.
S_193 Coming up, the final day of free health clinic in kansas city, missouri.

Figure 1. Two short closed-caption excerpts from television news programs, each containing a topic shift

The next step is to construct a graphical representation of the influence of terms throughout a document. When constructing topically coherent segments, we wish to assess coherence from one sentence to the next. We model similarity between successive sentences as a graph, in which each node represents both a term and a sentence that lies within its influence (that is, a sentence belonging to a relevance interval for that term). For example, if the term "drink" occurs in sentence 44, and its relevance interval extends to sentence 47, four nodes will be created for "drink", each corresponding to one sentence in that interval. The edges in the graph connect nodes in successive sentences. The weight of an edge between two terms t and t' consists not only of their relatedness, but is reinforced by the presence of other nodes in each sentence associated with terms related to t and t'.

The resulting graph thus consists of cohorts of nodes, one cohort associated with each sentence, and edges connecting nodes in one cohort to those in the next. Edges with a low weight are pruned from the graph. The algorithm for determining topic segment boundaries then seeks locations in which a relatively large number of relevance intervals for terms with relatively high relatedness end or begin.

In sum, we introduce two innovations here in computing topical coherence. One is that we use the extent of each term's relevance intervals to model the influence of that term, which thus extends beyond the sentences it occurs in. Second, we amplify the semantic relatedness of a term t to a term t' when there are other nearby terms related to t and t'. Related terms thereby reinforce one another in establishing coherence from one sentence to the next.

2.2 Constructing relevance intervals

As noted, the scope of a term's influence is captured through relevance intervals (RIs). We describe here how RIs are created. A corpus—in this case, seven years of *New York Times* text totaling approximately 325 million words—is run through a part-of-speech tagger. The pointwise mutual information between each pair of terms is computed using a 50-word window.[1]

PMI values provide a mechanism to measure relatedness between a term and terms occurring in nearby sentences of a document. When processing a document for segmentation, we first calculate RIs for all the terms in that document. An RI for a term t is built sentence-by-sentence, beginning with a sentence where t occurs. A sentence immediately succeeding or preceding the sentences already in the RI is added to that RI if it contains terms with sufficiently high PMI values with t. An adjacent sentence is also added to an RI if there is a pronominal believed to refer to t; the algorithm for determining pronominal reference is closely based on Kennedy and Boguraev (1996). Expansion of an RI is terminated if there are no motivations for expanding it further. Additional termination conditions can be included as well. For example, if large local voca-

[1] PMI values are constructed for all words other than those in a list of stopwords. They are also constructed for a limited set of about 100,000 frequent multi-word expressions. In our segmentation system, we use only the RIs for nouns and for multiword expressions.

bulary shifts or discourse cues signaling the start of end of a section are detected, RIs can be forced to end at those points. In one version of our system, we set these "hard" boundaries using an algorithm based on Choi (2000). In this paper we report segmentation results with and without this limited use of Choi's algorithm. Lastly, if two RIs for t are sufficiently close (i.e., the end of one lies within 150 words of the start of another), then the two RIs are merged.

The aim of constructing RIs is to determine which portions of a document are relevant to a particular term. While this is related to the goal of finding topically coherent segments, it is of course distinct, as a topic typically is determined by the influence of multiple terms. However, RIs do provide a rough indication of how far a term's influence extends or, put another way, of "smearing out" the occurrence of a term over an extended region.

2.3 From relevance intervals to graphs

Consider a sentence S_i, and its immediate successor S_{i+1}. Each of these sentences is contained in various relevance intervals; let W_i denote the set of terms with RIs containing S_i, and W_{i+1} denote the set containing S_{i+1}.

For each pair of terms a in W_i and b in W_{i+1}, we compute a connection strength $c(a,b)$, a non-negative real number that reflects how the two terms are related in the context of S_i and S_{i+1}. To include the context, we take into account that some terms in S_i may be closely related, and should support one another in their connections to terms in S_{i+1}, and vice versa, as suggested above. Here, we use PMI values between terms as the basis for connection strength, normalized to a similarity score that ranges between 0 and 1, as follows:

$$s(x,y) = 1 - \frac{1}{\exp(PMI(x,y))} \quad (1)$$

The similarity between two terms is set to 0 if this quantity is negative. Also, we assign the maximum value of 1 for self-similarity. We then define connection strength in the following way:

$$c(a,b) = \sum_{x \in W_i} s(x,a)s(x,b) + \sum_{y \in W_{i+1}} s(y,a)s(y,b) \quad (2)$$

That is, the similarity of another term in W_i or W_{i+1} to b or a respectively, will add to the connection strength between a and b, weighted by the similarity of that term to a or b respectively. Note that this formula also includes in the summation the similarity $s(a,b)$ between a and b themselves, when either x or y is set to either a or b.[2] Figure 2 illustrates this procedure. We normalize the connection strength by the total number of pairs in equation (2).

We note in passing that many possible modifications of this formula are easily imagined. One obvious alternative to using the product of two similarity scores is to use the minimum of the two scores. This gives more weight to pair values that are both moderately high, with respect to pairs where one is high and the other low. Apart from this, we could incorporate terms from RIs in sentences beyond these two adjoining sentences, we could weight individual terms in W_i or W_{i+1} according to some independent measure of topical salience, and so on.

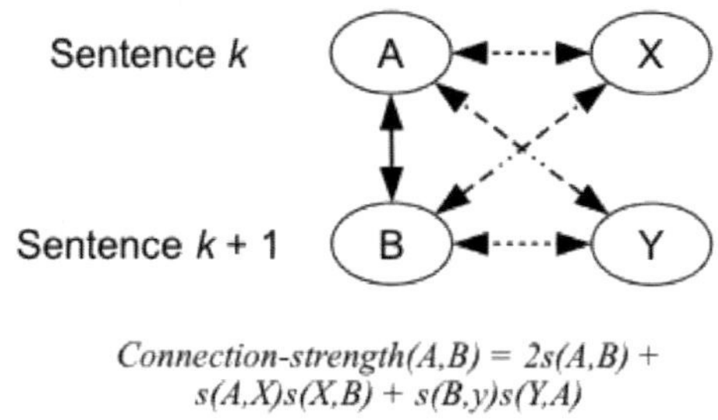

Figure 2. Calculation of connection strength between two nodes

What emerges from this procedure is a weighted graph of connections across slices of a document (sentences, in our experiments). Each node in the graph is labeled with a term and a sentence number, and represents a relevance interval for that term that includes the indicated sentence. The edges of the graph connect nodes associated with adjacent sentences, and are weighted by the connection strength. Because many weak connections are present in this graph, we remove edges that are unlikely to contribute to establishing topical coherence. There are various options for pruning: removing edges with connection strengths below a threshold, retaining only the top n edges, cutting the graph between two sentences where the total connection strength of edges connecting the sentences is small, and using an edge betweenness algorithm (e.g., Girvan and Newman, 2002) to remove edges that have high betweenness (and hence are indicative of a "thin" connection).

[2] In fact, the similarity $s(a_i,b_j)$ will be counted twice, once in each summation in the formula above; we retain this additional weighting of $s(a_i,b_j)$.

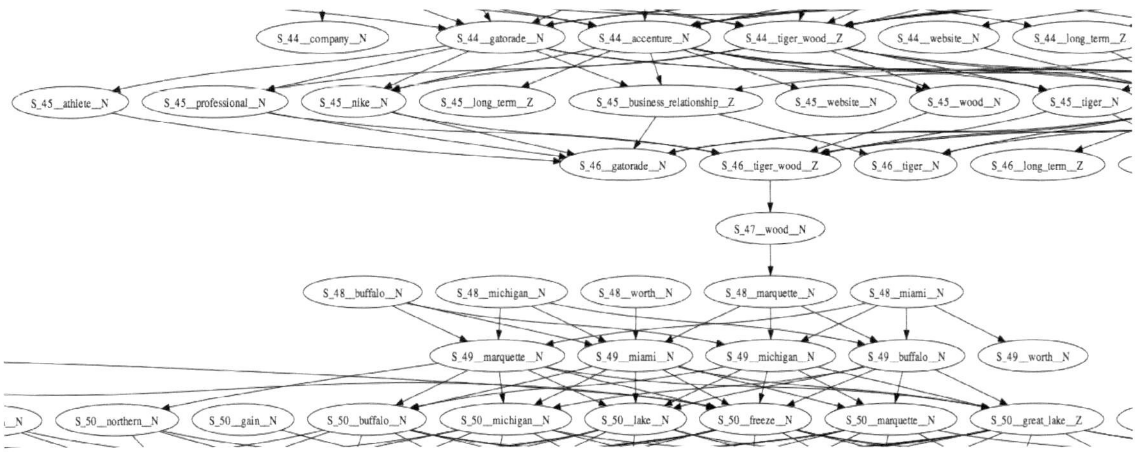

Figure 3. A portion of the graph generated from the first excerpt in Figure 1. Each node is labeled *S_i__term_pos,* where *i* indicates the sentence index

We have primarily investigated the first method, removing edges with a connection strength less than 0.5. Two samples of the graphs we produce, corresponding to the excerpts in figure 1, appear in figures 3 and 4.

2.4 Finding segment boundaries in graphs

Segment boundaries in these graphs are hypothesized where there are relatively few, relatively weak connections from a cohort of nodes associated with one sentence to the cohort of nodes associated with the following sentence. If a term has a node in one cohort and in the succeeding cohort (that is, its RI continues across the two corresponding sentences) it counts against a segment boundary at that location, whereas terms with nodes on only one side of the boundary count in favor of a segment. For example, in figure 3, a new set of RIs start in sentence 48, where we see nodes for "Buffalo", "Michigan", "Worth", Marquette", and "Miami", and RIs in preceding sentences for "Tiger Woods", "Gatorade", etc. end. Note that the corresponding excerpt in figure 1 shows a clear topic shift between a story on Tiger Woods ending at sentence 46, and a story about Great Lakes weather beginning at sentence 48.

Similarly, in figure 4, RIs for "Missouri", "city" and "health clinic" include sentences 190. 191, and 192; thus these are evidence against a segment boundary at this location. On the other hand, several other terms, such as "Oregon", "Ron", "Senator", and "bill", have RIs that end at sentence 191, which argues in favor of a boundary there. We present further details of our boundary heuristics in section 4.1.

3 Related Work

The literature on topic segmentation has mostly focused on detecting a set of segments, typically non-hierarchical and non-overlapping, exhaustively composing a document. Evaluation is then relatively simple, employing pseudo-documents constructed by concatenating a set of documents. This is a suitable technique for detecting coarse-grained topic shifts. As Ferret (2007) points out, approaches to the problem vary both in the kinds of knowledge they depend on, and on the kinds of features they employ.

Research on topic segmentation has exploited information internal to the corpus of documents to be segmented and information derived from external resources. If a corpus of documents pertinent to a domain is available, statistical topic models such as those developed by Beeferman et al. (1999) or Blei and Moreno (2001) can be tailored to documents of that type. Lexical cohesion techniques include similarity measures between adjacent blocks of text, as in TextTiling (Hearst, 1994, 1997) and lexical chains based on recurrences of a term or related terms, as in Morris and Hirst (1991), Kozima (1993), and Galley, et al. (2003). In Kan, et al. (1998) recurrences of the same term within a certain number of sentences are used for chains (the number varies with the type of term), and chains are based on entity reference as well as lexical identity. Our method is related to lexical chain techniques, in that the graphs we construct contain chains of nodes that extend the influence of a term beyond the site where it occurs. But we differ in that we do not require a term (or a semantically related term) to recur, in order to build such chains.

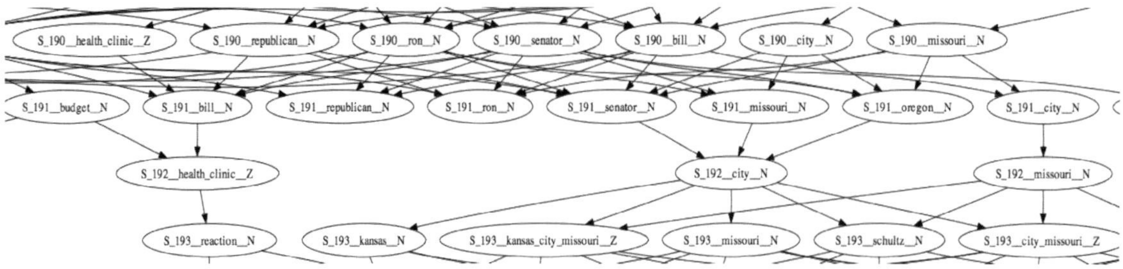

Figure 4. A portion of the graph generated from the second excerpt in Figure 1. Each node is labeled *S_i__term_pos,* where *i* indicates the sentence index

In this respect, our approach also resembles that of Matveeva and Levow (2007), who build semantic similarity among terms into their lexical cohesion model through latent semantic analysis. Our techniques differ in that we incorporate semantic relatedness between terms directly into a graph, rather than computing similarities between blocks of text.

In our experiments, we compare our method to C99 (Choi, 2000), an algorithm widely treated as a baseline. Choi's algorithm is based on a measure of local coherence; vocabulary similarity between each pair of sentences in a document is computed and the similarity scores of nearby sentences are ranked, with boundaries hypothesized where similarity across sentences is low.

4 Experiments, results, and evaluation

4.1 Systems compared

As noted above, we tested our system against the C99 segmentation algorithm (Choi, 2000). The implementation of C99 we use comes from the MorphAdorner website (Burns, 2006). We also compared our system to two simpler baseline systems without RIs. One uses graphs that do not represent a term's zone of influence, but contain just a single node for each occurrence of a term. The second represents a term's zone of influence in an extremely simple fashion, as a fixed number of sentences starting from each occurrence of that term. We tried several values ranging from 5 to 20 sentences for this extension. In addition, we varied two parameters to find the best-performing combination of settings: the threshold for pruning low-weight edges, and the threshold for positing a segment boundary. In both the single-node and fixed-extension systems, the connection strength between nodes is calculated in the same way as for our full system. These comparisons aim to demonstrate two things. First, segmentation is greatly improved when we extend the influence of terms beyond the sentences they occur in. Second, the RIs prove more effective than fixed-length extensions in modeling that influence accurately.

Lastly, to establish how much we can gain from using Choi's algorithm to determine termination points for RIs, we also compared two versions of our system: one in which RIs are calculated without information from Choi's algorithm and a second with these boundaries included.

Table 1 lists the systems we compare in the experiments described below.

C99	Implementation of Choi (2000)
SS+C	Our full Segmentation System, incorporating "hard" boundaries determined by modified Choi algorithm
SS	Our system, using RIs without "hard" boundaries determined by modified Choi algorithm
FE	Our system, using fixed extension of a term from its occurrence
SN	Our system, using a single node for each term occurrence (no extension)

Table 1. Systems compared in our experiments

4.2 Data and parameter settings

We tested our method on two sets of data. One set consists of concatenated news stories, following the approach of Choi (2000) and others since; the other consists of closed captions for twelve U.S. commercial television programs. Because the notion of a topic is inherently subjective, we follow many researchers who have reported results on "pseudo-documents"–documents formed by concatenating several randomly selected documents–so that the boundaries of segments are known, sharp, and not dependent on annotator variability (Choi, 2000). However, we also are interested in our system's performance on more realistic segmentation tasks, as noted in the introduction.

In testing our algorithm, we first generated graphs from the documents in each dataset, as described in section 2. We pruned edges in the graphs with connection strength of less than 0.5. To find segment boundaries, we seek locations where the number of common terms associated with successive sentences is at a minimum. This quantity needs to be normalized by some measure of how many nodes are present on either side of a potential boundary. We tested three normalization factors: the total number of nodes on both sides of the potential segment boundary, the maximum of the numbers of nodes on each side of the boundary, and the minimum of the numbers of nodes on each side of the boundary. The results for all three of these were very similar, so we report only those for the maximum. This measure provides a ranking of all possible boundaries in a document (that is, between each pair of consecutive sentences), with a value of 0 being most indicative of a boundary. After experimenting with a few threshold values, we selected a threshold of 0.6, and posit a boundary at each point where the measure falls below this threshold.

4.3 Evaluation metrics

We compute precision, recall, and F-measure based on exact boundary matches between the system and the reference segmentation. As numerous researchers have pointed out, this alone is not a perspicacious way to evaluate a segmentation algorithm, as a system that misses a gold-standard boundary by one sentence would be treated just like one that misses it by ten. We therefore computed two additional, widely used measures, P_k (Beeferman, et al., 1997) and WindowDiff (Pevzner and Hearst, 2002). P_k assesses a penalty against a system for each position of a sliding window across a document in which the system and the gold standard differ on the presence or absence of (at least one) segment boundary. WindowDiff is similar, but where the system differs from the gold standard, the penalty is equal to the difference in the number of boundaries between the two. This penalizes missed boundaries and "near-misses" less than P_k (but see Lamprier, et al., (2007) for further analysis and some criticism of WindowDiff). For both P_k and WindowDiff, we used a window size of half the average reference segment length, as suggested by Beeferman, et al. (1997). P_k and WindowDiff values range between 0 and 1, with lower values indicating better performance in detecting segment boundaries. Note that both P_k and WindowDiff are asymmetrical measures; different values will result if the system's and the gold-standard's boundaries are switched.

4.4 Concatenated *New York Times* articles

The concatenated pseudo-documents consist of *New York Times* articles selected at random from the *New York Times* Annotated Corpus.[3] Each pseudo-document contains twenty articles, with an average of 623.6 sentences. Our test set consists of 185 of these pseudo-documents.[4]

N = 185						
		Prec.	**Rec.**	**F**	**P_k**	**WD**
C99	μ	0.404	0.569	0.467	0.338	0.360
	s.d	0.106	0.121	0.105	0.109	0.135
SS	μ	0.566	0.383	0.448	0.292	0.317
	s.d.	0.176	0.135	0.140	0.070	0.084
SS +C	μ	0.578	0.535	0.537	0.262	0.283
	s.d.	0.148	0.197	0.150	0.081	0.098
FE	μ	0.265	0.140	0.176	0.478	0.536
	s.d.	0.123	0.042	0.055	0.055	0.076
SN	μ	0.096	0.112	0.099	0.570	0.702
	s.d.	0.040	0.024	0.027	0.072	0.164

Table 2. Performance of C99 and SS on segmentation of concatenated *New York Times* articles, without specifying a number of boundaries

Tables 2 and 3 provide summary results on the concatenated news articles. We ran the five systems listed in table 1 on the full dataset without any additional restrictions on the number of article boundaries to be detected. Means and standard deviations for each method on the five metrics are displayed in table 2. C99 typically finds many more boundaries than the 20 that are present (30.65 on average). Our SS system finds fewer than the true number of boundaries (14.52 on average), while the combined system SS+C finds almost precisely the correct number (19.98 on average). We used one-tailed paired t-tests of equal means to determine statistical significance at the 0.01 level. Although only SS+C's performance is significantly better in terms of F-

[3] www.ldc.upenn.edu/Catalog/CatalogEntry.jsp?catalogId=LDC2008T19

[4] Only article text is used, though occasionally some obvious heading material, such as book title, author and publisher at the beginning of a book review, is present also.

measure, both versions of our system outperform C99 according to P_k and WindowDiff.

Using the baseline single node system (SN) yields very poor performance. These results (table 2, row SN) are obtained with the edge-pruning threshold set to a connection strength of 0.9, and the boundary threshold set to 0.2, at which the average number of boundaries found is 26.86. Modeling the influence of terms beyond the sentences they occur in is obviously valuable.

The baseline fixed-length extensions system (FE) does better than SN but significantly worse than RIs. We found that, among the parameter settings yielding between 10 and 30 boundaries per document on average, the best results occur with the extension set to 6 sentences, the edge-pruning threshold set to a connection strength of 0.5, and the boundary threshold set to 0.7. The results for this setting are reported in table 2, row FE (the average number of segments per document is 12.5). Varying these parameters has only minor effects on performance, although the number of boundaries found can of course be tuned. RIs clearly provide a benefit over this type of system, by modeling a term's influence dynamically rather than as a fixed interval.

From here on, we report results only for the two systems: C99 and our best-performing system, SS+C.

For 86 of the documents, in which both C99 and SS+C found more than 20 boundaries, we also calculate the performance on the best-scoring 20 boundaries found by each system. These results are displayed in table 3. Note that when the number of boundaries to be found by each system is fixed at the actual number of boundaries, the values of precision and recall are necessarily identical. Here too our system outperforms C99, and the differences are statistically significant, according to a one-tailed paired t-test of equal means at the 0.01 level.

N = 86				
		Prec.=Rec.=F	P_k	WD
C99	μ	0.530	0.222	0.231
	s.d	0.105	0.070	0.074
SS + C	μ	0.643	0.192	0.201
	s.d.	0.130	0.076	0.085

Table 3. Performance of C99 and SS on segmentation of concatenated *New York Times* articles, selecting the 20 best-scoring boundaries

4.5 Human-annotated television program closed-captions

We selected twelve television programs for which we have closed-captions; they are a mix of headline news (3 shows), news commentary (4 shows), documentary/lifestyle (3 shows), one comedy/drama episode, and one talk show. Only the closed captions are used, no speaker intonation, video analysis, or metadata is employed. The closed captions are of variable quality, with numerous spelling errors.

Five annotators were instructed to indicate topic boundaries in the closed-caption text files. Their instructions were open-ended in the sense that they were not given any definition of what a topic or a topic shift should be, beyond two short examples, were not told to find a specific number of boundaries, but were allowed to indicate how important a topic was on a five-point scale, encouraging them to indicate minor segments or subtopics within major topics if they chose to do so. For some television programs, particularly the news shows, major boundaries between stories on disparate topics are likely be broadly agreed on, whereas in much of the remaining material the shifts may be more fine-grained and judgments varied. In addition, the scripted nature of television speech results in many carefully staged transitions and teasers for upcoming material, making boundaries more diffuse or confounded than in some other genres.

We combined the five annotators' segmentations, to produce a single set of boundaries as a reference. We used a three-sentence sliding window, and if three or more of the five annotators place a boundary in that window, we assign a boundary where the majority of them place it (in case of a tie, we choose one location arbitrarily). Although the annotators are rather inconsistent in their use of this rating system, a given annotator tends to be consistent in the granularity of segmentation employed across all documents. This observation is consistent with the remarks of Malioutov and Barzilay (2006) regarding varying topic granularity across human annotators on spoken material. We thus computed two versions of the combined boundaries, one in which all boundaries are used, and another in which we ignore minor boundaries—those the annotator assigned a score of 1 or 2. We ran our experiments with both versions of the combined boundaries as the reference segmentation.

We use P_k to assess inter-annotator agreement among our five annotators. Table 4 presents two

P_k values for each pair of annotators; one set of values is for all boundaries, while the other is for "major" boundaries, assigned an importance of 3 or greater on the five-point scale. The P_k value for each annotator with respect to the two reference segmentations is also provided.

	A	B	C	D	E	*Ref*
A		0.36 *0.48*	0.30 *0.45*	0.27 *0.44*	0.42 *0.67*	0.20 *0.38*
B	0.29 *0.40*		0.29 *0.32*	0.27 *0.33*	0.33 *0.55*	0.20 *0.25*
C	0.57 *0.48*	0.60 *0.44*		0.41 *0.20*	0.67 *0.61*	0.40 *0.18*
D	0.36 *0.46*	0.41 *0.46*	0.27 *0.20*		0.53 *0.63*	0.22 *0.26*
E	0.33 *0.35*	0.31 *0.34*	0.33 *0.30*	0.32 *0.31*		0.25 *0.27*
Ref	0.25 *0.39*	0.32 *0.35*	0.24 *0.17*	0.21 *0.22*	0.42 *0.58*	

Table 4. P_k values for the segmentations produced by each pair of annotators (A-E) and for the combined annotation described in section 4.5; upper values are for all boundaries and *lower values* are for boundaries of segments scored 3 or higher

These numbers are rather high, but comparable to those obtained by Malioutov and Barzilay (2006) in a somewhat similar task of segmenting video recordings of physics lectures. The P_k values are lower for the reference boundary set, which we therefore feel some confidence in using as a reference segmentation.

		Prec.	**Rec.**	**F**	P_k	**WD**
All topic boundaries						
C99	μ	0.197	0.186	0.184	0.476	0.507
	s.d	0.070	0.072	0.059	0.078	0.102
SS +C	μ	0.315	0.208	0.240	0.421	0.462
	s.d.	0.089	0.073	0.064	0.072	0.084
Major topic boundaries only						
C99	μ	0.170	0.296	0.201	0.637	0.812
	s.d.	0.063	0.134	0.060	0.180	0.405
SS +C	μ	0.271	0.316	0.271	0.463	0.621
	s.d.	0.102	0.138	0.077	0.162	0.445

Table 5. Performance of C99 and SS+C on segmentation of closed-captions for twelve television programs, with the two reference segmentations using "all topic boundaries" and "major topic boundaries only"

As the television closed-captions are noisy with respect to data quality and inter-annotator disagreement, the performance of both systems is worse than on the concatenated news articles, as expected. We present the summary performance of C99 and SS+C in table 5, again using two versions of the reference. Because of the small test set size, we cannot claim statistical significance for any of these results, but we note that on average SS+C outperforms C99 on all measures.

5 Conclusions and future work

We have presented an approach to text segmentation that relies on a novel graph based representation of document structure and semantics. It successfully models topical coherence using long-range influence of terms and a contextually determined measure of semantic relatedness. Relevance intervals, calculated using PMI and other criteria, furnish an effective model of a term's extent of influence for this purpose. Our measure of semantic relatedness reinforces global co-occurrence statistics with local contextual information, leading to an improved representation of topical coherence. We have demonstrated significantly improved segmentation resulting from this combination, not only on artificially constructed pseudo-documents, but also on noisy data with more diffuse boundaries, where inter-annotator agreement is fairly low.

Although the system we have described here is not trained in any way, it provides an extensive set of parameters that could be tuned to improve its performance. These include various techniques for calculating the similarity between terms and combining those similarities in connection strengths, heuristics for scoring potential boundaries, and thresholds for selecting those boundaries. Moreover, the graph representation lends itself to techniques for finding community structure and centrality, which may also prove useful in modeling topics and topic shifts.

We have also begun to explore segment labeling, identifying the most "central" terms in a graph according to their connection strengths. Those terms whose nodes are strongly connected to others within a segment appear to be good candidates for segment labels.

Finally, although we have so far applied this method only to linear segmentation, we plan to explore its application to hierarchical or overlapping topical structures. We surmise that strongly connected subgraphs may correspond to these more fine-grained aspects of discourse structure.

Acknowledgements

We thank our colleagues David Houghton, Olivier Jojic, and Robert Rubinoff, as well as the anonymous referees, for their comments and suggestions.

References

Doug Beeferman, Adam Berger, and John Lafferty. 1997. Text Segmentation Using Exponential Models. *Proceedings of the Second Conference on Empirical Methods in Natural Language Processing*, 35-46.

Doug Beeferman, Adam Berger, and John Lafferty. 1999. Statistical models for text segmentation. *Machine Learning*, 34(1):177–210.

David M. Blei and Pedro J. Moreno. 2001. Topic segmentation with an aspect hidden Markov model. *Proceedings of the 24th Annual Meeting of ACM SIGIR*, 343–348.

Burns, Philip R. 2006. MorphAdorner: Morphological Adorner for English Text. http://morphadorner.northwestern.edu/morphadorner/textsegmenter/.

Freddy Y.Y. Choi. 2000. Advances in domain independent linear text segmentation. *Proceedings of NAACL 2000*, 109-117.

Anthony Davis, Phil Rennert, Robert Rubinoff, Tim Sibley, and Evelyne Tzoukermann. 2004. Retrieving what's relevant in audio and video: statistics and linguistics in combination. *Proceedings of RIAO 2004*, 860-873.

Olivier Ferret. 2007. Finding document topics for improving topic segmentation. *Proceedings of the 45th Annual Meeting of the ACL*, 480–487.

Michel Galley, Kathleen McKeown, Eric Fosler-Lussier, and Hongyan Jing. 2003. Discourse Segmentation of Multi-Party Conversation. *Proceedings of the 41st Annual Meeting of the ACL*, 562-569.

Michelle Girvan and M.E.J. Newman. 2002. Community structure in social and biological networks. *Proceedings of the National Academy of Sciences*, 99:12, 7821-7826.

Marti A. Hearst. 1994. Multi-paragraph segmentation of expository text. *Proceedings of the 32nd Annual Meeting of the ACL*, 9-16.

Marti A. Hearst. 1997. TextTiling: Segmenting Text into Multi-Paragraph Subtopic Passages. *Computational Linguistics*, 23:1, 33-64.

Min-Yen Kan, Judith L. Klavans, and Kathleen R. McKeown. 1998. Linear Segmentation and Segment Significance. *Proceedings of the 6th International Workshop on Very Large Corpora*, 197-205.

Christopher Kennedy and Branimir Boguraev. 1996. Anaphora for Everyone: Pronominal Anaphora Resolution without a Parser. *Proceedings of the 16th International Conference on Computational Linguistics,* 113-118.

Hideki Kozima. 1993. Text segmentation based on similarity between words. *Proceedings of the 31st Annual Meeting of the ACL (Student Session)*, 286-288.

Sylvain Lamprier, Tassadit Amghar, Bernard Levrat and Frederic Saubion. 2007. On Evaluation Methodologies for Text Segmentation Algorithms. *Proceedings of the 19th IEEE International Conference on Tools with Artificial Intelligence*, 19-26.

Igor Malioutov and Regina Barzilay. 2006. Minimum Cut Model for Spoken Lecture Segmentation. *Proceedings of the 21st International Conference on Computational Linguistics and 44th Annual Meeting of the ACL*, 25–32.

Irina Matveeva and Gina-Anne Levow. 2007. Topic Segmentation with Hybrid Document Indexing. *Proceedings of the 2007 Joint Conference on Empirical Methods in Natural Language Processing and Computational Natural Language Learning*, 351–359,

David Milne and Ian H. Witten. 2009. An Open-Source Toolkit for Mining Wikipedia. http://www.cs.waikato.ac.nz/~dnk2/publications/AnOpenSourceToolkitForMiningWikipedia.pdf.

Jane Morris and Graeme Hirst. 1991. Lexical cohesion computed by thesaural relations. as an indicator of the structure of text. *Computational Linguistics*, 17:1, 21-48.

Lev Pevzner and Marti A. Hearst. 2002. A critique and improvement of an evaluation metric for text segmentation. *Computational Linguistics*, 28:1, 19–36.

MuLLinG: multilevel linguistic graphs for knowledge extraction

Vincent Archer
Laboratoire I3S (équipe RL), Université de Nice Sophia Antipolis
Sophia Antipolis, France
vincent.archer@unice.fr

Abstract

MuLLinG is a model for knowledge extraction (especially lexical extraction from corpora), based on multilevel graphs. Its aim is to allow large-scale data acquisition, by making it easy to realize automatically, and simple to configure by linguists with limited knowledge in computer programming. In MuLLinG, each new level represents the information in a different manner (more and more abstract). We also introduce several associated operators, written to be as generic as possible. They are independent of what nodes and edges represent, and of the task to achieve. Consequently, they allow the description of a complex extraction process as a succession of simple graph manipulations. Finally, we present an experiment of collocation extraction using MuLLinG model.

1 Introduction

Natural language processing systems often produce low-quality results, because of ambiguities and particular linguistic phenomena. One major reason is the lack of linguistic data needed to detect these phenomena or to solve ambiguities. To fill this lack, new linguistic resources should be produced. It could be done quickly with automatic processes, but quality would be unsatisfactory; on the contrary, manual work by linguists allows precise results, but takes lot of time. To get both rapidity and precision, we must combine machine and human abilities, by giving automatic processing tools to linguists, and allowing them to guide the process. Existing tools are often too centered on a task, and require too much knowledge in computer programming: they are not appropriate for linguists with few knowledge in coding. We should thus develop generic tools.

In this article, we first focus on how to make the resource gathering easier. Then, we introduce *MuLLinG*, our multilevel graph model for linguistic extraction, with several associated operations. Finally, we present an application of that model on collocation extraction.

2 Knowledge extraction

There are several manners to collect resources with automatic processes (machine learning, collaborative interfaces, etc.). We focus here on (linguistic and statistic) extraction of candidates. More precisely, our goal is to facilitate the large-scale production of candidates by extraction.

2.1 Simplify programming

Making a particular extraction task is not easy, as there is often no dedicated tool. It forces to write ad hoc tools (most of the time not unveiled). Moreover, ad hoc tools are not written to be universal. They generally depend on the data model, it is therefore difficult or impossible to use a new resource with a different format (such as an analysis from an other parser). To be really useful, an extraction tool should be *generic* (able to handle different data models) and *easy* to understand and to use. The data model on which the tool rely must be simple, expressive (complex structure should be represented easily), and universal (for monolingual or multilingual corpora, dictionaries, etc.). It should also provide simple generic, task-independent, high-level operations that can be combined to describe a complex task.

We choose to introduce a graph-based model. Graphs are understandable quickly by humans, easy to use in automatic processes, and flexible enough to represent various data types. Using graphs for knowledge extraction is quite classic. They can represent relations between words (produced by dependency analysers from corpora), and be used to produce semantically close terms (Widdows & Dorrow, 2002) or to group similar n-tuples (Hassan et al., 2006). Graphs also can be

Proceedings of the 2010 Workshop on Graph-based Methods for Natural Language Processing, ACL 2010, pages 69–73,
Uppsala, Sweden, 16 July 2010.

generated from dictionaries, and used to produce knowledge bases (Richardson et al., 1998) or proximity information (Gaume et al., 2006).

2.2 Existing graph models

Influenced by "existential graphs" (Peirce, 1931-1935) where relations between elements are represented by nodes, "conceptual graphs" (Sowa, 1976) are bipartite graphs with two node types: concepts and conceptual relations (edges only associate relations and concepts). That relation *materialization* is useful, as it allows to handle easily n-ary relations, without hypergraphs.

Another interesting network is the "lexical system" one (Polguère, 2006), defined as oriented, weighted, unhierarchical and, above all, *heterogeneous*: there is no constraint on what is modelized (it could be terms, meanings, collocations, etc.). It avoids the separation between dictionary-like and network-like lexical databases, and shows the same representation can be used for each kind of data and relation.

Finally, graphs can be *multilevel*, to represent different kinds of information. Links are generally allowed only in a same level or between two adjacent levels, like in "hypertexts" (Agosti and Crestani, 1993) made of three specified levels (documents, terms, concepts), or in Multi-Level Association Graphs (Witschel, 2007) in which there is no constraint on the number of levels. We believe that the use of several levels to represent various content types is pertinent in an extraction process, as it allows to handle both the occurrences of terms, and the terms themselves.

3 MuLLinG model

We introduce *MuLLinG* (Multi-Level Linguistic Graph), our own graph model. Divided in several ordered and distinct levels, it contains two kinds of edges: *intra-level* ones (between nodes from same level) and *inter-level* ones (from a node on level i to a node on level i+1). Intra-level edges are not unique (several edges are allowed between two nodes): every level is a multigraph. On the contrary, a node can be the source of only one inter-level edge; this association means that the target node (on the superior level) is a more global representation of the source node (it defines a hierarchy of precision).

Finally, in order to allow the heterogeneity of represented data, nodes and intra-level edges can carry any attribute (with no limit on kind or number). Figure 1 shows an example of a MuLLinG graph, in which 1st level contains occurrences of words, 2nd level contains lemmas, and 3rd level contains synonymy classes.

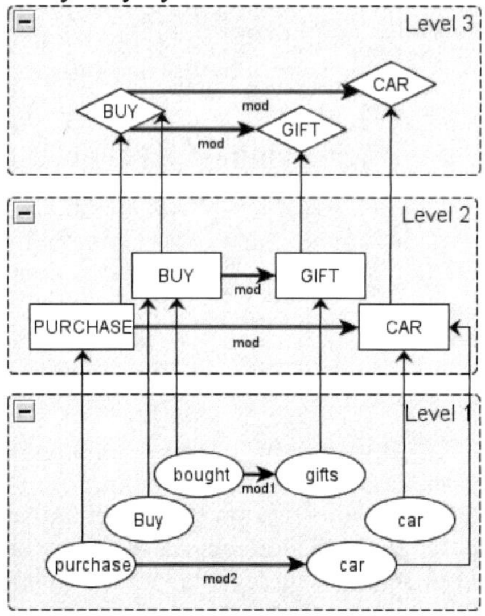

Figure 1. Example of 3-level MuLLinG graph

3.1 Definition

More precisely, a MuLLinG graph is an oriented multigraph $G^n = (V, E, F, A, \triangleleft, a_V, a_E)$ (for n levels) where:

- V: set of *nodes*, made of n disjoint subsets $V_1, \ldots, V_n$ (for the n levels);
- E: set of *intra-level edges*, made of n disjoint subsets $E_1, \ldots, E_n$; A: set of functions $\alpha_i : E_i \rightarrow V_i \times V_i \mid i \in \{1, \ldots, n\}$ associating an edge and its two extremities;
- F: set of *inter-level edges*, in *n-1* disjoint sets $F_1, \ldots, F_{n-1}$ defined as $F_i = \{\langle x, y\rangle \in V_i \times V_{i+1} \mid y = \varphi(x)\}$; $\triangleleft$: set of functions $\varphi_i : V_i \rightarrow V_{i+1} \mid i \in \{1, \ldots, n\}$, associating a node (on a given level) and a node on the superior level);
- $a_V = \{f : V \rightarrow \Sigma_V\}$, $a_E = \{f : E \rightarrow \Sigma_E\}$ (Σ_V, Σ_E are alphabets for attributes of objects from E and V) model attributes.

3.2 Associated operators

To manipulate MuLLinG graphs, we introduce several operations, designed for their particular structure. Some of them allow elementary manipulations: add or delete a node or an edge, clean a node (delete all edges of which it is a source or a target), delete a node and its "descendants" (the nodes linked *to* it by inter-level edges, and their own descendants). There are

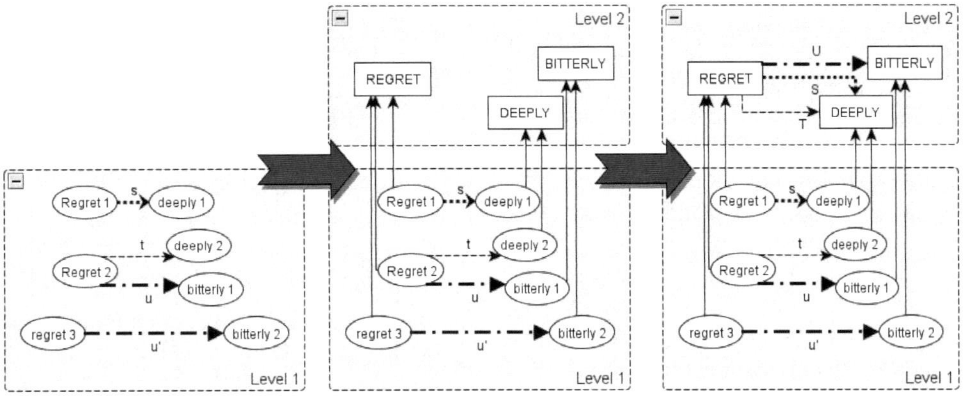

Figure 2. Two-steps emergence (nodes, then edges)

also operations to compute measures, to realize a *conditional manipulation* on nodes or edges (it can be use to *filter* the graph, by deleting nodes depending on the value of a given attribute). All these basic operations should not be directly used, but rather be called by more elaborate ones.

These operations (modifying the graph structure) take parameters fixed by the user: the level, the filtering function (which graph elements are concerned by the operation?), and computation functions (to produce attribute values for newly created elements). Graph coherence is guaranteed if the user provides correct parameters.

Emergence is the essential operation associated with MuLLinG. Its aim is to generate a superior level, by grouping elements (from the initial level) in equivalence classes. In the newly created level, each node (resp. edge) represent a equivalence class of nodes (resp. edges) from the initial level. The identification of equivalence classes is a parameter of the emergence (the user provides it). The operation goes in two steps:

- *node emergence*: for each equivalence class of nodes, it creates a node on the superior level to represent this class (and each node in the class is linked to the newly created node); figure 2 shows the emergence of nodes representing equivalence classes containing all occurrences of a same word;
- *edge emergence*: each edge added on the superior level between nodes *A* and *B* depict a set of equivalent edges between an element of *A* class and an element of *B* class; in figure 2, equivalent *u* and *u'* are grouped in a sole edge *U*, whereas *s* and *t* (not equivalent) are represented by two distinct edges *S* and *T*.

Finally, some other operations have been defined to mix information from two graphs in a third one. The *intersection* contain elements (nodes, edges) present in both graphs, with unification of identical elements. The *union* contain all elements from the two graphs, with unification of identical elements. The *difference* contain all elements from the first graph that are not identical to an element from the second one.

It is essential to recognize the identity between two nodes or two edges: *identity functions* are parameters for these "mix" operations, and should be provided by the user. Among parameters, there are also, depending on the case, functions for *fusion* (production of attributes for unified nodes or edges) or *copy* (production of attributes for elements present in only one graph).

To handle n-ary relations, we also provide a *complex* version of MuLLinG, where relations can be materialized. In that case, a relation is represented by a standard node and *numbered argument edges* linking that node to the arguments of the relation. It also allows the representation of relations between relations themselves.

We made an implementation of *MuLLinG* as a C++ library[1], based on *Boost* (open-source C++ libraries), especially for graph access and iterations. It can read and write MuLLinG graphs in GraphML format (Brandes et al., 2001).

4 Application to collocation extraction

4.1 Extraction process

We realized several experiments using our library. We remind the reader that our goal was not to obtain the more efficient method for extraction, but rather to introduce tools for simplifying the programming of extraction tasks. We present here experiments about collocation extraction. *Collocations* are particular expressions where a term is chosen arbitrarily, depending on the other

[1] Available at http://mulling.ligforge.imag.fr/ (under *CeCILL* free software license)

term, to express a particular meaning (like in "driving rain", where "driving" is used to express intensity). As the choice differs between languages[2], it causes big issues to machine translation systems (which lack resources to handle them correctly). In our experiment, the initial graph is made of relations produced by a dependency analyzer, on 1st level.

Firstly, we use the *filtering* operator to keep only pertinent relations (nouns modified by adjectives, like in figure 3, or verbs modified by adverbs), according to the analyzer. There are relations between term occurrences on 1st level, but we want relations between terms themselves: we generate them on 2nd level using emergence. So we proceed *node emergence* by considering that nodes with same attribute "lemma" are equivalent, then *edge emergence* by considering that edges expressing a modification are equivalent.

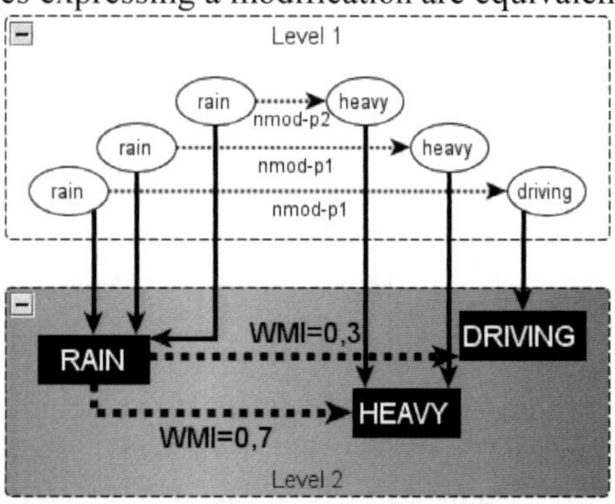

Figure 3. Collocations extraction with emergence (on 2nd level) and computation operations

The "collocation" candidates are all 2nd-level edges created during the emergence. To rank them, we use the *computation* operation (with occurrence and co-occurrence frequencies) to fix an association measure on those nodes. Figure 3 shows an example of a MuLLinG graph after emergence and computation operations.

To facilitate the description, our library contains lots of pre-defined generic functions. By example, a filter (used as a parameter of emergence) can be based on an excepted value, a threshold, etc. We also described numerous association measures; for now, new ones should be written in the C++ program.

We used our library to carry out the extraction as described previously, with LeMonde95 corpus (news articles) analyzed by Xerox's XIP parser. Thanks to MuLLinG structure, it is very easy to get all potential collocations (*heavy/driving* rain): these are the relations of which it is the source.

[2]By example, a "*heavy* smoker" is *big* in French ("*gros* fumeur") and *strong* in German ("starker Raucher").

Experiments		*verb-adverb*	*noun-adjective*
Level 1	nodes	1 155 824	1 319 474
	edges	1 780 759	2 009 051
Level 2	nodes	6 813	33 132
	edges	144 586	273 655

Table 1. Nodes and edges produced during experiments on collocation extraction

4.2 Advantages and drawbacks

With MuLLinG library, we reproduced *exactly* some experiments on collocation extraction we made before (with ad hoc programs): results are obviously coherent. The production is currently slightly slower (around 20% more time) but speed is not crucial, and could be optimized. MuLLinG has a great advantage while writing the program: it only calls functions (and declare parameters). Consequently, task description with our library is much faster (source lines of code are divided by 5), it also avoids errors. It requires less knowledge in programming, so it is far more accessible. Nevertheless, usability should still be improved: we must describe a high-level language (we believe it should be a request one). Furthermore, there is no constraint on input resources, so programs could easily be re-used with other relations (from other parsers). Finally, as graphs with millions of elements can reach RAM limits, we plan to allow database storage.

We also made bilingual experiments on collocations, taking advantage of MuLLinG complex version to materialize monolingual "collocation" nodes, and to describe bilingual relations between collocations as edges between them.

5 Conclusion

Facing the lack of tools for extraction of lexical knowledge, we looked for a new one, simple and generic. We specified MuLLinG, multilevel graph model (with no constraint on the data), associated with several simple manipulation operations (which could be combined to realize complex tasks). The ensuing tool allows to program linguistic tasks in a resource-independent manner, simpler and more efficient. One major prospect of this work concerns its implementation. As explained before, we must provide a high-level language. It is also necessary to facilitate the import and to optimize memory management. In order to provide a less NLP-centered tool, we should extend it with new operations, and with algorithms related to classic problems of graph theory. It would also be interesting to interact with semantic web tools (RDF/SPARQL).

References

Maristella Agosti and Fabio Crestani. 1993. A Methodology for the Automatic Construction of a Hypertext for Information Retrieval. In *Proceedings of 1993 ACM Symposium on Applied Computing*, 745-753.

Ulrik Brandes, Markus Eiglsperger, Ivan Herman, Michael Himsolt and M. Scott Marshall. 2001. GraphML Progress Report - Structural Layer Proposal. In *Proceedings of 9th International Symposium Graph Drawing (GD'01)*, 501-512.

Hany Hassan, Ahmed Hassan and Sara Noeman. 2006. Graph based semi-supervised approach for information extraction. In *Proceedings of HLT-NAACL-07 Workshop on Textgraphs-06*, 9-16.

Bruno Gaume, Karine Duvignau and Martine Vanhove. 2008. Semantic associations and confluences in paradigmatic networks. In Martine Vanhove (Ed.), *From Polysemy to Semantic Change Towards a typology of lexical semantic associations*, John Benjamins, 233-264.

Charles Sanders Peirce. 1931-1935. *Collected Papers of C. S. Peirce* (C. Hartshorne & P. Weiss, eds.), Cambridge: Harvard University Press.

Alain Polguère. 2006. Structural Properties of Lexical Systems: Monolingual and Multilingual Perspectives. In *Proceedings of Workshop on Multilingual Language Resources and Interoperability (COLING/ACL 2006)*, 50-59.

Stephen D. Richardson, William B. Dolan, and Lucy Vanderwende. 1998. MindNet: acquiring and structuring semantic information from text. In *Proceedings of COLING 1998*. 1098-1102.

John F. Sowa. 1976. Conceptual graphs for a database interface. *IBM Journal of Research and Development 20:4*, 336-357.

Dominic Widdows and Beate Dorow. 2002. A Graph Model for Unsupervised Lexical Acquisition. In *Proceedings of 19th International Conference on Computational Linguistics(COLING 2002)*. 1093-1099.

Hans Friedrich Witschel. 2007. Multi-level Association Graphs - A New Graph-Based Model for Information Retrieval. In *Proceedings of HLT-NAACL-07 Workshop on Textgraphs-07*, 9-16.

Experiments with CST-based Multidocument Summarization

Maria Lucía del Rosario Castro Jorge, Thiago Alexandre Salgueiro Pardo
Núcleo Interinstitucional de Lingüística Computacional (NILC)
Instituto de Ciências Matemáticas e de Computação, Universidade de São Paulo
Avenida Trabalhador são-carlense, 400 - Centro
P.O.Box 668. 13560-970, São Carlos/SP, Brazil
{mluciacj,taspardo}@icmc.usp.br

Abstract

Recently, with the huge amount of growing information in the web and the little available time to read and process all this information, automatic summaries have become very important resources. In this work, we evaluate deep content selection methods for multidocument summarization based on the CST model (Cross-document Structure Theory). Our methods consider summarization preferences and focus on the overall main problems of multidocument treatment: redundancy, complementarity, and contradiction among different information sources. We also evaluate the impact of the CST model over superficial summarization systems. Our results show that the use of CST model helps to improve informativeness and quality in automatic summaries.

1 Introduction

In the last years there has been a considerable increase in the amount of online information and consequently the task of processing this information has become more difficult. Just to have an idea, recent studies conducted by IDC showed that 800 exabytes of information were produced in 2009, and it is estimated that in 2012 it will be produced 3 times more. Among all of this information, there is a lot of related content that comes from different sources and that presents similarities and differences. Reading and dealing with this is not straightforward. In this scenario, multidocument summarization has become an important task.

Multidocument summarization consists in producing a unique summary from a set of documents on the same topics (Mani, 2001). A multidocument summary must contain the most relevant information from the documents. For example, we may want to produce a multidocument summary from all the documents telling about the recent world economical crisis or the terrorism in some region. As an example, Figure 1 reproduces a summary from Radev and Mckeown (1998), which contains the main facts from 4 news sources.

> Reuters reported that 18 people were killed in a Jerusalem bombing Sunday. The next day, a bomb in Tel Aviv killed at least 10 people and wounded 30 according to Israel radio. Reuters reported that at least 12 people were killed and 105 wounded. Later the same day, Reuters reported that the radical Muslim group Hamas had claimed responsibility for the act.

Figure 1: Example of multidocument summary (Radev and Mckeown, 1998, p. 478)

Multidocument summarization has to deal not only with the fact of showing relevant information but also with some multidocument phenomena such as redundancy, complementarity, contradiction, information ordering, source identification, temporal resolution, etc. It is also interesting to notice that, instead of only generic summaries (as the one in the example), summaries may be produced considering user preferences. For example, one may prefer summaries including information attributed to particular sources (if one trusts more in some sources) or more context information (considering a reader that has not accompanied some recent important news), among other possibilities.

Proceedings of the 2010 Workshop on Graph-based Methods for Natural Language Processing, ACL 2010, pages 74–82,
Uppsala, Sweden, 16 July 2010.

There are two main approaches for multidocument summarization (Mani and Maybury, 1999): the superficial and the deep approaches. Superficial approach uses little linguistic knowledge to produce summaries. This approach usually has low cost and is more robust, but it produces poor results. On the other hand, deep approaches use more linguistic knowledge to produce summaries. In general terms, in this approach it is commonly used syntactical, semantic and discourse parsers to analyze the original documents. A very common way to analyze documents consists in establishing semantic relations among the documents parts, which helps identifying commonalities and differences in information. Within this context, discourse models as CST (Cross-document Structure Theory) (Radev, 2000) are useful (see, e.g., Afantenos et al., 2004; Afantenos, 2007; Jorge and Pardo, 2009, 2010; Radev and Mckeown, 1998; Radev et al., 2001; Zhang et al., 2002).

It was proposed in Mani and Maybury (1999) a general architecture for multidocument summarization, with analysis, transformation, and synthesis stages. The first stage consists in analyzing and formally representing the content of the original documents. The second stage consists mainly in transforming the represented content into a condensed content that will be included in the final summary. One of the most important tasks in this stage is the content selection process, which consists in selecting the most relevant information. Finally, the third stage expresses the condensed content in natural language, producing the summary.

In this paper, we explore a CST-based summarization method and evaluate the corresponding prototype system for multidocument summarization. Our system, called CSTSumm (CST-based SUMMarizer), produces multidocument summaries from input CST-analyzed news documents. We mainly investigate content selection methods for producing both generic and preference-based summaries. Particularly, we formalize and codify our content selection strategies as operators that perform the previously cited transformation stage. We run our experiments with Brazilian Portuguese news texts (previously analyzed according to CST by human experts) and show that we produce more informative summaries in comparison with some superficial summarizers (Pardo, 2005; Radev et al., 2000). We also use CST to enrich these superficial summarizers, showing that the results also improve. Our general hypothesis for this work is that the deep knowledge provided by CST helps to improve information and quality in summaries.

This work is organized as follows. In Section 2, the main concepts of the CST model are introduced and the works that have already used CST for multidocument summarization are reviewed. In Section 3, we present CSTSumm, while its evaluation is reported in Section 4. Some final remarks are presented in Section 5.

2 Related Work

2.1 Cross-document Structure Theory

Radev (2000) proposed CST model with a set of 24 relations for multidocument treatment in any domain. Table 1 lists these relations.

Table 1: CST original relations

Identity	Judgment
Equivalence	Fulfillment
Translation	Description
Subsumption	Reader profile
Contradiction	Contrast
Historical background	Parallel
Modality	Cross-reference
Attribution	Citation
Summary	Refinement
Follow-up	Agreement
Elaboration	Generalization
Indirect speech	Change of perspective

The established relations may have (or not) directionality, e.g., the equivalence relation (which states that two text segments have similar content) has no directionality while the historical background relation (which states that a segment provides historical information about other) has. Figure 2 shows examples of these two relations among sentences from different sources.

As part of the model, the author proposes a general schema that reveals the possibility of relationship at any level of linguistic analysis. Figure 3 (reproduced from Radev, 2000) illustrates this schema. According to this schema, the documents with CST relations are represented as a graph, whose nodes are text segments (of possibly any level) and the edges are relations. This graph is possibly disconnected, since not all segments present relations with other segments. It is important to say that, in general, only one analysis level is treated. In this work, we only deal with sentences from the input documents, since sentences are well delimited and are standard segments in discourse analysis.

Equivalence relation

Sentence 1: Nine people died, three of them children, and 25 others were wounded last Monday in a blast at a market in Moscow, police said.

Sentence 2: Nine people died, including three children, and 25 others were injured last Monday in an explosion that happened at a market in Moscow, police of Moscow informed.

Historical background relation
(directionality: from Sentence 2 to 1)

Sentence 1: An airplane accident in Bukavu, east of Democratic Republic of Congo, killed 13 people this Thursday in the afternoon.

Sentence 2: Congo has a history of more than 30 airplane tragedies.

Figure 2: Examples of CST relations

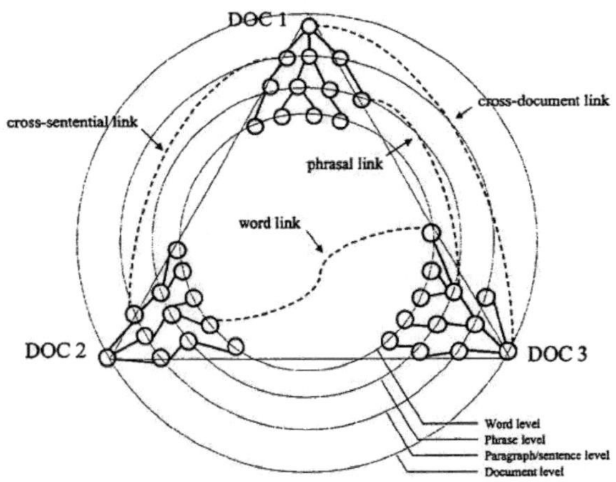

Figure 3: CST general schema (Radev, 2000, p. 78)

2.2 Multidocument Summarization

A few works explored CST for multidocument summarization. A 4-stage multidocument summarization methodology was proposed in Radev (2000). In this methodology, the first stage consists in clustering documents according to their topics. In the second stage, internal analysis (syntactical and semantic, for instance) of the texts may be performed. In the third stage, CST relations are established among texts. Finally, in the fourth stage, information is selected to produce the final summary. For this methodology the author suggests using operators activated by user summarization preferences such as authorship (i.e., reporting the information sources) or contradictory information preference. The author also says that it may be possible to produce generic summaries without considering a particular preference. In this case the criterion used to select information is based on the number of CST relations that a segment has. This criterion is based on the idea that relevant information is more repeated/elaborated and related to other segments across documents. This may be easily verified in practice. In this paper we follow such ideas.

A methodology for enriching multidocument summaries produced by superficial summarizers was proposed by Zhang et al. (2002). The authors incorporated the information given by CST relations to MEAD (Radev et al., 2000) summarization process, showing that giving preference to segments with CST relations produces better summaries. Otterbacher et al. (2002) investigated how CST relations may improve cohesion in summaries, which was tested by ordering sentences in summaries according to CST relations. The idea used behind this ordering is that sentences related by CST relations should appear closer in the final summaries as well as should respect possible temporal constraints indicated by some relations.

Afantenos et al. (2004) proposed another summarization methodology that extracts message templates from the texts (using information extraction tools) and, according to the type of CST relation between two templates, produces a unified message that would represent the summary content. The authors did not fully implement this method.

3 CSTSumm

In this paper we evaluate a CST-based multidocument summarization method by implementing and testing a prototype system, called CSTSumm. It performs content selection operations over a group of texts on the same topic that were previously annotated according to CST. For the moment, we are using manually annotated texts, i.e., the analysis stage of multidocument summarization is only simulated. In the future, texts may be automatically annotated, since a CST parser is under development for Brazilian Portuguese language (Maziero et al., 2010).

Initially, the system receives as input the CST-annotated texts, which are structured as a graph. An initial rank of sentences is then built: the sentences are ordered according to the number of CST relations they present; the more relations a sentence presents, better ranked it will be. Having the initial rank, content selection is performed. In this work, following the idea of Jorge and Pardo (2010), we represent and codify each content selection strategy as an operator. A content selection operator tells how to rearrange the sentences in the rank in order to produce summaries that better satisfy the corresponding user preferences. For instance, if a user requires more context information in the summary, the corresponding operator is activated. Such operator will (i) select in the rank all the sentences that present historical background and elaboration CST relations with better ranked sentences and (ii) improve their position in the rank by putting them immediately after the better ranked sentences with which they are related. This final action would give to these "contextual" sentences more preference for being in the summary, since they are better positioned in the refined rank. Figure 4 shows an example of a hypothetical CST graph (derived from a group of texts), the corresponding initial rank (with relations preserved for clarification) and the transformation that the context operator would do for producing the new/refined rank. It is possible to see that sentence 1, that presents historical information about the sentence 4, gets a better position in the rank (immediately after sentence 4), receiving some privilege to be in the summary.

Besides the context operator, we also have other 3 operators: the contradiction operator (which looks for the contradiction CST relation in order to include in the summary every contradiction in the texts), the authorship operator (which looks for the citation and attribution CST relations in order to include in the summary possible sources that provided the available information), and the evolving events operator (which looks for historical background and follow-up CST relations in order to present the development of the events during a time period).

Independently from the user preference, an extra operator is always applied: the redundancy operator. It removes from the rank all sentences whose information is already expressed in other better ranked sentences. Redundancy is represented by the identity, equivalence, and subsumption CST relations.

After the content selection process, in the last stage – the synthesis stage – the system selects as many sentences from the rank as allowed by the specified compression rate. The compression rate (provided by the user) informs the size of the summary. For instance, a 70% rate indicates that the summary must have at most 30% of the number of words in a text. In this work, given the multidocument nature of the task, we compute the compression rate over the size of the longest text in the group.

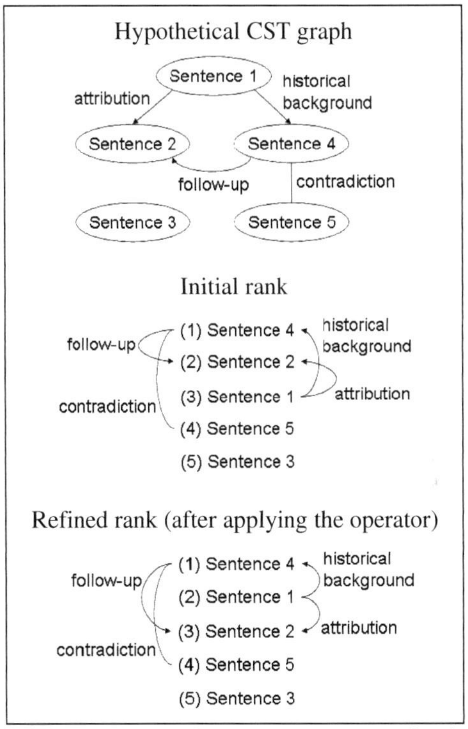

Figure 4: Example of context operator application

Synthesis stage also orders the selected sentences according to a simple criterion that only considers the position of the sentences in the original documents: first sentences appear first in the summary. If two sentences have the same position but in different documents, then the sentences are ordered according to the document number. Finally, we apply a sentence fusion system (Seno and Nunes, 2009) to some selected sentences. This is done when sentences with overlap CST relation among them are selected to the summary. The overlap relation indicates that the sentences have similar content, but also that both present unique content. In this case, it is desired that the sentences become only one with the union of their contents. The fusion system that we use does that. Figure 5 illustrates the fusion process, with the original sentences and a resulting fusion.

Figure 6 shows the general architecture of CSTSumm, which summarizes the whole process described before. Each operator is codified in

XML, where it is specified which relations should be looked in the rank in order to have the correspondent sentences better ranked. It is important to notice that, excepting the redundancy operator, our system was designed to allow the application of only one content selection operator at a time. If more than one operator is applied, the application of the following operator may probably rewrite the modifications in the rank that the previous operator has done. For instance, the application of the contradiction operator after the context operator might include sentences with contradiction above sentences with context information in the rank, altering therefore the rank produced by the context operator. One simple alternative to this design choice is to ask the user to rank his preferences and, then, to apply the corresponding operators in the opposite order, so that the rank produced by the most important preference will not be further altered. Other alternative is to produce more complex operators that combine preferences (and the corresponding CST relations), but some preference on the relations should still be specified.

Sentence 1: According to a spokesman from United Nations, the plane was trying to land at the airport in Bukavu in the middle of a storm.

Sentence 2: Everyone died when the plane, hampered by bad weather, failed to reach the runway and crashed in a forest 15 kilometers from the airport in Bukavu.

Fusion: According to a spokesman for the United Nations, everyone died when a plane that was trying to land at Bukavu airport, hampered by bad weather, failed to reach the runway and crashed in a forest 15 kilometers from the airport.

Figure 5: Example of sentence fusion

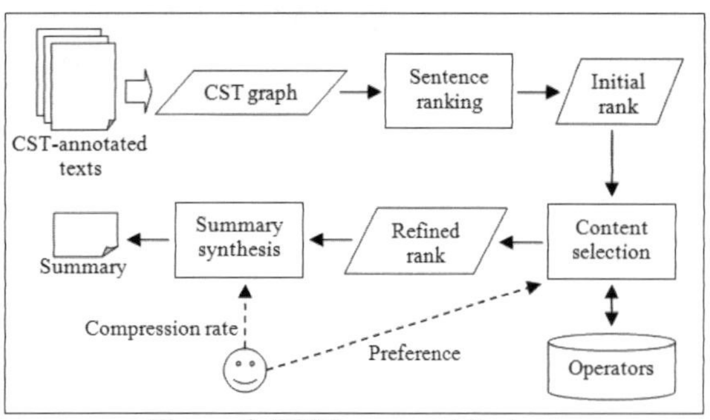

Figure 6: CSTSumm architecture

In Figure 7 we show the algorithm for the application of operators during content selection process. It is important to notice that the selected operator looks for its relations in all pairs of sentences in the rank. Once it finds the relations, it rearranges the rank appropriately, by putting the related sentence more above in the rank.

procedure for application of content selection operators
input data: initial rank, user summarization preference, operators
output data: refined rank
apply the redundancy operator
select one operator according to the user summarization preference
for i=sentence at the first position in the rank to the last but one sentence
    for j=sentence at position i+1 in the rank to the last sentence
        if the operator relations happen among sentences i and j, rearrange the rank appropriately

Figure 7: Algorithm for application of content selection operators

As an illustration of the results of our system, Figure 8 shows an automatic summary produced from a group of 3 texts with the application of the context operator (after redundancy operator was applied) and a 70% compression rate. The summary was translated from Portuguese, the language with which the summarizer was tested.

The Brazilian volleyball team has won on Friday the seventh consecutive victory in the World League, defeating Finland by 3 sets to 0 - partials of 25/17, 25/22 and 25/21 - in a match in the Tampere city, Finland. The first set remained balanced until the middle, when André Heller went to serve. In the last part, Finland again paired the game with Brazil, but after a sequence of Brazilians points Finland failed to respond and lost by 25 to 21. The Brazilian team has won five times the World League in 1993, 2001, 2003, 2004 and 2005.

Figure 8: Example of multidocument summary with context information

4 Evaluation

Our main research question in this work was how helpful CST would be for producing better summaries. CSTSumm enables us to assess the summaries and content selection strategies, but a comparison of these summaries with summaries produced by superficial methods is still necessary. In fact, we not only proceeded to such comparison, but also improved the superficial methods with CST knowledge.

As superficial summarizers, we selected MEAD (Radev et al., 2000) and GistSumm (Pardo et al., 2003; Pardo, 2005) summarizers. MEAD works as follows. Initially, MEAD builds an initial rank of sentences according to a score based on three parameters: position of the sentence in the text, lexical distance of the sentence to the centroid of the text, and the size of the sentence. These three elements are linearly combined for producing the score. GistSumm, on the other side, is very simple: the system juxtaposes all the source texts and gives a score to each sentence according to the presence of frequent words (following the approach of Luhn, 1958) or by using TF-ISF (Term Frequency – Inverse Sentence Frequency, as proposed in Larroca et al., 2000). Following the work of Zhang et al. (2002), we decided to use CST to rearrange (and supposedly improve) the sentence ranks produced by MEAD and GistSumm. We simply add to each sentence score the number of CST relations that the sentence presents:

new sentence score = old sentence score + number of CST relations

The number of sentences is retrieved from the CST graph. This way, the sentence positions in the rank are changed.

For our experiments, we used the CSTNews corpus (Aleixo and Pardo, 2008), which is a corpus of news texts written in Brazilian Portuguese. The corpus contains 50 clusters of texts. Each group has from 2 to 4 texts on the same topic annotated according to CST by human experts, as well as a manual generic summary with 70% compression rate (in relation to the longest text). The annotation process was carried out by 4 humans, with satisfactory agreement, which demonstrated that the annotation task was well defined and performed. More details about the corpus and its annotation process are presented by Maziero et al. (2010).

For each cluster of CSTNews corpus, it was produced a set of automatic summaries corresponding to each method that was explored in this work. To evaluate the informativity and quality of the summaries, we used two types of evaluation: automatic evaluation and human evaluation. For the automatic evaluation we used ROUGE (Lin, 2004) informativity measure, which compares automatic summaries with human summaries in terms of the n-grams that they have in common, resulting in precision, recall and f-measure numbers between 0 (the worst) and 1 (the best), which indicate how much information the summary presents. Precision indicates the amount of relevant information that the automatic summary contains; recall indicates how much information from the human summary is reproduced in the automatic summary; f-measure is a unique performance measure that combines precision and recall. Although it looks simple, ROUGE author has showed that it performs as well as humans in differentiating summary informativeness, which caused the measure to be widely used in the area. In particular, for this work, we considered only unigram comparison, since the author of the measure demonstrated that unigrams are enough for differentiating summary quality. For computing ROUGE, we compared each automatic summary with the corresponding human summary in the corpus.

We computed ROUGE for every summary we produced through several strategies: using only the initial rank, only the redundancy operator, and the remaining preference operators (applied after the redundancy operator). Is is important to notice that it is only fair to use ROUGE to evaluate the summaries produced by the initial rank and by the redundancy operator, since the human summary (to which ROUGE compares the automatic summaries) are generic, produced with no preference in mind. We only computed ROUGE for the preference-biased summaries in order to have a measure of how informative they are. Ideally, these preference-biased summaries should not only mirror the user preference, but also contain the main information from the source texts.

On the other hand, we used human evaluation to measure the quality of the summaries in terms of coherence, cohesion and redundancy, factors that ROUGE is not sensitive enough to capture. By coherence, we mean the characteristic of a text having a meaning and being understandable. By cohesion, we mean the superficial makers of coherence, i.e., the sequence of text elements that connect the ideas in the text, as punctuation, discourse markers, anaphors, etc.

For each one of the above evaluation factors, a human evaluator was asked to assign one of five values: very bad (score 0), bad (score 1), regular (score 2), good (score 3), and excellent (score 4). We also asked humans to evaluate informativity in the preference-biased summaries produced by our system, which is a more fair evaluation than the automatic one described above. The user should score each summary (using the same values above) according to how much he was satisfied with the actual content of the summary in face of the preference made. The user had access to the source texts for performing the evaluation.

Table 2 shows the ROUGE scores for the summaries produced by the initial rank, by the application of the operators, by the superficial summarizers, and by the CST-enriched superficial summarizers. It is important to say that these results are the average results obtained for the automatic summaries generated for all the clusters in the CSTNews corpus.

Table 2: ROUGE results

Content selection method	Precision	Recall	F-measure
Initial rank	0.5564	0.5303	0.5356
Redundancy treatment (only)	0.5761	0.5065	0.5297
Context information	0.5196	0.4938	0.4994
Authorship information	0.5563	0.5224	0.5310
Contradiction information	0.5503	0.5379	0.5355
Evolving events information	0.5159	0.5222	0.5140
MEAD without CST	0.5242	0.4602	0.4869
MEAD with CST	0.5599	0.4988	0.5230
GistSumm without CST	0.3599	0.6643	0.4599
GistSumm with CST	0.4945	0.5089	0.4994

As expected, it may be observed that the best results were achieved by the initial rank (since it produces generic summaries, as happens to the human summaries to which they are compared), which does not consider any summarization preference at all. It is also possible to see that: (a) the superficial summarizers are outperformed by the CST-based methods and (b) CST-enriched superficial summarizers produced better results than the superficial summarizers.

Results for human evaluation are shown in Table 3. These results show the average value for each factor evaluated for a sample group of 48 texts randomly selected from the corpus. We also associated to each value the closest concept in our evaluation. We could not perform the evaluation for the whole corpus due to the high cost and time-demanding nature of the human evaluation. Six humans carried out this evaluation. Each human evaluated eight summaries, and each summary was evaluated by three humans.

Table 3: Results for human evaluation

Content selection method	Coherence	Cohesion	Redundancy	Informativity
Initial rank	3.6 Excellent	3.2 Good	1.8 Regular	3.6 Excellent
Context	2.1 Regular	2.7 Good	3.6 Excellent	2.2 Regular
Authorship	3.3 Good	2.4 Regular	2.8 Good	3 Good
Contradiction	2.4 Regular	2.7 Good	2.5 Regular	3.7 Excellent
Evolving events	2.1 Regular	2.5 Regular	2.6 Good	3.2 Good

It may be observed that informativity factor results are quite satisfactory, since more than 50% of the judges considered that the performance was excellent. For coherence, cohesion and redundancy factors, results were not excellent in all the cases, but they were not bad either. We consider that one of the things that could have had an influence in this case is the performance of the fusion system, since it may generate sentences with some problems of coherence and cohesion. There are also other things that may influence these results, such as the method for ordering sentences that we used in this work. This method does not follow any deep criteria to order sentences and may also lead to coherence and cohesion problems.

These results show that CSTSumm is capable of producing summaries with good informativity and quality. In fact, the results validate our hypothesis that deep knowledge may improve the results, since it deals better with the multidocument phenomena, as the presence of redundant, complementary and contradictory information.

5 Final Remarks

Although we consider that very good results were achieved, there is still room for improvements. Future works include the investigation of better sentence ordering methods, as well as more investigation on how to jointly apply more than one content selection operator.

For the moment, CSTSumm assumes that the texts to be summarized must be already annotated with CST. In the future, as soon as an automatic CST parser is available for Portuguese, it should provide the suitable input to the summarizer.

Finally, it is interesting to notice that, although we have tested our methods with Brazilian Portuguese texts, they are robust and generic enough to be applied to any other language, since both our methods and CST model are language independent.

Acknowledgments

The authors are grateful to FAPESP and CNPq for supporting this work.

References

Afantenos, S.D.; Doura, I.; Kapellou, E.; Karkaletsis, V. 2004. Exploiting Cross-Document Relations for Multi-document Evolving Summarization. In the *Proceedings of SETN*, pp. 410-419.

Afantenos, S.D. 2007. Reflections on the Task of Content Determination in the Context of Multi-Document Summarization of Evolving Events. In *Recent Advances on Natural Language Processing*. Borovets, Bulgaria.

Aleixo, P. and Pardo, T.A.S. 2008. *CSTNews: Um Córpus de Textos Journalísticos Anotados segundo a Teoria Discursiva CST (Cross-Document Structure Theory).* Série de Relatórios Técnicos do Instituto de Ciências Matemáticas e de Computação, Universidade de São Paulo no. 326. São Carlos, Brazil .

Jorge, M.L.C and Pardo, T.A.S. 2009. Content Selection Operators for Multidocument Summarization based on Cross-document Structure Theory. In the *Proceedings of the 7th Brazilian Symposium in Information and Human Language Technology*. São Carlos, Brazil.

Jorge, M.L.C. and Pardo, T.A.S. 2010. Formalizing CST-based Content Selection Operations. In the *Proceedings of the 9th International Conference on Computational Processing of Portuguese Language* (Lecture Notes in Artificial Intelligence 6001), pp. 25-29. Porto Alegre, Brazil.

Larocca Neto, J.; Santos, A.D.; Kaestner, A.A.; Freitas, A.A. 2000. Generating Text Summaries through the Relative Importance of Topics. In M.C. Monard and J.S. Sichman (eds.), *Lecture Notes in Artificial Intelligence*, N. 1952, pp. 300-309. Springer, Verlag.

Lin, C-Y. 2004. ROUGE: a Package for Automatic Evaluation of Summaries. In the *Proceedings of the Workshop on Text Summarization Branches Out*. Barcelona, Spain.

Luhn, H.P. 1958. The automatic creation of literature abstracts. *IBM Journal of Research and Development*, Vol. 2, pp. 159-165. Barcelona, Spain.

Mani, I. and Maybury, M. T. 1999. *Advances in automatic text summarization*. MIT Press, Cambridge, MA.

Mani, I. 2001. *Automatic Summarization*. John Benjamins Publishing Co. Amsterdam.

Maziero, E.G.; Jorge, M.L.C.; Pardo, T.A.S. 2010. Identifying Multidocument Relations. In the *Proceedings of the 7th International Workshop on Natural Language Processing and Cognitive Science*. June 8-12, Funchal/Madeira, Portugal.

Otterbacher, J.C.; Radev, D.R.; Luo, A. 2002. Revisions that improve cohesion in multi-document summaries: a preliminary study. In the *Proceedings of the Workshop on Automatic Summarization*, pp 27-36. Philadelphia.

Pardo, T.A.S.; Rino, L.H.M.; Nunes, M.G.V. 2003. GistSumm: A Summarization Tool Based on a New Extractive Method. In N.J. Mamede, J. Baptista, I. Trancoso, M.G.V. Nunes (eds.), *6th Workshop on Computational Processing of the Portuguese Language - Written and Spoken* (Lecture Notes in Artificial Intelligence 2721), pp. 210-218. Faro, Portugal.

Pardo, T.A.S. 2005. *GistSumm - GIST SUMMarizer: Extensões e Novas Funcionalidades*. Série de Relatórios do NILC. NILC-TR-05-05. São Carlos, Brazil.

Radev, D. and McKeown, K. 1998. Generating natural language summaries from multiple on-line sources. *Computational Linguistics*, Vol. 24, N. 3, pp. 469-500.

Radev, D.R. 2000. A common theory of information fusion from multiple text sources, step one: Cross-document structure. In the *Proceedings of the 1st ACL SIGDIAL Workshop on Discourse and Dialogue*. Hong Kong.

Radev, D.R.; Jing, H.; Budzikowska, M. 2000. Centroid-based summarization of multiple documents: sentence extraction, utility-based evaluation and user studies. In the *Proceedings of the ANLP/NAACL Workshop*, pp. 21-29.

Radev, D.R.; Blair-Goldensohn, S.; Zhang, Z. 2001. Experiments in single and multi-document summarization using MEAD. In the *Proceedings of the 1st Document Understanding Conference*. New Orleans, LA.

Seno, E.R.M. and Nunes, M.G.V. 2009. Reconhecimento de Informações Comuns para a Fusão de Sentenças Comparáveis do Português. *Linguamática*, Vol. 1, pp. 71-87.

Zhang, Z.; Goldenshon, S.B.; Radev, D.R. 2002. Towards CST-Enhanced Sumarization. In the *Proceedings of the 18th National Conference on Artificial Intelligence*. Edmonton.

Distinguishing between Positive and Negative Opinions with Complex Network Features

Diego R. Amancio, Renato Fabbri, Osvaldo N. Oliveira Jr.,
Maria G. V. Nunes and Luciano da F. Costa
University of São Paulo, São Carlos, São Paulo, Brazil
diego.amancio@usp.br, renato.fabbri@gmail.com, chu@ifsc.usp.br,
gracan@icmc.usp.br, ldfcosta@gmail.com

Abstract

Topological and dynamic features of complex networks have proven to be suitable for capturing text characteristics in recent years, with various applications in natural language processing. In this article we show that texts with positive and negative opinions can be distinguished from each other when represented as complex networks. The distinction was possible by obtaining several metrics of the networks, including the in-degree, out-degree, shortest paths, clustering coefficient, betweenness and global efficiency. For visualization, the obtained multidimensional dataset was projected into a 2-dimensional space with the canonical variable analysis. The distinction was quantified using machine learning algorithms, which allowed an recall of 70% in the automatic discrimination for the negative opinions, even without attempts to optimize the pattern recognition process.

1 Introduction

The use of statistical methods is well established for a number of natural language processing tasks (Manning and Schuetze, 2007), in some cases combined with a deep linguistic treatment in hybrid approaches. Representing text as graphs (Antiqueira et al., 2007), in particular, has become popular with the advent of complex networks (CN) (Newman, 2003; Albert and Barabasi, 2002), especially after it was shown that large pieces of text generate scale-free networks (Ferrer i Cancho and Sole, 2001; Barabasi, 2009). This scale-free nature of such networks is probably the main reason why complex networks concepts are capable of capturing features of text, even in the absence of any linguistic treatment. Significantly, the scale-free property has also allowed CN to be applied in diverse fields (Costa et al., 2008), from neuroscience (Sporns, 2002) to physics (Gfeller, 2007), from linguistics (Dorogovtsev and Mendes, 2001) to computer science (Moura et al., 2003), to mention a few areas. Other frequently observed unifying principles that natural networks exhibit are short paths between any two nodes and high clustering coefficients (i.e. the so-called small-world property), correlations in node degrees, and a large number of cycles or specific motifs.

The topology and the dynamics of CN can be exploited in natural language processing, which has led to several contributions in the literature. For instance, metrics of CN have been used to assess the quality of written essays by high school students (Antiqueira et al., 2007). Furthermore, degrees, shortest paths and other metrics of CN were used to produce strategies for automatic summarization (Antiqueira et al., 2009), whose results are among the best for methods that only employ statistics. The quality of machine translation systems can be examined using local mappings of local measures (Amancio et al., 2008). Other related applications include lexical resources analysis (Sigman and Cecchi, 2002), human-induced words association (Costa, 2004), language evolution (Dorogovtsev and Mendes, 2002), and authorship recognition (Antiqueira et al., 2006).

In this paper, we model texts as complex networks with each word being represented by a node and co-occurrences of words defining the edges (see next section). Unlike traditional methods of text mining and sentiment detection of reviews (Tang et al., 2009; Pennebaker et al., 2003), the method described here only takes into account the relationships between concepts, regardless of the semantics related to each word. Specifically, we analyze the topology of the networks in order to distinguish between texts with positive and negative opinions. Using a corpus of 290 pieces of

Proceedings of the 2010 Workshop on Graph-based Methods for Natural Language Processing, ACL 2010, pages 83–87,
Uppsala, Sweden, 16 July 2010.

Before pre-processing	*After pre-processing*
The projection of the network data into two dimensions is crucial for big networks	projection network data two dimension be crucial big network

Table 1: *Adjacency list obtained from the sentence "The projection of the network data into two dimensions is crucial for big networks".*

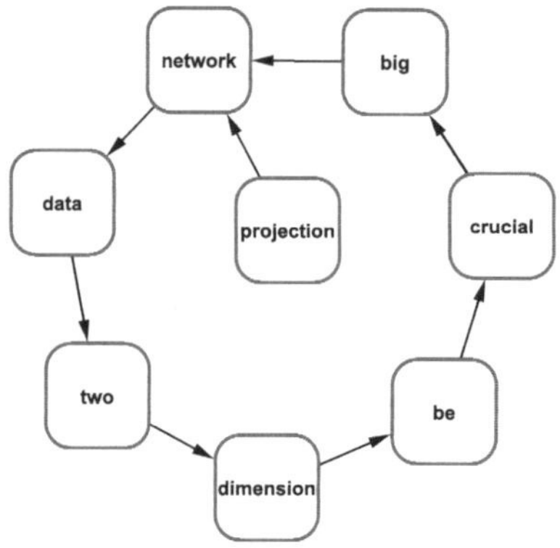

Figure 1: *Network obtained from the sentence "The projection of the network data into two dimensions is crucial for big networks".*

text with half of positive opinions, we show that the network features allows one to achieve a reasonable distinction.

2 Methodology

2.1 Representing texts as complex networks

Texts are modeled as complex networks here by considering each word (concept) as a node and establishing links by co-occurrence of words, disregarding the punctuation. In selecting the nodes, the stopwords were removed and the remaining words were lemmatized to combine words with the same canonical form but different inflections into a single node. Additionally, the texts were labeled using the MXPost part-of-speech Tagger based on the Ratnaparki's model (Ratnaparki, 1996), which helps to resolve problems of ambiguity. This is useful because the words with the same canonical form and same meaning are grouped into a single node, while words that have the same canonical form but distinct meanings generate distinct nodes. This pre-processing is done by accessing a computational lexicon, where each word has an associated rule for the generation of the canonical form. For illustrative means, Table 1 shows the pre-processed form of the sentence "The projection of the network data into two dimensions is crucial for big networks" and Figure 1 shows the network obtained for the same sentence.

Several CN metrics have been used to analyze textual characteristics, the most common of which are out-degree (k_{out}), in-degree (k_{in}), cluster coefficient (C) and shortest paths (l). Here we also use the betweenness (ϱ) and the global efficiency (η). The out-degree corresponds to the number of edges emanating from a given node, where the weight of each link between any two nodes may also be considered, being referred to as out-strength. Analogously, the node's in-degree is defined as the number of edges arriving at a given node. The network's k_{out} and k_{in} are evaluated by calculating the average among all the nodes, note that such global measures k_{out} and k_{in} are always equal. Regarding the adjacency matrix to represent the network, for a given node i, its k_{out} and k_{in} are calculated by eqs 1 and 2, where N represents the number of distinct words in the pre-processed text:

$$k_{out}(i) = \sum_{j=1}^{N} W_{ji} \quad (1)$$

$$k_{in}(i) = \sum_{j=1}^{N} W_{ij} \quad (2)$$

The cluster coefficient (C) is defined as follows. Let S be the set formed by nodes receiving edges of a given node i, and N_c is the cardinality of this set. If the nodes of this set form a completely connected set, then there are $N_c(N_c$-1) edges in this sub graph. However, if there are only B edges, then the coefficient is given by eq. (3):

$$C(i) = \frac{B}{N_c(N_c - 1)} \quad (3)$$

If N_c is less than 1, then C is defined as zero. Note that this measure quantifies how the nodes connected to a specific node are linked to each other, with its value varying between zero and one.

The shortest paths are calculated from all pairs of nodes within the network. Let d_{ij} be the minimum distance between any two words i and j in the network. The shortest path length l of a node i is given in equation 4.

$$l(i) = \frac{1}{N-1} \sum_{j \neq i} d_{ij} \quad (4)$$

Another measure often used in network analysis is the global efficiency (η), which is defined in equation 5, and may be interpreted as the speed with which information is exchanged between any two nodes, since a short distance d_{ij} contributes more significantly than a long distance. Note that the formula below prevents divergence; therefore, it is especially useful for networks with two or more components. The inverse of η, named *harmonic mean of geodesic distances*, has also been used to characterize complex networks.

$$\eta = \frac{1}{N(N-1)} \sum_{i \neq j} \frac{1}{d_{ij}} \quad (5)$$

While l and η use the length of shortest paths, the betweenness uses the number of shortest paths. Formally, the betweenness centrality for a given vertex v is given in equation 6, where the numerator represents the number of shortest paths passing through the vertices i, v and j and the denominator represents the number of shortest paths passing through the vertices i and j. In other words, if there are many shortest paths passing through a given node, this node will receive a high betweenness centrality.

$$\varrho(v) = \sum_i \sum_j \frac{\sigma(i,v,j)}{\sigma(i,j)} \quad (6)$$

2.2 Corpus

The corpus used in the experiments was obtained from the Brazilian newspaper Folha de São Paulo[1], from which we selected 290 articles over a 10-year period from a special section where a positive opinion is confronted with a negative opinion about a given topic. For this study, we selected the 145 longest texts with positive opinion and the 145 longest text with negative opinions[2], in order to have meaningful statistical data for the CN analysis.

2.3 Machine Learning Methods

In order to discriminate the topological features from distinct networks we first applied a technique for reducing the dimension of the dataset, the canonical variable analysis (McLachlan, 2004). The projection of network data into a lower dimension is crucial for visualization, in addition to avoids the so-called "curse of dimensionality" (Bishop, 2006). To calculate the axes points for projecting the data, a criterion must be established with which the distances between data points are defined. Let S be the overall dispersion of the measurements, as shown in equation 7, where ζ is the number of instances (ζ = 290), $\overrightarrow{x_c}$ is the set of metrics for a particular instance and $\langle \overrightarrow{x} \rangle$ is the average of all $\overrightarrow{x_c}$.

$$S = \sum_{c=1}^{\zeta} \left(\overrightarrow{x_c} - \langle \overrightarrow{x} \rangle\right)\left(\overrightarrow{x_c} - \langle \overrightarrow{x} \rangle\right)^T \quad (7)$$

Considering that two classes (C_1 = positive opinions and C_2 = negative opinions) are used, the scatter matrix S_i is obtained for each class C_i, according to equation 8, where $\langle \overrightarrow{x} \rangle_i$ is the analogous of $\langle \overrightarrow{x} \rangle$ when only the instances belonging to class C_i is taken into account.

$$S_i = \sum_{c \in C_i} \left(\overrightarrow{x_c} - \langle \overrightarrow{x} \rangle_i\right)\left(\overrightarrow{x_c} - \langle \overrightarrow{x} \rangle_i\right)^T \quad (8)$$

The intraclass matrix, i.e. the matrix that gives the dispersion inside C_1 and C_2, is defined as in equation 9. Additionally, we define the interclass matrix, i.e. the matrix that provides the dispersion between C_1 and C_2, as shown in equation 10.

$$S_{intra} = S_1 + S_2 \quad (9)$$

$$S_{inter} = S - S_{intra} \quad (10)$$

The principal axes for the projection are then obtained by computing the eigenvector associated with the largest eigenvalues of the matrix Λ (McLachlan, 2004) defined in equation 11. Since the data were projected in a two-dimensional space, the two principal axes were selected, corresponding to the two largest eigenvalues.

$$\Lambda = S_{intra}^{-1} S_{inter} \quad (11)$$

Finally, to quantify the efficiency of separation with the projection using canonical variable analysis, we implemented three machine learning algorithms (decision tree, using the C4.5 algorithm (Quinlan, 1993); rules of decision, using the

[1] http://www.folha.com.br

[2] The average size of the selected corpus is 600 words.

RIP algorithm (Cohen, 1995), and Naive Bayes algorithm (John and Langley, 1995)) and evaluated the accuracy rate using the 10-fold-cross-validation (Kohavi, 1995).

3 Results and Discussion

The metrics out-degree (k_{out}), in-degree (k_{in}), shortest paths (l), cluster coefficient (C), betweenness (ϱ) and global efficiency (η) were computed for each of the 145 texts for positive and negative opinions, as described in the Methodology. The mean values and the standard deviations of these metrics were used as attributes for each text. This generated a dataset described in 10 attributes, since the average k_{in} is equal to the average k_{out} and the standard deviation of η is not defined (in other words, it is always zero). Figure 2 shows the projection of the dataset obtained with canonical variable analysis, illustrating that texts with different opinions can be distinguished to a certain extent. That is to say, the topological features of networks representing positive opinion tend to differ from those of texts with negative opinion.

The efficiency of this methodology for characterizing different opinions can be quantified using machine learning algorithms to process the data from the projection. The results are illustrated in Table 2. Again, the distinction between classes is reasonably good, since the accuracy rate reached 62%. Indeed, this rate seems to be a good result, since the baseline method[3] tested showed an accuracy rate of 53%. One also should highlight the coverage found for the class of negative reviews by using the C4.5 algorithm, for which a value of 82% (result not shown in the Table 2) was obtained. This means that if an opinion is negative, the probability of being classified as negative is only 18%. Thus, our method seems especially useful when a negative view should be classified correctly.

Method	*Correctly classified*
C4.5	58%
Rip	60%
Naive Bayes	62%

Table 2: *Percentage of correctly classified instances.*

[3]The baseline method used as attributes the frequency of each word in each text. Then, the algorithm C4.5 was run with the same parameters used for the methodology based on complex networks.

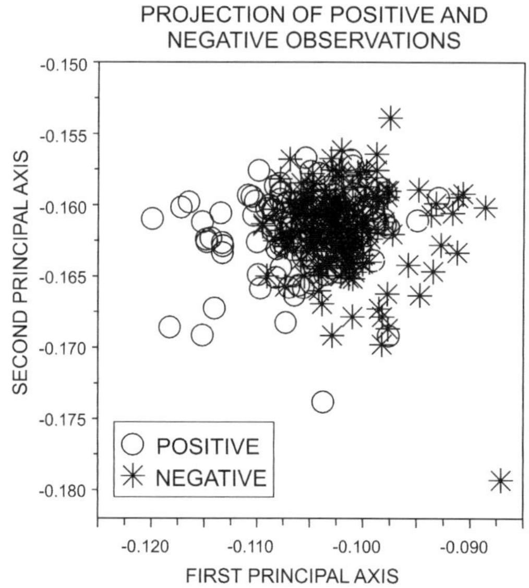

Figure 2: *Projection obtained by using the method of canonical variables. A reasonable distinction could be achieved between positive and negative opinions.*

4 Conclusion and Further Work

The topological features of complex networks generated with texts appear to be efficient in distinguishing between attitudes, as indicated here where texts conveying positive opinions could be distinguished from those of negative opinions. The metrics of the CN combined with a projection technique allowed a reasonable separation of the two types of text, and this was confirmed with machine learning algorithms. An 62% accuracy was achieved (the baseline reached 53%), even though there was no attempt to optimize the metrics or the methods of analysis. These promising results are motivation to evaluate other types of subtleties in texts, including emotional states, which is presently being performed in our group.

Acknowledgements: Luciano da F. Costa is grateful to FAPESP (05/00587-5) and CNPq (301303/06-1 and 573583/2008-0) for the financial support. Diego R. Amancio is grateful to FAPESP sponsorship (proc. 09/02941-1) and Renato Fabbri is grateful to CAPES sponsorship. We also thank Dr. Oto Araujo Vale very much for supplying the corpus.

References

C. D. Manning and H. Schuetze. 1999. Foundations of Statistical Natural Language Processing. *The MIT Press*, First Edition.

L. Antiqueira, M. G. V. Nunes, O. N. Oliveira Jr. and L. da F. Costa. 2007. Strong correlations between text quality and complex networks features. *Physica A*, 373:811–820.

M. E. J. Newman. 2003. The Structure and Function of Complex Networks. *SIAM Review*, 45:167–256.

R. Z. Albert and A.L. Barabasi. 2002. Statistical Mechanics of Complex Networks. *Rev. Modern Phys.*, 74:47–97.

R. Ferrer i Cancho and R. V. Sole. 2001. The small world of human language. *Proceedings of the Royal Society of London B*, 268:2261.

A.L. Barabasi. 2009. Scale-Free Networks: a decade and beyond. *Science*, 24 325 5939 412–413.

L. F. da Costa, O. N. Oliveira Jr., G. Travieso, F. A. Rodrigues, P. R. Villas Boas, L. Antiqueira, M. P. Viana, L. E. C. da Rocha. 2008. Analyzing and Modeling Real-World Phenomena with Complex Networks: A Survey of Applications. *arXiv* 0711.3199.

O. Sporns. 2002. Network analysis, complexity, and brain function. *Complexity*, 8(1):56–60.

D. Gfeller, P. LosRios, A. Caflisch and F. Rao. 2007. Complex network analysis of free-energy landscapes. *Proceedings of the National Academy of Science USA*, 104 (6):1817–1822

S. N. Dorogovtsev and J. F. F.Mendes. 2001. Language as an evolving word web. *Proceedings of the Royal Society of London B*, 268:2603.

A. P. S. de Moura, Y. C. Lai and A. E. Motter. 2003. Signatures of small-world and scale-free properties in large computer programs. *Physical Review E*, 68(1):017102.

L. Antiqueira, O. N. Oliveira Jr., L. da F. Costa and M. G. V. Nunes. 2009. A Complex Network Approach to Text Summarization. *Information Sciences*, 179:(5) 584–599.

M. Sigman and G.A. Cecchi. 2002. Global Organization of the Wordnet Lexicon. *Proceedings of the National Academy of Sciences*, 99:1742–1747.

L. F. Costa. 2004. What's in a name ? *International Journal of Modern Physics C*, 15:371–379.

S. N. Dorogovtsev and J. F. F. Mendes. 2002. Evolution of networks. *Advances in Physics*, 51:1079–1187.

L. Antiqueira, T. A. S. Pardo, M. G. V. Nunes, O. N. Oliveira Jr. and L. F. Costa. 2006. Some issues on complex networks for author characterization. *Proceeedings of the Workshop in Information and Human Language Technology*.

H. Tang, S. Tan and X. Cheng. 2009. A survey on sentiment detection of reviews. *Expert Systems with Applications*, 36:7 10760–10773.

J. W. Pennebaker, M. R. Mehl and K. G. Niederhoffer. 2003. Psychological aspects of natural language. use: our words, our selves. *Annual review of psychology*, 54 547-77.

D. R. Amancio, L. Antiqueira, T. A. S. Pardo, L. F. Costa, O. N. Oliveira Jr. and M. G. V. Nunes. 2008. Complex networks analysis of manual and machine translations. *International Journal of Modern Physics C*, 19(4):583-598.

A. Ratnaparki. 1996. A Maximum Entropy Part-Of-Speech Tagger. *Proceedings of the Empirical Methods in Natural Language Processing Conference, University of Pennsylvania*.

G. J. McLachlan. 2004. Discriminant Analysis and Statistical Pattern Recognition. *Wiley*.

C. M. Bishop. 2006. Pattern Recognition and Machine Learning. *Springer-Verlag New York*.

R. Quinlan. 1993. C4.5: Programs for Machine Learning. *Morgan Kaufmann Publishers*.

W. W. Cohen. 1995. Fast Effective Rule Induction. *12 International converence on Machine Learning*, 115–223.

G. H. John and P. Langley. 1995. Estimating Continuous Distribution in Bayesian Classifiers. *11 Conference on Uncertainty in Artificial Intelligence*, 338–345.

R. Kohavi. 1995. A study of cross-validation and bootstrap for accuracy estimation and model selection. *Proceedings of the Fourteenth International Joint Conference on Artificial Intelligence 2*, 12:1137-1143.

Image and Collateral Text in Support of Auto-annotation and Sentiment Analysis

Pamela Zontone and **Giulia Boato**
University of Trento
Trento, Italy.
{zontone|boato}@disi.unitn.it

Jonathon Hare and **Paul Lewis**
University of Southampton
Southampton, United Kingdom
{jsh2|phl}@ecs.soton.ac.uk

Stefan Siersdorfer and **Enrico Minack**
L3S Research Centre
Hannover, Germany
{siersdorfer|minack}@l3s.de

Abstract

We present a brief overview of the way in which image analysis, coupled with associated collateral text, is being used for auto-annotation and sentiment analysis. In particular, we describe our approach to auto-annotation using the graph-theoretic dominant set clustering algorithm and the annotation of images with sentiment scores from SentiWordNet. Preliminary results are given for both, and our planned work aims to explore synergies between the two approaches.

1 Automatic annotation of images using graph-theoretic clustering

Recently, graph-theoretic approaches have become popular in the computer vision field. There exist different graph-theoretic clustering algorithms such as minimum cut, spectral clustering, dominant set clustering. Among all these algorithms, the Dominant Set Clustering (DSC) is a promising graph-theoretic approach based on the notion of a *dominant set* that has been proposed for different applications, such as image segmentation (Pavan and Pelillo, 2003), video summarization (Besiris et al., 2009), etc. Here we describe the application of DSC to image annotation.

1.1 Dominant Set Clustering

The definition of Dominant Set (DS) was introduced in (Pavan and Pelillo, 2003). Let us consider a set of data samples that have to be clustered. These samples can be represented as an undirected edge-weighted (similarity) graph with no self-loops $G = (V, E, w)$, where $V = 1, \ldots, n$ is the vertex set, $E \subseteq V \times V$ is the edge set, and $w : E \rightarrow \mathbb{R}_+^*$ is the (positive) weight function. Vertices in G represent the data points, whereas edges represent neighborhood relationships, and finally edge-weights reflect similarity between pairs of linked vertices. An $n \times n$ symmetric matrix $A = (a_{ij})$, called affinity (or similarity) matrix, can be used to represent the graph G, where $a_{ij} = w(i, j)$ if $(i, j) \in E$, and $a_{ij} = 0$ if $i = j$. To define formally a Dominant Set, other parameters have to be introduced. Let S be a non-empty subset of vertices, with $S \subseteq V$, and $i \in S$. The (average) weighted degree of i relative to S is defined as:

$$\text{awdeg}_S(i) = \frac{1}{|S|} \sum_{j \in S} a_{ij}$$

where $|S|$ denotes the number of elements in S. It can be observed that $\text{awdeg}_{\{i\}}(i) = 0$ for any $i \in V$. If $j \notin S$ we can define the parameter $\phi_S(i, j) = a_{ij} - \text{awdeg}_S(i)$ that is the similarity between nodes j and i with respect to the average similarity between node i and its neighbors in S. It can be noted that $\phi_{\{i\}}(i, j) = a_{ij}$, for all $i, j \in V$ with $i \neq j$. Now, if $i \in S$, the weight $w_S(i)$ of i relative to S is:

$$w_S(i) = \begin{cases} 1 & \text{if } |S| = 1 \\ \sum_{j \in S \setminus \{j\}} \phi_{S \setminus \{i\}}(j, i) w_{S \setminus \{i\}}(j) & \text{otherwise.} \end{cases}$$

This is a recursive equation where to calculate $w_S(i)$ the weights of the set $S \setminus \{i\}$ are needed. We can deduce that $w_S(i)$ is a measure of the overall similarity between the node i and the other nodes in $S \setminus \{i\}$, considering the overall similarity among the nodes in $S \setminus \{i\}$. So, the total weight of S can be defined as:

$$W(S) = \sum_{i \in S} w_S(i).$$

A non-empty subset of vertices $S \subseteq V$ such that $W(T) > 0$ for any non-empty $T \subseteq S$ is defined as a *dominant set* if the following two conditions

Proceedings of the 2010 Workshop on Graph-based Methods for Natural Language Processing, ACL 2010, pages 88–92,
Uppsala, Sweden, 16 July 2010. ©2010 Association for Computational Linguistics

are satisfied: 1. $\forall i \in S$, $w_S(i) > 0$; and 2.$\forall i \notin S$, $w_{S\cup\{i\}}(i) < 0$. These conditions characterize the internal homogeneity of the cluster and the external inhomogeneity of S. As a consequence of this definition, a dominant set cluster can be derived from a graph by means of a quadratic program (Pavan and Pelillo, 2003). Let $\mathbf{x}$ be an n-dimensional vector, where n is the number of vertices of the graph and its components indicate the presence of nodes in the cluster. Let A be the affinity matrix of the graph. Let us consider the following standard quadratic program:

$$\begin{aligned} \max\ f(\mathbf{x}) &= \mathbf{x}^T A\mathbf{x} \\ s.t. \quad \mathbf{x} &\in \Delta \end{aligned} \tag{1}$$

where $\Delta = \{\mathbf{x} \geq 0 \text{ and } e^T\mathbf{x} = 1\}$ is the standard simplex of $\mathbb{R}^n$. If a point $\mathbf{x}^* \in \Delta$ is a local maximum of f, and $\sigma(\mathbf{x}*) = \{i \in V : x_i^* > 0\}$ is the support of $\mathbf{x}^*$, it can be shown that the support $\sigma(\mathbf{x}*)$ is a dominant set for the graph. So, a dominant set can be derived by solving the equation (1). The following iterative equation can be used to solve (1):

$$x_i(t+1) = x_i(t)\frac{(A\mathbf{x}(t))_i}{\mathbf{x}(t)^T A\mathbf{x}(t)}$$

where t denotes the number of iterations. To summarize the algorithm, a dominant set is found and removed from the graph. A second dominant cluster is extracted from the remaining part of the graph, and so on. This procedure finishes when all the elements in the graph have been assigned to a cluster.

1.2 Image annotation using DSC

Here we present an approach to automatically annotate images using the DSC algorithm. In the initialization phase (training) the image database is split into L smaller subsets, corresponding to the different image categories or visual concepts that characterize the images in the database. In this process only tags are exploited: an image is included in all subsets corresponding to its tags. Given a subset l, the corresponding affinity matrix A_l is calculated and used by the DSC algorithm. Following (Wang et al., 2008), the elements of the affinity matrix $A_l = (a_{ij})$ are defined as $a_{ij} = \mathrm{e}^{-w(i,j)/r^2}$ where $w(i,j)$ represents the similarity function between images i and j in the considered subset l, and $r > 0$ is the scaling factor used as an adjustment function that allows the control of clustering sensitivity. We use the MPEG.7 descriptors (Sikora, 2001) as features for computing the similarity between images. Following the DSC approach, we can construct all clusters of subset l with similar images, and associate them with the tag of subset l.

In the test phase, a new image is annotated associating to it the tag of the cluster that best matches the image. To do this, we use a decision algorithm based on the computation of the MSE (Mean Square Error), where for each cluster we derive a feature vector that represents all the images in that cluster (e.g., the average of all the feature vectors). The tag of the cluster with smaller MSE is used for the annotation.

For our experiments, we consider a subset of the Corel database, that consists of 4287 images in 49 categories ($L = 49$). The 10% of images in each category have been randomly selected from the database and used only for testing. In Figure 1 we report the annotation accuracy results obtained on 15 different classes with optimal parameter $r = 0.2$. For some classes the accuracy is very high, whereas for others the accuracy is very low (under 30%). The total annotation accuracy considering all the 49 classes is roughly 69%.

In a second set of experiments we consider a set of 6531 images from the MIR Flickr database (Huiskes and Lew, 2008), where each image is tagged with at least one of the chosen 30 visual concepts ($L = 30$). Images are characterized by multiple tags associated to them, thus an image is included in all the corresponding subsets. For testing we use 875 images. To evaluate the annotation accuracy we compare the automatically associated tag with the user defined tags of that image. In Figure 1 we report the annotation accuracy obtained for the 30 different categories, with the optimal parameter $r = 0.2$. The total annotation accuracy is about 87%.

Further simulations are in progress to evaluate the accuracy of multiple tags that can be associated to the test set in the MIR Flickr database. Indeed, our idea is to annotate the images considering the other common tags of the images belonging to each cluster.

2 Annotating Sentiment

In the previous section we were concerned with annotating images with visual concepts, typically object names or descriptors. A separate strand of

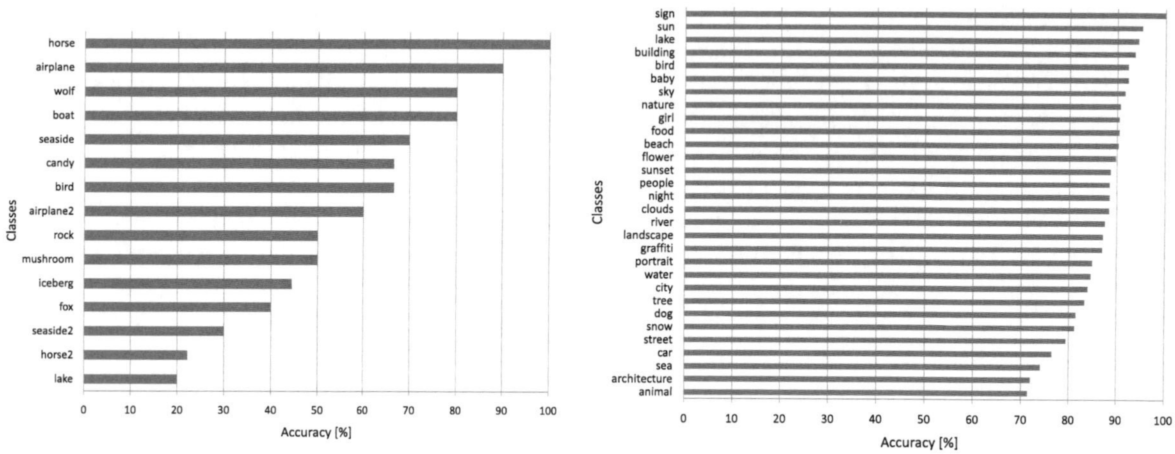

Figure 1: Annotation accuracy for 15 classes of the Corel database (left) and for 30 classes of the MIR Flickr database (right).

our work is concerned with opinion analysis in multimedia information and the automatic identification of sentiment. The study of image indexing and retrieval in the library and information science fields has long recognized the importance of sentiment in image retrieval (Jörgensen, 2003; Neal, 2006). It is only recently however, that researchers interested in automated image analysis and retrieval have become interested in the sentiment associated with images (Wang and He, 2008).

To date, investigations that have looked at the association between sentiment and image content have been limited to small datasets (typically much less than 1000) and rather specific, specially designed image features. Recently, we have started to explore how sentiment is related to image content using much more generic visual-term based features and much larger datasets collected with the aid of lexical resources such as SentiWordNet.

2.1 SentiWordNet and Image Databases

SentiWordNet (Esuli and Sebastiani, 2006) is a lexical resource built on top of WordNet. WordNet (Fellbaum, 1998) is a thesaurus containing textual descriptions of terms and relationships between terms (examples are hypernyms: "car" is a subconcept of "vehicle" or synonyms: "car" describes the same concept as "automobile"). WordNet distinguishes between different part-of-speech types (verb, noun, adjective, etc.). A *synset* in WordNet comprises all terms referring to the same concept (e.g., $\{car, automobile\}$). In SentiWordNet a triple of three *senti-values* (pos, neg, obj) (corresponding to positive, negative, or rather neutral sentiment flavor of a word respectively) are assigned to each WordNet synset (and, thus, to each term in the synset). The senti-values are in the range of $[0, 1]$ and sum up to 1 for each triple. For instance $(pos, neg, obj) = (0.875, 0.0, 0.125)$ for the term "good" or $(0.25, 0.375, 0.375)$ for the term "ill". Senti-values were partly created by human assessors and partly automatically assigned using an ensemble of different classifiers (see (Esuli, 2008) for an evaluation of these methods).

Popular social websites, such as Flickr, contain massive amounts of visual information in the form of photographs. Many of these photographs have been collectively tagged and annotated by members of the respective community. Recently in the image analysis community it has become popular to use Flickr as a resource for building datasets to experiment with. We have been exploring how we can crawl Flickr for images that have a strong (positive or negative) sentiment associated with them. Our initial explorations have been based around crawling Flickr for images tagged with words that have very high positive or negative sentiment according to their SentiWordNet classification.

Our image dataset has been refined by assigning an overall sentiment value to each image based on its textual metadata and discarding images with low overall sentiment. At the simplest level we use a dictionary of clearly positive and negative SentiWords, with which we assign a positive (+1) sentiment value if the text representation only con-

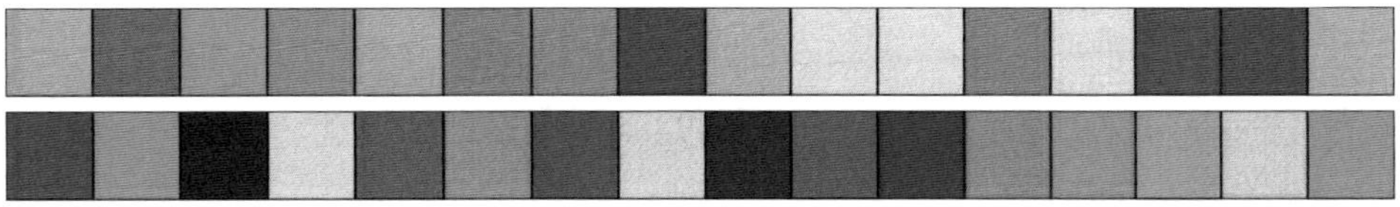

Figure 2: Top 16 most discriminative colours (from left to right) for positive and negative sentiment classes.

tains positive sentiment terms, and a negative (-1) sentiment value if it only contains negative sentiment terms. We discarded images with neither a positive nor negative score. Currently we are also exploring more powerful ways to assign sentiment values to images.

2.2 Combining Senti-values and Visual Terms

In the future we intend to exploit the use of techniques such as the one described in Section 1.2 in order to develop systems that are able to predict sentiment from image features. However, as a preliminary study, we have performed some small-scale experiments on a collection of 10000 images crawled from Flickr in order to try and see whether a primitive visual-bag-of-terms (Sivic and Zisserman, 2003; Hare and Lewis, 2005) can be associated with positive and negative sentiment values using a linear Support Vector Machine and Support Vector Regression. The visual-term bag-of-words for the study was based upon a quantisation of each pixel in the images into a set of 64 discrete colours (i.e., each pixel corresponds to one of 64 possible visual terms). Our initial results look promising and indicate a considerable correlation between the visual bag-of-words and the sentiment scores.

Discriminative Analysis of Visual Features. In our small-scale study we have also performed some analysis in order to investigate which visual-term features are most predictive of the positive and negative sentiment classes. For this analysis we have used the Mutual Information (MI) measure (Manning and Schuetze, 1999; Yang and Pedersen, 1997) from information theory which can be interpreted as a measure of how much the joint distribution of features (colour-based visual-terms in our case) deviate from a hypothetical distribution in which features and categories ("positive" and "negative" sentiment) are independent of each other.

Figure 2 illustrates the 16 most discriminative colours for the positive and negative classes. The dominant visual-term features for positive sentiment are dominated by earthy colours and skin tones. Conversely, the features for negative sentiment are dominated by blue and green tones. Interestingly, this association can be explained through intuition because it mirrors human perception of warm (positive) and cold (negative) colours.

Currently we are working on expanding our preliminary experiments to a much larger image dataset of over half a million images and incorporating more powerful visual-term based image features. In addition to seeking improved ways of determining image sentiment for the training set we are planning to combine the dominant set clustering approach to annotation presented in Section 1.2 with the sentiment annotation task of this section and compare the combined approach with other state of the art approaches as a step towards achieving robust image sentiment annotation.

3 Conclusions

The use of dominant set clustering as a basis for auto-annotation has shown promise on image collections from both Corel and from Flickr. We have also shown how that visual-term feature representations show some promise as indicators of sentiment in images. In future work we plan to combine these approaches to provide better support for opinion analysis of multimedia web documents.

Acknowledgments

This work was supported by the European Union under the Seventh Framework Programme (FP7/2007-2013) project LivingKnowledge (FP7-IST-231126), and the LiveMemories project, graciously funded by the Autonomous Province of Trento (Italy). The authors are also grateful to the creators of Flickr for providing an API that can be used in scientific evaluations and the broader Flickr community for making images and metadata available.

References

D. Besiris, A. Makedonas, G. Economou, and S. Fotopoulos. 2009. Combining graph connectivity and dominant set clustering for video summarization. *Multimedia Tools and Applications*, 44 (2):161–186.

A. Esuli and F. Sebastiani. 2006. Sentiwordnet: A publicly available lexical resource for opinion mining. *LREC*, 6.

Andrea Esuli. 2008. *Automatic Generation of Lexical Resources for Opinion Mining: Models, Algorithms and Applications*. PhD in Information Engineering, PhD School "Leonardo da Vinci", University of Pisa.

C. Fellbaum. 1998. *WordNet: An Electronic Lexical Database*. MIT Press.

Jonathon S. Hare and Paul H. Lewis. 2005. On image retrieval using salient regions with vector-spaces and latent semantics. In Wee Kheng Leow, Michael S. Lew, Tat-Seng Chua, Wei-Ying Ma, Lekha Chaisorn, and Erwin M. Bakker, editors, *CIVR*, volume 3568 of *LNCS*, pages 540–549, Singapore. Springer.

Mark J. Huiskes and Michael S. Lew. 2008. The MIR Flickr Retrieval Evaluation. In *MIR '08: Proceedings of the 2008 ACM International Conference on Multimedia Information Retrieval*, New York, NY, USA. ACM.

Corinne Jörgensen. 2003. *Image Retrieval: Theory and Research*. Scarecrow Press, Lanham, MD.

C. Manning and H. Schuetze. 1999. *Foundations of Statistical Natural Language Processing*. MIT Press.

Diane Neal. 2006. *News Photography Image Retrieval Practices: Locus of Control in Two Contexts*. Ph.D. thesis, University of North Texas, Denton, TX.

M. Pavan and M. Pelillo. 2003. A new graph-theoretic approach to clustering and segmentation. *IEEE Conf. Computer Vision and Pattern Recognition*, 1:145–152.

Thomas Sikora. 2001. The mpeg-7 visual standard for content description - an overview. *IEEE Trans. Circuits and Systems for Video Technology*, 11 (6):262–282.

J Sivic and A Zisserman. 2003. Video google: A text retrieval approach to object matching in videos. In *ICCV*, pages 1470–1477, October.

Weining Wang and Qianhua He. 2008. A survey on emotional semantic image retrieval. In *ICIP*, pages 117–120, San Diego, USA. IEEE.

M. Wang, Z. Ye, Y. Wang, and S. Wang. 2008. Dominant sets clustering for image retrieval. *Signal Processing*, 88 (11):2843–2849.

Yiming Yang and Jan O. Pedersen. 1997. A comparative study on feature selection in text categorization. In *ICML*, pages 412–420.

Aggregating opinions: Explorations into Graphs and Media Content Analysis

Gabriele Tatzl
SORA
Institute for Social Research & Analysis
Vienna, Austria
gt@sora.at

Christoph Waldhauser
SORA
Institute for Social Research & Analysis
Vienna, Austria
chw@sora.at

Abstract

Understanding, as opposed to reading is vital for the extraction of opinions out of a text. This is especially true, as an author's opinion is not always clearly marked. Finding the overall opinion in a text can be challenging to both human readers and computers alike. Media Content Analysis is a popular method of extracting information out of a text, by means of human coders. We describe the difficulties humans have and the process they use to extract opinions and offer a formalization that could help to automate opinion extraction within the Media Content Analysis framework.

1 Introduction

When humans read, they try to not only decode the written language, but also link it with external information. This gives them access to meaning and opinion of a text, that remain hidden from a mere decoder. This process of reading can be organized scientifically within the framework of Media Content Analysis (MCA). Reading, however, is expensive in terms of time and money. Yet the volume of textual data that is available for research grows seemingly without bounds. Automating reading, indeed doing MCA – at least to some degree – is a very desirable advance for any practitioner in the field.

The purpose of this short positional paper is to introduce MCA as we use it in our day-to-day lives and discuss challenges and possible solutions for them, with regards to automation.

The remainder of this paper is organized as follows. First we give a brief introduction to Media Content Analysis and it's applications in the social sciences in general. We will then focus on opinion mining as an important task within the general MCA framework. Special emphasis will be put on the challenges humans (and computers alike) face, when extracting opinions from a document. As a contribution to the effort of overcoming these obstacles, we offer a formalized interpretation of the MCA opinion extraction process in section 4. Finally, some concluding remarks and suggestions for an algorithmic implementation are made.

2 Media Content Analysis

Media Content Analysis from a social science perspective is driven by research questions (e.g. *How does the perception of migrant groups vary in different media?*) and practical questions of private and public clients (e.g. *In which context do negative opinions about a corporation occur?*) in order to investigate and evaluate the content of communication.

Media Content analysis can be generally described as "systematic reading of a body of texts, images, and symbolic matter" (Krippendorf, 2004). It "is applied to a wide variety of printed matter, such as textbooks, comic strips, speeches, and print advertising" (Krippendorf, 2004) or more generally to any cultural artifact[1]. Additionally, Content Analysis is defined as an empirical method for (I) systematic and inter-subjective understandable description of textual and formal characteristics and (II) for inquiring into social reality that consists of inferring features of a non-manifest context from features of a manifest written text and other meaningful matters (Merten, 1995; Krippendorf, 2004; Früh, 2007).

There is a wide range of methods of research,

> "(...) from simple and extensive classifications of types of content for organizational or descriptive purposes to

[1] MCA is e.g. also used for comparing representations of groups, issues and events to their real-world occurrences.

Proceedings of the 2010 Workshop on Graph-based Methods for Natural Language Processing, ACL 2010, pages 93–97, Uppsala, Sweden, 16 July 2010.

deeply interpretative enquiries into specific examples of content, designed to uncover subtle and hidden potential meanings" (McQuail, 2005).

The methodology we use is based upon a broad foundation of recent and widely approved literature (Riffe et al., 1998; Franzosi, 2008; Kaplan, 2004; Merten, 1995; Roberts, 2001; Krippendorf, 2004; Neuendorf, 2007; Rössler, 2005; Früh, 2007; Weerakkody, 2009): The analysis typically starts from the formulation of some specific research questions, in terms of topics, actors and patterns of interpretation that need to be investigated. Based on theoretical foundations and operationalisation, categories (theoretically or empirically grounded) and indicators are defined. All categories together make up the codebook, which is the instrument for the manual coding of text. The codebook consists of different characteristics for every variable and of instructions for the manual coding. One can compare the codebook to the perhaps more familiar questionnaire used in empirical quantitative social science. In this understanding, the codebook is little more than questions on the text and some hints on how to answer them. For instance, a question might concern a statement's speaker or subject actor and the way she is arguing her opinion: Is the argumentation of SACT in the statement rational?; possible answer codes are 1—the argumentation is consistent and rational, 2—the argumentation is not consistent and not well explained, and 3—no valuation possible.

In particular, variables are extracted on different levels of the documents: some address the whole document (article) and its source, some focus on claims to be able to answer all the different research questions. A core point in conducting empirical research is the demand for validity (external and internal) and reliability[2] (pre-tests). These quality checks have to be done carefully (Krippendorf, 2004).

The work proceeds with the identification (the manual annotation) of specific variables and indicators by turning text into numbers and fill out the codebook's answer sheet (data entry mask). The turning of text into numbers (coding process) is at the moment a very cumbersome task, as it is done manually. Humans, so called coders (usually trained junior researchers), have to read each article and de facto answer questions (the codebook) on the text afterwards. Last but not least, the final data file (cleaned manual codings) is used in statistical analysis in order to answer the research questions. The significance of this methodology lies precisely in its capacity to describe the mediated public discourse and various forms and aspects of diversity (i.e. diversity of opinions).

It should be considered that we conduct neither discourse analysis (e.g. Hajer and Versteeg, 2005) nor linguistic analysis (e.g. Livesey, 2001). Our approach is an analysis of mediated public discourse (see inter alia Gerhards et al., 2007), which implies certain methodological differences. This methodology is especially useful for the analysis of web media content and can be combined with other approaches. In the LivingKnowledge project[3], the analysis of the mediated public discourse is combined with Multimodal Genre Analysis (Baldry and Thibault, 2005).

3 Opinion Mining in MCA

Determining the degree to which a whole article (entire content) or a statement in a text (part of content) is positive, negative or neutral is not the only but a very essential reason for conducting Media Content Analysis. Applying the kind of Media Content Analysis mentioned above, we are able to describe the polarity of an opinion and the degree of correlation between the polarity of an opinion and the context of the opinion holder. An opinion holder could be considered as the speaker (person or organization) of a statement in the text. The human coders are instructed by the codebook (rules for coding) how opinions should be detected and ranked (five point-scale[4]). We are firmly convinced that it is not possible to detect opinions across different use cases only by means of polar words or opinion bearing words, because meaning of these words is always dependent on the con-

[2]Reliability in Content Analysis is the amount of agreement or correspondence among two or more coders (Krippendorf, 2004; Neuendorf, 2007).

[3]The research leading to these results has received funding from the European Community's Seventh Framework Programme (FP7/2007-2013) under grant agreement n°231126 Living Knowledge: Living Knowledge – Facts, Opinions and Bias in Time.

[4]Rate the opinion according to your interpretation of the article: The overall opinion is very positive, if the topic is mentioned with positive attributes and/or if a really positive outcome of an event is reported and not criticized and/or if the author of the article or more than half of the speakers talking about a certain topic evaluates it as very positive (1 = very positive).

tent's context. If you only have a short view on parts of the text, it can result in narrow incomplete interpretations. Besides that, additional information (which is not in the text) is often required to interpret an opinion and to understand the elements of social structure. It must be pointed out that when human coders read an article, there is a process of automatic inference. The proverbial concept of reading vs. understanding captures this notion with surprising accuracy. Correspondingly, sentiment analysis is a rather challenging process for humans as well as for computers.

4 Structuring opinions

In the following we will try to formalize what usually happens inside a human coder, coding an article. A typical research question in this sense might be: *is the opinion of article X, Θ_x positive, neutral, or negative towards a topic Y*[5]*?* The tricky part lies in the fact, that very few articles state their opinions expressis verbis. Rather, articles contain a number of statements on diverse facets of the article's topic. These statements in turn are again composed of reported actions or speech of subject actors[6] (SACTs). All these elements can be thought of as nodes in a tree: article being the root node containing M statement nodes and N SACT nodes. Note, that the N SACT nodes need not be uniformly distributed between the M statement nodes. Figure 1 displays the tree structure inherent to Media Content Analysis.

Each node has a number of attributes, variables in the codebook terminology, such as the name of the author or SACT. Next to these obvious attributes there are also latent ones, which are only accessible by analyzing all child nodes and aggregating the results (possibly with using external information). Opinions of articles are one example of latent attributes in Media Content Analysis. The process of aggregating all of a statement's SACTs' opinions (θ_{mn}) into a single statement opinion (θ_m), and further aggregating all of an article's statement opinions into a single article opinion, lies at the hearth of opinion mining within the Media Content Analysis framework. Figure 2

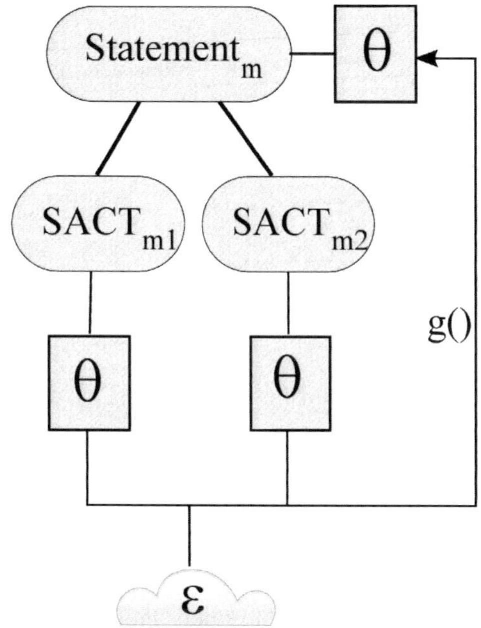

Figure 2: Aggregating SACTs' opinions into a statement opinion within the MCA framework

depicts the aggregating of SACTs' opinions into a statement opinion as a subtree.

To return to the more formalized notation introduced above, $\Theta_x = f(g_1, g_2, \ldots, g_m)$, with $g_k(\theta_{m1}, \theta_{m2}, \ldots, \theta_{mn}, \epsilon)$. A description of these two classes of functions is not trivial. A function (f) that aggregates statement opinions (g_k, themselves aggregates of their SACTs' opinions) into an overall article opinion (θ) requires to take into account not only the opinion attributes of its statement arguments, but also their relationships, an assessment of their equal presentation and take hints at the author's intentions. This function will typically be a weighted mean of the values for the opinion variable for the contained statements:

$$\widehat{\Theta_x} = \frac{\sum_{k=1}^{M} w_k g_k}{\sum_{k=1}^{M} w_k}$$

Estimating the weights w_k needs to include the aforementioned interstatement relationships and presentation. For instance, in the aggregation of two mildly negative statements and a very positive one, do these opinions really cancel out? Difficult as this may be, aggregating SACTs' opinions into a single statement opinion is even more difficult. Here, external information (ϵ) plays a crucial role, e.g. can the three SACTs Bill Gates, Linus Torvalds and an unnamed undergraduate computer science student be equal contributors to any

[5] Selecting only statements that deal with a certain topic Y is beyond the scope of this paper. However, automating topic selection is rather feasible by including background knowledge on the topic itself. Background knowledge that is readily available at a very early stage of MCA research question formulation.

[6] A subject actor is the person that effects a claim, e.g. if the claim is a statement, it is the speaker

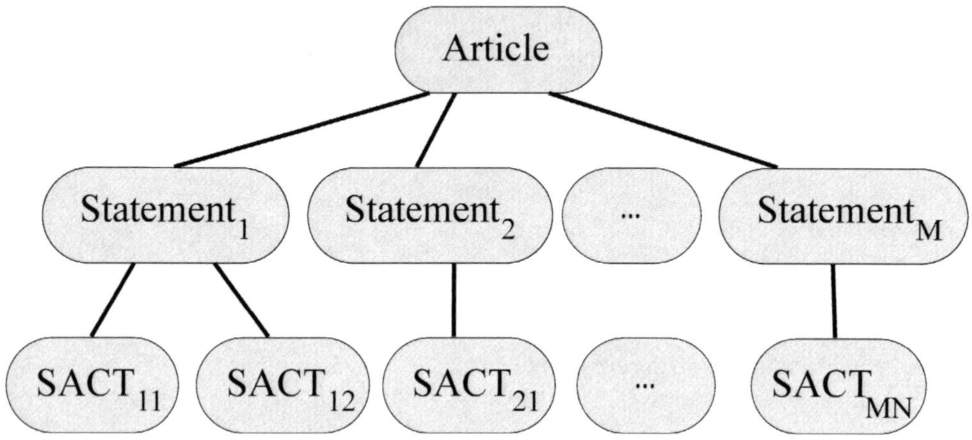

Figure 1: Relationship among levels of a document

given statement. In structure, this class of functions is also based on the weighted mean concept. However, in estimating the weights, notions of speaker interaction, speaker significance and effectiveness come into play. Many of these concepts cannot be sufficiently included by means of analyzing the text. Further, external information is required. This information can be thought of as an ontology or metadata, giving meaning to the actions and speech of a SACT. In a manual coding process, this information has been learned by the human coders through their past experience in reading texts. This is one of the reasons junior researchers, and not e.g. unskilled laborers, are used for this task. External knowledge, quite often to a substantial part, is critical in understanding a text.

5 Conclusion

Reading and understanding text is daunting task for humans. It requires years if not decades of training and experience to uncover hidden meanings and latent opinions. However, the process of reading is rather simple. We formalized this process by focusing on the example of extracting and aggregating opinions of an article. By rethinking reading and understanding opinions as a tree, we were able to structure the way humans use automatic inference to weight arguments and form opinions. The aggregating functions are simple themselves, however, estimating the right arguments is tricky. It requires the inclusion of massive amounts of external knowledge. In our opinion, this knowledge is currently not available in machine accessible form. With the ever increasing diffusion of semantic web data and ongoing efforts to create substantial ontologies of external knowledge, the future certainly will show interesting developments in this field.

In the meantime, thinking opinion extracting as traversing a tree might help to create software that helps human coders in their work. Also, large training sets of manually coded articles could be used to estimate the weights required to aggregate opinions on higher levels of analysis. However, achieving acceptable performance across diverse topics and usecases seems unlikely at this time.

References

Anthony Baldry and Paul J Thibault. 2005. *Multimodal Transcription and Text Analysis*. Equinox, London and Oakville.

Roberto Franzosi. 2008. *Content analysis*, volume 1 of *Sage benchmarks in social research methods*. Sage, Los Angeles.

Werner Früh. 2007. *Inhaltanalyse. Theorie und Praxis*. UVK, Konstanz, 6. rev. ed. edition.

Jürgen Gerhards, Anke Offerhaus, and Jochen Roose. 2007. The public attrobution of responsibility. developing an instrument for content analysis. *Kölner Zeitschrift für Soziologie und Sozialpsychologie*, 59:105–125.

Marteen Hajer and Wytske Versteeg. 2005. A decade of discourse analysis of environmental politics: Achievements, challenges, perspectives. *Journal of Environmental Policy and Planning*, 7(3):175–184.

David Kaplan, editor. 2004. *The SAGE handbook of quantitative methodology for the social sciences*. Sage, Thousand Oaks.

Klaus Krippendorf. 2004. *Content analysis. An introduction to its methodology*. Sage, London, 2. ed edition.

Sharon M Livesey. 2001. Eco-identity as discursive struggle: Royal dutch/shell, brent spar and nigeria. *Journal of Business Communication*, 38(1):58–91.

Denis McQuail. 2005. *McQuail's Mass Communication Theory*. Sage, London, 5. ed edition.

Klaus Merten. 1995. *Inhaltsanalyse. Einführung in Theorie, Methode und Praxis*. Westdt. Verlag, Opladen.

Kimberly A Neuendorf. 2007. *The content analysis guidebook*. Sage, Thousand Oaks.

Daniel Riffe, Stephen Lacy, and Frederick Fico. 1998. *Analyzing media messages: using quantitative content analysis in research*. Erlbaum, Mahwah.

C W Roberts. 2001. Content analysis. In Smelser and Baltes (Smelser and Baltes, 2001).

Patrick Rössler. 2005. *Inhaltsanalyse*. UVK, Konstanz.

Neil J Smelser and Paul B Baltes, editors. 2001. *International Encyclopedia of the Social & Behavioral Science*. Elsevier, Amsterdam.

Niranjala Weerakkody. 2009. *Research Methods for Media and Communication*. Oxford University Press, Oxford.

Eliminating Redundancy by Spectral Relaxation for Multi-Document Summarization

Fumiyo Fukumoto **Akina Sakai** **Yoshimi Suzuki**
Interdisciplinary Graduate School of Medicine and Engineering
University of Yamanashi
{fukumoto, t05kg014, ysuzuki}@yamanashi.ac.jp

Abstract

This paper focuses on redundancy, overlapping information in multi-documents, and presents a method for detecting salient, *key* sentences from documents that discuss the same event. To eliminate redundancy, we used spectral clustering and classified each sentence into groups, each of which consists of semantically related sentences. Then, we applied link analysis, the Markov Random Walk (MRW) Model to deciding the importance of a sentence within documents. The method was tested on the NTCIR evaluation data, and the result shows the effectiveness of the method.

1 Introduction

With the exponential growth of information on the Internet, it is becoming increasingly difficult for a user to read and understand all the materials from a series of large-scale document streams that is potentially of interest. Multi-document summarization is an issue to attack the problem. It differs from single document summarization in that it is important to identify differences and similarities across documents. Graph-based ranking methods, such as PageRank (Page et al., 1998) and HITS (Kleinberg, 1999) have recently applied and been successfully used for multi-document summarization (Erkan and Radev, 2004; Mihalcea and Tarau, 2005). Given a set of documents, the model constructs graph consisting vertices and edges where vertices are sentences and edges reflect the relationships between sentences. The model then applies a graph-based ranking method to obtain the rank scores for the sentences. Finally, the sentences with large rank scores are chosen into the summary. However, when they are strung together, the resulting summary still contains much overlapping information. Because all the sentences are ranked based on a sentence as unit of information. Therefore, for example, semantically related two sentences with "high recommendation" are ranked with high score, and thus are regarded as a summary sentence. To attack the problem, Wan *et al.* proposed two models, *i.e.*, the Cluster-based conditional Markov Random Walk model and the Cluster-based HITS model, both make use of the theme clusters in the document set (Wan and Yang, 2008). Their model first groups documents into theme clusters by using a simple clustering method, k-means. Next, the model constructs a directed or undirected graph to reflect the relationships between sentences and clusters by using link analysis. They reported that the results on the DUC2001 and DUC2002 datasets showed the effectiveness of their models. However, one of the problems using multivariate clustering such as k-means is that it is something of a black art when applied to high-dimensional data. The available techniques for searching this large space do not offer guarantees of global optimality, thus the resulting summary still contains much overlapping information, especially for a large amount of documents.

This paper focuses extractive summarization, and present a method for detecting key sentences from documents that discuss the same event. Like Wan *et al.*'s approach, we applied link analysis, the Markov Random Walk (MRW) model (Bremaud, 1999) to a graph consisting sentences and clusters. To attack the problem dealing with the high dimensional spaces, we applied spectral clustering technique (Ng et al., 2002) to the sentences from a document set. Spectral clustering is a transformation of the original sentences into a set of orthogonal eigenvectors. We worked in the space defined by the first few eigenvectors, using standard clustering techniques in the transformed space.

Proceedings of the 2010 Workshop on Graph-based Methods for Natural Language Processing, ACL 2010, pages 98–102,
Uppsala, Sweden, 16 July 2010. ©2010 Association for Computational Linguistics

2 Spectral Clustering

Similar to other clustering algorithms, the spectral clustering takes as input a matrix formed from a pairwise similarity function over a set of data points. Given a set of points $S = \{s_1, \cdots, s_n\}$ in a high dimensional space, the algorithm is as follows:

1. Form a distance matrix $D \in R^2$. We used cosine similarity as a distance measure.
2. D is transformed to an affinity matrix A_{ij}.

$$A_{ij} = \begin{cases} exp(-\frac{D_{ij}^2}{\sigma^2}), & \text{if } i \neq j \\ 0, & \text{otherwise.} \end{cases}$$

   σ^2 is a parameter and controls the rate at which affinity drops off with distance.

3. The matrix $L = D^{-1/2}AD^{-1/2}$ is created. D is a diagonal matrix whose (i,i) element is the sum of A's i-th row.
4. The eigenvectors and eigenvalues of L are computed, and a new matrix is created from the vectors associated with the number of l largest eigenvalues.
5. Each item now has a vector of l coordinates in the transformed space. These vectors are normalized to unit length.
6. K-means is applied to S in the l-dimensional space.

3 Cluster-based Link Analysis

The link analysis we used is an approach presented by Wan *et. al* (Wan and Yang, 2008). The model called "Cluster-based Conditional Markov Random Walk Model" incorporates the cluster-level information into the process of sentence ranking. The model is summarized as follows: Let $\pi(clus(s_i)) \in [0, 1]$ be the importance of cluster $clus(s_i)$ in the whole document set D. Let also $\omega(s_i, clus(s_i)) \in [0, 1]$ denote the strength of the correlation between sentence s_i and its cluster $clus(s_i)$. $clus(s_i)$ refers to the cluster containing sentence s_i. The transition probability from s_i to s_j is defined by formula (1).

$$p(i \rightarrow j | clus(s_i), clus(s_j)) = \begin{cases} \frac{f(i \rightarrow j | clus(s_i), clus(s_j))}{\sum_{k=1}^{|S|} f(i \rightarrow k | clus(s_i), clus(s_k))}, & \text{if } \Sigma f \neq 0 \\ 0, & \text{otherwise.} \end{cases} \quad (1)$$

$f(i \rightarrow j \mid clus(s_i), clus(s_j))$ in formula (1) refers to the weight between two sentences s_i and s_j, conditioned on the two clusters containing the two sentences, and defined by formula (2).

$$f(i \rightarrow j | clus(s_i), clus(s_j)) = f(i \rightarrow j) \cdot \{\lambda \cdot \pi(clus(s_i)) \cdot \omega(clus(s_i)) + (1 - \lambda) \cdot \pi(clus(s_j)) \cdot \omega(clus(s_j))\} \quad (2)$$

$\lambda \in [0, 1]$ in formula (2) is the combination weight controlling the relative contributions from the source cluster and the destination cluster. $\pi(clus(s_i))$ denotes the value indicating the importance of the cluster $clus(s_i)$ in the document set D. Similarly, $\omega(s_i, clus(s_i))$ refers to the similarity value between the sentence s_i and its cluster $clus(s_i)$. These values are obtained by using the cosine similarity. The new row-normalized matrix M is defined by formula (3).

$$M_{ij} = p(i \rightarrow j \mid clus(s_i), clus(s_j)) \quad (3)$$

The saliency scores for the sentences are computed based on formula (3) by using the iterative form in formula (4).

$$Score(s_i) = \mu \sum_{all j \neq i} Score(s_j) \cdot M_{ji} + \frac{(1 - \mu)}{\mid S \mid} \quad (4)$$

μ in formula (4) is the damping factor, which we set to 0.85. The above process can be considered as a Markov chain by taking the sentences as the states and the final transition matrix is given by formula (5), and each score of the sentences is obtained by the principle eigenvector of the new transition matrix A.

$$A = \mu M^T + \frac{(1 - \mu)}{\mid V \mid} \vec{e}\vec{e}^T \quad (5)$$

$\vec{e}$ in formula (5) is a column vector with all elements equal to 1. We selected a certain number of sentences according to rank score into the summary.

4 Experiments

We had an experiment by using the NTCIR-3[1] SUMM to evaluate our approach. NTCIR-3 has two tasks, single, and multi-document summarization. The data is collected from two years(1998-1999) Mainichi Japanese Newspaper articles. We used multi-document summarization task. There are two types of gold standard data provided to human judges, FBFREE DryRun and FormalRun, each of which consists of 30 topics. There are two types of correct summary according to the character length, *i.e.*, "long" and "short". All documents were tagged by a morphological analysis, ChaSen (Matsumoto et al., 1997) and noun words are extracted.

We used FormalRun consisting of 30 topics as a test data. Similarly, we randomly chose 10 topics from the FBFREE DryRun data to tuning a parameter σ in Spectral Clustering, and the number of l in the l-dimensional space obtained by the Spectral Clustering. σ is searched in steps of 0.01 from 1.0 to 5.0. l in the l-dimensional space is searched in steps 10% from 0 to 80% against the total number of words in the training data. The size that optimized the average F-score of 10 topics was chosen. Here, F-score is the standard measure used in the clustering algorithm, and it combines recall and precision with an equal weight. Precision is a ratio of the number of correct pair of sentences obtained by the k-means divided by the total number of pairs obtained by the k-means. Recall indicates a ratio of the number of correct pair of sentences obtained by the k-means divided by the total number of correct pairs. As a result, σ and l are set to 4.5 and 80%, respectively.

It is difficult to predict the actual cluster number k in a given input sentences to produce optimal results. The usual drawback in many clustering algorithms is that they cannot give a valid criterion for measuring class structure. Therefore, similar to Wan *et. al*'s method (Wan and Yang, 2008), we typically set the number of k of expected clusters as $\sqrt{N}$ where N is the number of all sentences in the document set. We used these values of the parameters and evaluated by using test data.

We used two evaluation measures. One is cosine similarity between the generated summary by the system and the human generated summary. Another is ROUGE score used in DUC (Liu and Hovy, 2003).

[1]http://research.nii.ac.jp/ntcir/

$$ROUGE = \frac{\sum_{s \in Cand} \sum_{ngram \in s} Count_{match}(ngram)}{\sum_{s \in Cand} \sum_{ngram \in s} Count(ngram)} \quad (6)$$

We used a word instead of n-gram sequence in formula (6). The results are shown in Table 1. "# of doc" and "# of sent" refer to the average number of documents and sentences, respectively. "# of sum" denotes to the average number of summary sentences provided by NTCIR3 SUMM. "cos" and "ROUGE" refer to the results evaluated by using cosine, and ROUGE score, respectively. "MRW" indicates the results obtained by directly applying MRW model to the input sentences.

We can see from Table 1 that our approach (Spectral) outperforms the baselines, "MRW" and "k-means", regardless of the types of summary (long/short) and evaluation measures (cosine/ROUGE). The results obtained by three approaches show that "short" was better than "long". This indicates that the rank score of correct sentences within the candidate sentences obtained by the MRW model works well. Comparing the results evaluated by "ROUGE" were worse than those of "cos" at any approaches. One reason is that the difference of summarization technique, *i.e.*, our work is extractive summarization, while the gold standard data provided by NTCIR-3 SUMM is the abstracts written by human professionals. As a result, a large number of words in a candidate summary are extracted by our approaches. For future work, it is necessary to extend our method to involve paraphrasing for extracted key sentences to reduce the gap between automatically generated summaries and human-written abstracts (Barzilay et al., 1993; Carenini and Cheung, 2008).

It is interesting to note how our approach affects for the number of sentences as an input. Figure 1 illustrates the results of summary "long" with evaluated ROUGE score. We can see from Figure 1 that our approach is more robust than k-means and the MRW model, even for a large number of input data. We have seen the same observations from other three results, *i.e.*, the results of short and long with evaluated cos and short with evaluated ROUGE.

We recall that the cluster number k is set to the square root of the sentence number. We tested different number of k to see how the cluster number

Table 1: Results against 30 topics

	# of doc	# of sent	# of sum	cos			ROUGE		
				MRW	k-means	Spectral	MRW	k-means	Spectral
Short	7.5	83.0	11.9	0.431	0.575	0.632	0.330	0.334	0.360
Long			20.4	0.371	0.408	0.477	0.180	0.186	0.209

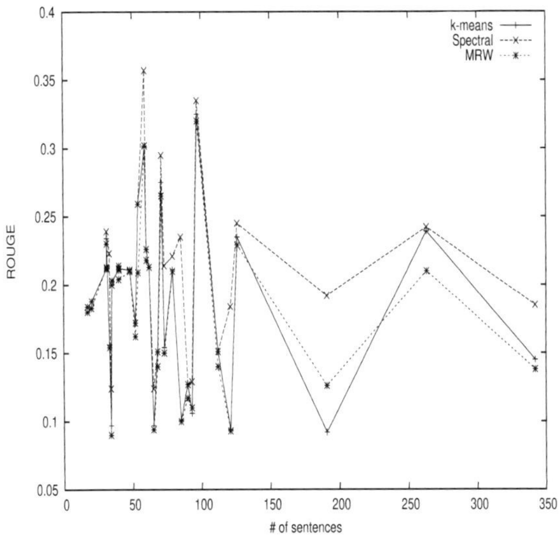

Figure 1: Long with ROUGE vs. # of sentences

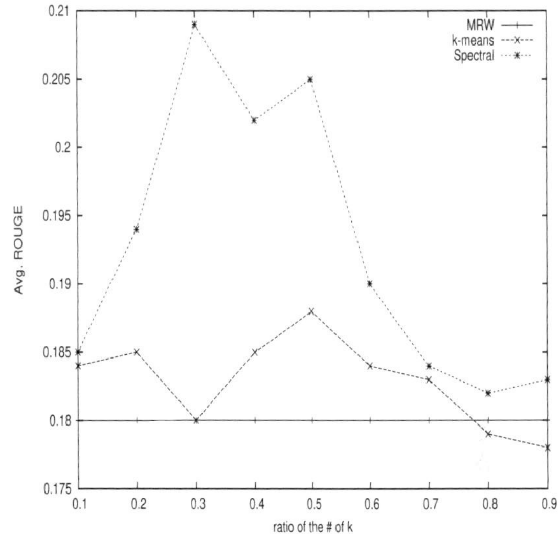

Figure 2: Long with ROUGE score measure vs. # of k

affects the summarization performance. In the experiment, we set $k = r* \mid N \mid$ where r is a parameter ranged from 0 to 1 (Wan and Yang, 2008). Because of space is limited, we report only the result with summary "long" and ROUGE score. The result is shown in Figure 2.

Overall the results obtained by our approach and k-means outperformed the results obtained by directly applying MRW model, while the results by k-means was worse than the results by MRW model when the ratio of the number of sentences was larger than 0.8. This shows that cluster-based summarization is effective reduce redundancy, overlapping information. Figure 2 also shows that our approach always outperforms, regardless of how many number of sentences were used. This indicates that the MRW model with spectral clustering is more robust than that with the baseline, k-means, with respect to the different number of clusters.

5 Conclusion

We have developed an approach to detect salient sentences from documents that discuss the same event. The results showed the effectiveness of the method. Future work will include: (i) comparing other approaches that uses link analysis to reduce redundancy, such as (Zhu et al., 2007), (ii) applying the method to the DUC evaluation data for quantitative evaluation, and (iii) extending the method to classify sentences into more than one classes by using soft-clustering techniques such as EM (Dempster et al., 1977) and fuzzy c-means algorithms (Zhang and Wang, 2007).

References

R. Barzilay, K. R. McKeown, and M. Elhadad. 1993. Information Fusion in the Context of Multi-document Summarization. In *Proc. of the 37th Annual Meeting of the Association for Computational Linguistics*, pages 550–557.

P. Bremaud. 1999. *Markov Chains: Gibbs Fields, Monte Carlo Simulation, and Queues*. Springer-Verlag.

G. Carenini and J. C. K. Cheung. 2008. Extractive vs. NLG-based Abstractive Summarization of Evaluative Text: The Effect of Corpus Controversiality.

In *Proc. of the 5th International Natural Language Generation Conference*, pages 33–41.

A. P. Dempster, N. M. Laird, and D. B. Rubin. 1977. Maximum Likelihood from Incomplete Data Via the EM Algorithm. *Royal Statistical Society*, 39(B):1–38.

G. Erkan and D. Radev. 2004. LexPageRank: Prestige in Multi-document Text Summarization. In *Proc. of the 2004 Conference on Empirical Methods in Natural Language Processing*, pages 365–371.

J. M. Kleinberg. 1999. Authoritative Sources in a Hyperlinked Environment. *ACM*, 46(5):604–632.

C-Y. Liu and E. H. Hovy. 2003. Automatic Evaluation of Summaries Using N-gram Co-occurrence Statistics. In *Proc. of Human Language Technologies: The Annual Conference of the North American Chapter of the Association for Computational Linguistics*, pages 71–78.

Y. Matsumoto, A. Kitauchi, T. Yamashita, Y. Haruno, O. Imaichi, and T. Imamura. 1997. *Japanese Morphological Analysis System Chasen Mannual.*

R. Mihalcea and P. Tarau. 2005. Language Independent Extractive Summarization. In *In Proc. of the 43nd Annual Meeting of the Association for Computational Linguistics*, pages 49–52.

A. Y. Ng, M. I. Jordan, and Y. Weiss. 2002. *On Spectral Clustering: Analysis and an Algorithm*, volume 14. MIT Press.

L. Page, S. Brin, R. Motwani, and T. Winograd. 1998. The Pagerank Citation Ranking: Bringing Order to the Web. In *Technical report, Stanford Digital Libraries.*

X. Wan and J. Yang. 2008. Multi-document Summarization Using Cluster-based Link Analysis. In *Proc. of the 31st Annual International ACM SIGIR Conference on Research and Development in Information Retrieval*, pages 299–306.

Z. Zhang and R. Wang. 2007. Identification of Overlapping Community Structure in Complex Networks using Fuzzy C-means Clustering. *PHYSICA*, A(374):483–490.

X. Zhu, A. Goldberg, J. V. Gael, and D. Andrzejewski. 2007. Improving Diversity in Ranking using Absorbing Random Walks. In *In Human Language technologies: The Annual Conference of the North American Chapter of the Association for Computational Linguistics*, pages 97–104.

Computing Word Senses by Semantic Mirroring and Spectral Graph Partitioning

Martin Fagerlund
Linköping University
Linköping, Sweden
marfa229@student.liu.se

Magnus Merkel
Linköping University
Linköping, Sweden
magnus.merkel@liu.se

Lars Eldén
Linköping University
Linköping, Sweden
lars.elden@liu.se

Lars Ahrenberg
Linköping University
Linköping, Sweden
lars.ahrenberg@liu.se

Abstract

Using the technique of "semantic mirroring" a graph is obtained that represents words and their translations from a parallel corpus or a bilingual lexicon. The connectedness of the graph holds information about the different meanings of words that occur in the translations. Spectral graph theory is used to partition the graph, which leads to a grouping of the words according to different senses. We also report results from an evaluation using a small sample of seed words from a lexicon of Swedish and English adjectives.

1 Introduction

A great deal of linguistic knowledge is encoded implicitly in bilingual resources such as parallel texts and bilingual dictionaries. Dyvik (1998, 2005) has provided a knowledge discovery method based on the semantic relationship between words in a source language and words in a target language, as manifested in parallel texts. His method is called Semantic mirroring and the approach utilizes the way that different languages encode lexical meaning by mirroring source words and target words back and forth, in order to establish semantic relations like synonymy and hyponymy. Work in this area is strongly related to work within Word Sense Disambiguation (WSD) and the observation that translations are a good source for detecting such distinctions (Resnik & Yarowsky 1999, Ide 2000, Diab & Resnik 2002). A word that has multiple meanings in one language is likely to have different translations in other languages. This means that translations serve as sense indicators for a particular source word, and make it possible to divide a given word into different senses.

In this paper we propose a new graph-based approach to the analysis of semantic mirrors. The objective is to find a viable way to discover synonyms and group them into different senses. The method has been applied to a bilingual dictionary of English and Swedish adjectives.

2 Preparations

2.1 The Translation Matrix

In these experiments we have worked with a English-Swedish lexicon consisting of 14850 English adjectives, and their corresponding Swedish translations. Out of the lexicon was created a translation matrix $\mathbf{B}$, and two lists with all the words, one for English and one for Swedish. $\mathbf{B}$ is defined as

$$\mathbf{B}(\mathbf{i},\mathbf{j}) = \begin{cases} 1, & \text{if } i \sim j, \\ 0, & \text{otherwise.} \end{cases}$$

The relation $i \sim j$ means that word i translates to word j.

2.2 Translation

Translation is performed as follows. From the word i to be translated, we create a vector $\bar{e}_i$, with a one in position i, and zeros everywhere else. Then perform the matrix multiplication $\mathbf{B}\bar{e}_i$ if it is a Swedish word to be translated, or $\mathbf{B}^T\bar{e}_i$ if it is an English word to be translated. $\bar{e}_i$ has the same length as the list in which the word i can be found.

3 Semantic Mirroring

We start with an English word, called *eng1*[1]. We look up its Swedish translations. Then we look up

[1] Short for english1. We will use swe for Swedish words.

Proceedings of the 2010 Workshop on Graph-based Methods for Natural Language Processing, ACL 2010, pages 103–107, Uppsala, Sweden, 16 July 2010.

the English translations of each of those Swedish words. We have now performed one "mirror-operation". In mathematical notation:

$$f = \mathbf{B}\mathbf{B}^T\bar{e}_{eng1}.$$

The non-zero elements in the vector f represent English words that are semantically related to $eng1$. Dyvik (1998) calls the set of words that we get after two translations the *inverse t-image*. But there is one problem. The original word should not be here. Therefore, in the last translation, we modify the matrix $\mathbf{B}$, by replacing the row in $\mathbf{B}$ corresponding to *eng1*, with an all-zero row. Call this new modified matrix $\mathbf{B}_{mod1}$. So instead of the matrix multiplication performed above, we start over with the following one:

$$\mathbf{B}_{mod1}\mathbf{B}^T\bar{e}_{eng1}. \quad (1)$$

To make it clearer from a linguistic perspective, consider the following figure[2].

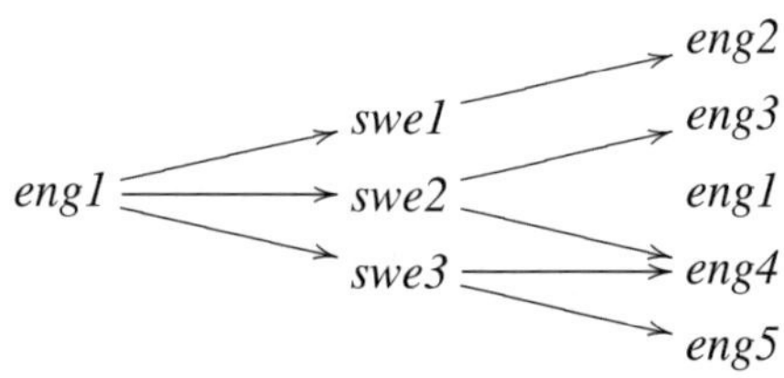

The words to the right in the picture above (*eng2,...,eng5*) are the words we want to divide into senses. To do this, we need some kind of relation between the words. Therefore we continue to translate, and perform a second "mirror operation". To keep track of what each word in the inverse t-image translates to, we must first make a small modification. We have so far done the operation (1), which gave us a vector, call it $e \in \mathbb{R}^{14850\times 1}$. The vector e consists of nonzero integers in the positions corresponding to the words in the invers t-image, and zeros everywhere else. We make a new matrix $\mathbf{E}$, with the same number of rows as e, and the same number of columns as there are nonzeros in e. Now go through every element in e, and when finding a nonzero element in row i, and if it is the j:th nonzero element, then put a one in position (i, j) in $\mathbf{E}$. The procedure is illustrated in (2).

[2]The arrows indicate translation.

$$\begin{pmatrix} 1 \\ 0 \\ 2 \\ 1 \\ 0 \\ 3 \end{pmatrix} \longrightarrow \begin{pmatrix} 1 & 0 & 0 & 0 \\ 0 & 0 & 0 & 0 \\ 0 & 1 & 0 & 0 \\ 0 & 0 & 1 & 0 \\ 0 & 0 & 0 & 0 \\ 0 & 0 & 0 & 1 \end{pmatrix} \quad (2)$$

When doing our second "mirror operation", we do not want to translate through the Swedish words *swe1,...,swe3*. We once again modify the matrix $\mathbf{B}$, this time replacing the columns of $\mathbf{B}$ corresponding to the Swedish words *swe1,...,swe3*, with zeros. Call this second modified matrix $\mathbf{B}_{mod2}$. With the matrix $\mathbf{E}$ from (2), we now get:

$$\mathbf{B}_{mod2}\mathbf{B}^T_{mod2}\mathbf{E} \quad (3)$$

We illustrate the operation (3):

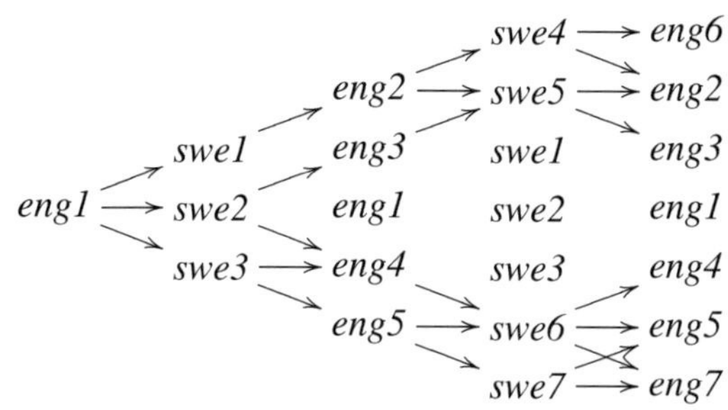

Now we have got the desired relation between *eng2,...eng5*. In (3) we keep only the rows corresponding to *eng2,...eng5*, and get a symmetric matrix $\mathbf{A}$, which can be considered as the adjacency matrix of a graph. The adjacency matrix and the graph of our example are illustrated below.

$$\mathbf{A} = \begin{pmatrix} 2 & 1 & 0 & 0 \\ 1 & 1 & 0 & 0 \\ 0 & 0 & 1 & 1 \\ 0 & 0 & 1 & 2 \end{pmatrix} \quad (4)$$

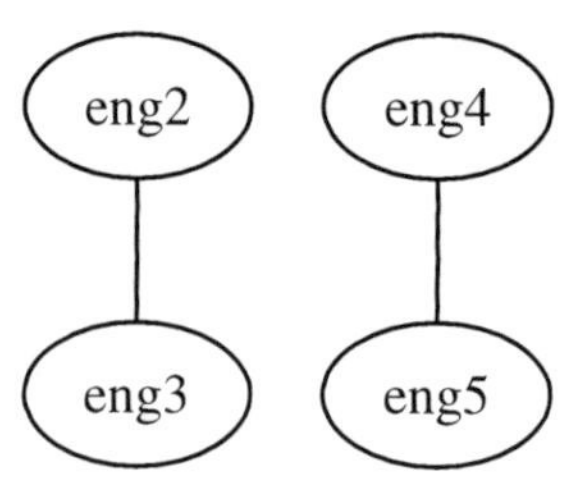

Figure 1: The graph to the matrix in (4).

The adjacency matrix should be interpreted in the following way. The rows and the columns correspond to the words in the inverse t-image. Following our example, *eng2* corresponds to row 1 and column 1, *eng3* corresponds to row 2 and column 2, and so on. The elements on position (i, i) in **A** are the vertex weights. The vertex weight associated with a word, describes how many translations that word has in the other language, e.g. *eng2* translates to *swe4* and *swe5* that is translated back to *eng2*. So the vertex weight for *eng2* is 2, as also can be seen in position $(1, 1)$ in (4). A high vertex weight tells us that the word has a high number of translations, and therefore probably a wide meaning.

The elements in the adjacency matrix on position $(i, j), i \neq j$ are the edge weights. These weights are associated with two words, and describe how many words in the other language that both word i and j are translated to. E.g. *eng5* and *eng4* are both translated to *swe6*, and it follows that the weight, w(*eng4*,*eng5*) = 1. If we instead would take *eng5* and *eng7*, we see that they both translate to *swe6* and *swe7*, so the weight between those words, w(*eng5*,*eng7*) = 2. (But this is not shown in the adjacency matrix, since *eng7* is not a word in the inverse t-image). A high edge weight between two words tells us that they share a high number of translations, and therefore probably have the same meanings.

4 Graph Partitioning

The example illustrated in Figure 1 gave as a result two graphs that are not connected. Dyvik argues that in such a case the graphs represent two groups of words of different senses. In a larger and more realistic example one is likely to obtain a graph that is connected, but which can be partitioned into two subgraphs without breaking more than a small number of edges. Then it is reasonable to ask whether such a partitioning has a similar effect in that it represents a partitioning of the words into different senses.

We describe the mathematical procedure of partitioning a graph into subgraphs, using spectral graph theory (Chung, 1997). First, define the degree $d(i)$ of a vertex i to be

$$d(i) = \sum_j A(i, j).$$

Let D be the diagonal matrix defined by

$$D(i, j) = \begin{cases} d(i), & \text{if } i = j, \\ 0, & \text{otherwise.} \end{cases}$$

The Laplacian L is defined as

$$L = D - A.$$

We define the normalised Laplacian $\mathcal{L}$ to be

$$\mathcal{L} = D^{-\frac{1}{2}} L D^{-\frac{1}{2}}.$$

Now calculate the eigenvalues $\lambda_0, \ldots, \lambda_{n-1}$, and the eigenvectors of $\mathcal{L}$. The smallest eigenvalue, λ_0, is always equal to zero, as shown by Chung (1997). The multiplicity of zero among the eigenvalues is equal to the number of connected components in the graph, as shown by Spielman (2009). We will look at the eigenvector belonging to the second smallest eigenvalue, λ_1. This eigenpair is often referred to as the *Fiedler value* and the *Fiedler vector*. The entries in the Fiedler vector corresponds to the vertices in the graph. (We will assume that there is only one component in the graph. If not, chose the component with the largest number of vertices). Sort the Fiedler vector, and thus sorting the vertices in the graph. Then make $n - 1$ cuts along the Fiedler vector, dividing the elements of the vector into two sets, and for each cut compute the conductance, $\phi(S)$, defined as

$$\phi(S) = d(V) \frac{| \partial(S, \bar{S}) |}{d(S) d(\bar{S})}, \tag{5}$$

where $d(S) = \sum_{i \in S} d(i)$. $| \partial(S, \bar{S}) |$ is the total weight of the edges with one end in S and one end in $\bar{S}$, and $V = S + \bar{S}$ is the set of all vertices in the graph. Another measure used is the sparsity, $sp(S)$, defined as

$$sp(S) = \frac{| \partial(S, \bar{S}) |}{\min(d(S), d(\bar{S}))} \tag{6}$$

For details, see (Spielman, 2009). Choose the cut with the smallest conductance, and in the graph, delete the edges with one end in S and the other end in $\bar{S}$. The procedure is then carried out until the conductance, $\phi(S)$, reaches a tolerance. The tolerance is decided by human evaluators, performing experiments on test data.

5 Example

We start with the word *slithery*, and after the mirroring operation (3) we get three groups of words in the inverse t-image, shown in Table 1. After two partitionings of the graph to *slithery*, using the method described in section 4, we get five sense groups, shown in Table 2.

smooth slick lubricious	slimy smooth-faced oleaginous	saponaceous
slippery glib sleek	oily greasy	slippy

Table 1: The three groups of words after the mirroring operation.

slimy smooth-faced smooth sleek	glib slippery lubricious slick	oleaginous oily greasy
saponaceous	slippy	

Table 2: The five sense groups of *slithery* after two partitionings.

6 Evaluation

A small evaluation was performed using a random sample of 10 Swedish adjectives. We generated sets under four different conditions. For the first, using conductance (5). For the second, using sparsity (6). For the third and fourth, we set the diagonal entries in the adjacency matrix to zero. These entries tell us very little of how the words are connected to each other, but they may effect how the partitioning is made. So for the third, we used conductance and no vertex weights, and for the fourth we used sparsity and no vertex weights. There were only small differences in results due to the conditions, so we report results only for one of them, the one using vertex weights and sparsity.

Generated sets, with singletons removed, were evaluated from two perspectives: consistency and synonymy with the seed word. For consistency a three-valued scheme was used: (i) the set forms a single synset, (ii) at least two thirds of the words form a single synset, and (iii) none of these. Synonymy with the seed word was judged as either yes or no.

Two evaluators first judged all sets independently and then coordinated their judgements. The criterion for consistency was that at least one domain, such as personality, taste, manner, can be found where all adjectives in the set are interchangeable. Results are shown in Table 3.

Depending on how we count partially consistent groups this gives a precision in the range 0.57 to 0.78. We have made no attempt to measure recall.

	Count	**Average**	**Percentage**
All groups	58	5.8	100
Consistent groups	33	3.3	57
2/3 consistency	12	1.2	21
Synonymy with seed word	14	1.4	24

Table 3: Classified output with frequencies from one type of partition

It may be noted that group size varies. There are often several small groups with just 2 or 3 words, but sometimes as many as 10-15 words make up a group. For large groups, even though they are not fully consistent, the words tend to be drawn from two or three synsets.

7 Conclusion

So far we have performed a relatively limited number of tests of the method. Those tests indicate that semantic mirroring coupled with spectral graph partitioning is a useful method for computing word senses, which can be developed further using refined graph theoretic and linguistic techniques in conjunction.

8 Future work

There is room for many more investigations of the approach outlined in this paper. We would like to explore the possibility to have a vertex (word) belong to multiple synsets, instead of having discrete cuts between synsets. In the present solution a vertex belongs to only one partition of a graph, making it impossible to having the same word belong to several synsets. We would also like to investigate the properties of graphs to see whether it is possible to automatically measure how close a seed word is to a particular synset. Furthermore, more thorough evaluations of larger data sets would give us more information on how to combine similar synsets which were generated from distinct seed words and explore more complex semantic fields. In our future research we will test the method also on other lexica, and perform experiments with the different tolerances involved. We will also perform extensive tests assessing the results using a panel of human evaluators.

References

Daniel A. Spielman. 2009. *Spectral Graph theory*. Lecture notes.

Daniel A. Spielman, S. -H. Teng. 2006. *Spectral partitioning works: Planar graphs and finite element meshes*. Elsevier Inc.

Diab, M. Resnik, P. 2002. *An Unsupervised Method for Word Sense Tagging using Parallel Corpora*. Proceedings of the 40th Annual Meeting of the Association for Computational Linguistics. 255-262.

Fan R. K. Chung. 1997. *Spectral Graph Theory*. American Mathematical Society, Providence, Rhode Island.

H. Dyvik. 1998. *A Translational Basis for Semantics*. In: Stig Johansson and Signe Oksefjell (eds.): Corpora and Crosslinguistic Research: Theory, Method and Case Studies, pp. 51-86. Rodopi.

H. Dyvik. 2005. *Translations as a Semantic Knowledge Source*. Proceedings of the Second Baltic Conference on Human Language Technologies, Tallinn.

Nancy Ide. 2000. *Cross-lingual sense determination: Can it work?* Computers and the Humanities: Special issue on SENSEVAL, 34:223–234.

Philip Resnik , David Yarowsky. *Distinguishing systems and distinguishing senses: new evaluation methods for Word Sense Disambiguation* Natural Language Engineering, v.5 n.2, p.113-133, June 1999

Author Index